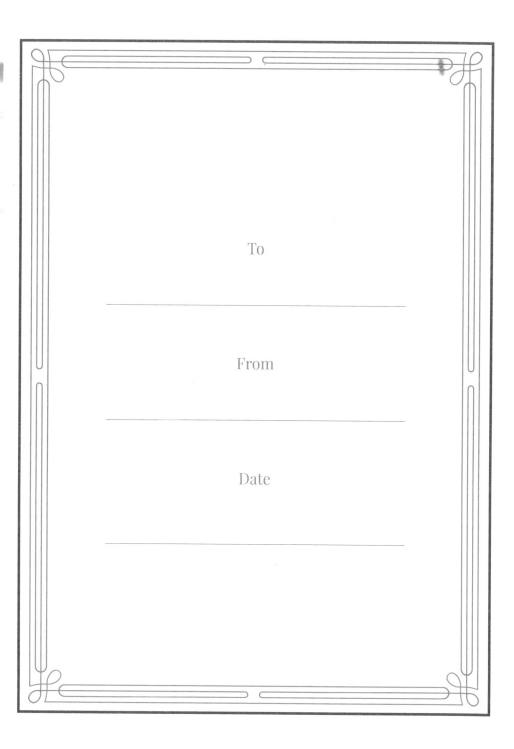

To

_____

From

_____

Date

_____

Visit Christian Art Gifts, Inc., at www.christianartgifts.com.

Ten Minutes with God for Women: 365 Daily Devotions

Published by Christian Art Gifts, Inc., Bloomingdale, IL, USA.

© 2024 by Debbie Alsdorf. All rights reserved.

The author is represented by Books & Such, Inc., www.booksandsuch.com.

First edition 2024.

Designed by Christian Art Gifts, Inc.

Cover and interior images used under license from Shutterstock.com.

Unless otherwise indicated, all Scripture quotations are taken from The Holy Bible, New International Version®, NIV®, Copyright © 1973, 1978, 1984, 2011 by Biblica, Inc.® Used by permission. All rights reserved worldwide.

Scripture quotations marked AMP are taken from The Amplified Bible, Copyright © 2015 by The Lockman Foundation, La Habra, CA 90631. All rights reserved.

Scripture quotations marked CEV are taken from Contemporary English Version® Copyright © 1995 American Bible Society. All rights reserved.

Scripture quotations marked ESV are taken from The ESV® Bible (The Holy Bible, English Standard Version®). ESV® Text Edition: 2016. Copyright © 2001 by Crossway, a publishing ministry of Good News Publishers.

Scripture quotations marked MSG are taken from THE MESSAGE, copyright © 1993, 2002, 2018 by Eugene H. Peterson. Used by permission of NavPress. All rights reserved. Represented by Tyndale House Publishers, Inc.

Scripture quotations marked NASB (1995) are taken from New American Standard Bible®, Copyright © 1960, 1971, 1977, 1995 by The Lockman Foundation. All rights reserved.

Scripture quotations marked NIV (1984) are taken from Holy Bible, New International Version®, NIV® Copyright ©1973, 1978, 1984 by Biblica, Inc.® Used by permission. All rights reserved worldwide.

Scripture quotations marked NKJV are taken from the New King James Version®. Copyright © 1982 by Thomas Nelson. Used by permission. All rights reserved.

Scripture quotations marked NLT are taken from the Holy Bible, New Living Translation, copyright © 1996, 2004, 2015 by Tyndale House Foundation. Used by permission of Tyndale House Publishers, Inc., Carol Stream, Illinois 60188. All rights reserved.

Words studies based on *Vines Expository Dictionary of Biblical Words* (Nashville TN: Thomas Nelson, 1985).

ISBN 978-1-63952-762-5 (DEV298)
        978-1-63952-820-2 (DEV302)

Printed in China.

29 28 27 26 25 24
10 9 8 7 6 5 4 3 2 1

365 DEVOTIONS

Ten Minutes
WITH GOD
— FOR WOMEN —

DEBBIE ALSDORF

Christian Art
PUBLISHERS

Dedicated to the ones who call me Grammy:
Easton, Jessa, Pierce, McCartney, Declan,
Jace, Jalen, Karis, Lennox, Jenson, Jayelle.

Dear Friend,

I am glad you picked up this devotional. These pages are written woman to woman. I don't write because I have the answers. I write knowing I desperately need Jesus. I pray that each of the 365 daily thoughts about life, learning, and Scripture will help draw you closer to Jesus, give you a daily starting point, and help you know you are not alone. From personal experience, I know that staying connected to Jesus each day changes my perspective and attitude—which changes everything. Though circumstances might be unpredictable, we can practice tethering ourselves to the one true God who never changes.

Each month has a focus. Let that be in the forefront of your mind as you walk through each day of the month—practicing new habits of thinking, believing, and living based on the Scriptures and focused theme of the month. The goal is to commit ten minutes each day to focus our hearts upward. After reading the devotional, reflect on what God might be saying to you personally. Stop to pray, and then carry the Scripture, the points to remember, and the prayer prompt into your day. Watch and see how God shows up and how He speaks to you, leading you, one day at a time.

We are busy women, and God invites us to meet with Him daily, ushering His presence into all that we do. Ten minutes with God will start a change in our lives, helping us develop habits of focusing on biblical truth, prayer, and daily application of God's Word.

Taking the ten-minute walk with you,
Debbie Alsdorf

January

LIVING LOVED

"Though our feelings come and go, [God's] love for us does not."[1]
C. S. Lewis

---

1 C. S. Lewis, *Mere Christianity* (New York: Macmillan, 1967), 118.

BEAUTIFUL IN HIS SIGHT

You are precious and honored in my sight...because I love you.
ISAIAH 43:4

Twirling and giggling in her new princess dress, her arms were outstretched with a "Ta-da!" At three, she was feeling beautiful—as if a fairy godmother touched her, creating the best and most beautiful version of her preschool self. Wrapping my arms around her pint-sized body, I spoke into her little ears, "you are beautiful," and with that, it was settled. For the next hour she walked out that beauty—a little sweeter and with a smile big enough to express her happiness at being declared beautiful by her Grammy.

It wasn't the sparkling tiara, wobbly plastic princess heels, or blue tulle satin dress that made her beautiful. It was simply her—a little girl formed miraculously by God. My whisper wasn't "you are beautiful in that dress," but simply, "You are beautiful."

God whispers the same to us grown-up girls. He calls us by name and calls out our beauty. He reminds us that our beauty is not dependent on size, fashion, or age. He knows that we were once little girls who secretly hoped they were beautiful—without props or the validation of good looks or behavior. He declares us beautiful just because—wobbly, worn-out heels and all. We are beauties created by God, and we are His—treasured and greatly loved.

Today I will remember:
- I am precious to God.
- He calls me by name and calls out beauty in me.
- He honors me with His love.

Lord, from the very beginning, You have held me
and called me Your own. Now You whisper Your love into this
grown-up girl's ears. Knowing I am important to You fills me with joy.

HE DELIGHTS IN ME

He rescued me because he delighted in me.

PSALM 18:19

This is a psalm of praise, written after the Lord rescued David from his enemies. Do you have enemies or situations that are too much to handle? Have you ever felt hemmed in or stuck in your circumstances? I have felt stuck and overwhelmed on many occasions, and God has faithfully pulled me out of every pit that I've found myself in.

God wants to be our support. When we call to Him, He hears us. When our lives are entangled with difficulties, He shields us. When we are backed into a corner, He moves on our behalf to bring us to a spacious place of blessing. He doesn't do this because we've earned it, deserve it, or are good enough. He does all this because of who He is, not based on who we are.

Friend, He delights in you. He stands in every gap. Life is not perfect, but a loving God will draw you out of deep waters and troubles too big for your own strength. God is your rock; you are secure in His strength. God is your shield; you are covered. God is your stronghold; you can trust in His grip on your life.

Today I will remember:
- God rescues me because He delights in me.
- When I call out for help, He hears and moves on my behalf.
- He is everything I will ever need.

Lord, You rescue me from the messes in life and cause me to
stand firm even when my feet are tired and life is confusing.
May I always look first to You with every need.

DON'T FORGET HIS LOVE

Be careful that you do not forget the Lord...
DEUTERONOMY 8:11

Do you ever walk into a room and forget why? How about losing your car in a parking lot? I sure do. It's comforting to know that most people occasionally forget things. There are apps to help us find our car, our phone, and even our friends. But what about when we forget the Lord and His goodness? What happens then? According to Scripture, when we forget the Lord, our hearts become proud, self-focused, and self-sufficient.[2] Not a good look, considering God opposes the proud but gives grace to the humble.[3]

In light of the possibility of developing a proud heart, it's probably best to make a practice of remembering God every day. This happens as you remind yourself of who Scripture declares God to be. Look for creative ways to keep the truth of God's goodness in front of you.

Psalm 103:2-5 breaks it down by giving a list of the things we are told not to forget: "Praise the Lord, my soul, and forget not all his benefits..." He forgives all your sins. He heals all your diseases. He redeems your life from the pit. He crowns you with love and compassion. He satisfies your desires with good things. He renews your youth.

Most girls grow up playing with princess crowns. But, friend, the crown you are given is not make-believe. God crowns you with His love and with His compassion. A double crown. There is nothing better.

Today I will remember:
- I am crowned with love.
- I am being renewed daily.
- He satisfies me with good things.

Lord, You are healing, redemption, provision, and all things good.
Even when things don't go as I had hoped, You are still good.

---

2 See Deuteronomy 8:14.
3 See James 4:6.

HE KNOWS MY NAME

I have summoned you by name; you are mine.

ISAIAH 43:1

I can remember a face but often forget a name. When someone remembers my name, it touches me and makes me feel connected. God calls us by name. He takes it a step further to tell us we belong—in this place—to Him—for His purpose. And as those belonging to Him, He promises to hold us through the details of our circumstances. If you feel alone in this world, alone in a crowd, or alone in your problems, you're not. Though we might feel alone sometimes, God is near and knows us completely.

My friend, God is writing your story and my story. He is leading us along paths that will take us where He has planned for us to be. Our story is not our own, and our life belongs to a God who loves us, watches over us, and guides us through life. This is a God we can trust with all the details—the fears, insecurities, uncertainties, hurts, and the hope of healing from every hard place in the path. This is a God who says, *you are mine*. Let that sink in today.

Today I will remember:
- I am God's beloved child.
- I am called by name, for His purposes.
- I am never alone in this world and belong because I am part of His plan.

Lord, may I walk loved, known, and seen today.
May I walk in my true identity today—Your daughter.
In a sea of faces, You know me, and my name is forever on Your lips.

HIS

For you are a people holy to the Lord your God.
The Lord your God has chosen you out of all the peoples on
the face of the earth to be his people, his treasured possession.

DEUTERONOMY 7:6

I never thought much about being chosen by God—being His. Even as a Christian, being His was not my core identity. Ministry, serving, motherhood, and being a good wife were what identified me. Then my life fell apart. After going through an unwanted divorce and a terrible season of depression, I came to know Jesus as the lover of my soul—and myself as His. Gone were the lights, the people, and the accolades. Gone were my dreams of happily ever after. My days were spent shuffling between shift work, single parenting, and a desperate desire to believe that Jesus still had hold of my life. He did and still does.

What defines you? The sweetest name you and I can ever embrace is being His. We are His treasured possession. We belong to the God of all power and might. We are not our own. It might sound heavy but, friend, this identity lightens every load. Knowing the love of our burden bearer is the greatest thing imaginable. We come to believe that we have value because we know we are His treasure and His woman.

Today I will remember:
- God calls me holy, a treasure, and His.
- My core identity is that I am a woman who belongs to God.
- Because I am His, He will lead me and guide me through a life that is often hard.

Lord, in a world of uncertainty I can be certain that two
things will never change: my value and Your love for me.

WHO HE IS AND HOW HE LOVES

The Lord is compassionate and gracious,
slow to anger, abounding in love.
PSALM 103:8

Knowing the nature of God is important for your faith walk. Psalm 103 will help you remember who He is and how He loves. Then when life hits hard, you will know where God stands concerning you. Here in this one verse are four powerful truths for us to remember: God is compassionate, God is gracious, God is slow to anger, and God is abounding in love toward us.

It's often easy to believe these things for others, but harder to hold them close to our own heart. We need to know that God is compassionate toward us because then we will exhale all the shame of our imperfections and shortcomings. Compassionate means He is concerned for the suffering and misfortunes we go through—even if we are going through something we caused. That is where slow to anger and abounding in love come in. We may blow it, but He never blows us off. His love goes beyond us, and He carries a commitment to love us throughout our life. What a relief to know that this is the nature of God. People may not be these things toward us, but God is. In the end, it is the love of God that makes all the difference. It's important to remember who He is and how He loves us.

Today I will remember:
- God is compassionate—tender and caring.
- God is gracious—forgiving my failures and faults.
- God is abounding in love—committed to me until my very last breath.

Lord, please silence all other voices and make Your voice
the soundtrack of my life and the music of my soul.

CARRIED BY GOD

I have upheld [you] since your birth, and have carried [you]
since you were born. Even to your old age and gray hairs I am he,
I am he who will sustain you. I have made you and I will carry you.

ISAIAH 46:3-4

As women, there are a multitude of things we can do to disguise our age. I get my roots painted brown every few weeks, but God knows the silver threads underneath and promises to sustain me as I grow older. Age is not important to Him, as He promises to carry us from beginning to end. This brings such peace and is life-giving.

To know that God holds us since conception and still carries us to old age brings a relief that I cannot adequately express. The fact that God reminds us that He made us is a beautiful thing. Especially in our culture of self-made everything, it's easy to let the foundational and beautiful truth of being created by God and for God slip from our thoughts. And yet, it is because He made us that He is so deeply committed to us.

Sustain and carry are important here as well. To sustain is to give support, nourish, handle, tolerate, and abide. To carry is to move while supporting, to hold the weight or burden of. I love that God says He carries us—holding the weight of our problems and the challenges of our lives. Whatever burden you are holding today, know that God is holding you. There is so much beauty here. Let it sink in.

Today I will remember:
• God made me—exactly as I am—for His plan.
• God carries me from conception to last breath.
• God sustains me by nourishing me and supporting me in this life.

Lord, as I let this truth of Your care wash over my heart today,
I am humbled by Your involvement in my life.
Thank You for always being with me, from start to finish.

SEEN AND KNOWN

*You have searched me, Lord, and you know me. You know when I sit
and when I rise; you perceive my thoughts from afar. You discern my
going out and my lying down; you are familiar with all my ways.*

PSALM 139:1-3

During a season of depression, it occurred to me that I was getting tired of my own sad, bad story. Each time I repeated it, I felt another stab to the heart. One afternoon as I was reading Psalm 139, a new thought occurred to me. God knew my story. He knew details that I didn't even understand. He had been with me every step of the way. And not only did He know the current hurt that brought me face-to-face with a counselor, He knew my full story and the wounding that ultimately made me act and react the way I do. I sighed with relief that afternoon and began to trust the process of healing with a God who understands me completely.

The word familiar means one who is well acquainted with something. I found hope in connecting that truth to the dots in my life. God was well acquainted with everything about me, all the things that trigger me, my childhood trauma, and my adult hurts and hang-ups. He has been with me through it all.

Maybe you need to know that you are seen and known today. Even if people have hurt or disappointed you, God sees, and He knows. And because He completely gets you, He knows exactly what you need to move forward.

Today I will remember:
• God knows me.
• He knows my thoughts, even the thoughts that drift in and out.
• He is intimately acquainted with me and my history.

*Father, You know everything about me—the stories, the hurts,
and the happy times. You know what triggers me and what makes
me tick. Because You know me fully, I now trust You completely.*

THE MIRACLE OF LIFE

For in him we live and move and have our being.
ACTS 17:28

Pictures of new babies fill my social media feed. I catch myself smiling at each one. *Such a miracle*, I think to myself. In those first days and months after birth, we revel in the miracle of life represented in these tiny new humans, but over time we don't think about it as often—they are cute and we love them, but miracle?

Our life is a miracle. Yes, our less-than-perfect, sometimes broken-down life, is a miracle! I didn't raise my children reminding them they were a miracle. I applauded what they did, helped them advance to the next step in their development, and before long they were grown. Growing up in a culture of self-made people it's easy to leave the most important thing out of the equation—we were created by God and for God. It's because of Him that we exist, living with the breath He supplies.

Why is this important? Because when this biblical view becomes our reality we will be able to live with purpose until our very last breath. A biblical view of the miracle of our one and only life will push us past insecurities about being good enough and all the other nonsense we grow up battling. Pure and simple, we are created by God, and we continue living because He truly is the breath and life within us.

Today I will remember:
- God created me, and I live because it is His plan for me to be here.
- I move about because God has given me the ability to do so.
- My very being is wrapped up in being a miracle of God's creation.

Lord, may I live fully aware of the miracle of life—mine and others.

HE CROWNS ME

*Praise the Lord...who redeems your life from
the pit and crowns you with love and compassion.*
PSALM 103:2, 4

Excited to be crowned homecoming queen, I couldn't wait to show my mom the sparkling tiara. The next morning, I ran into the room where my mom was having her coffee, twirling in excitement. I held out the crown and exclaimed, "Look, Mom, I'm the Queen!"

She put her cup down and looked at me and said, "They must have miscounted the votes." I knew then that I would never be enough. My mother, if given the chance, would not have voted for me.

I became chronically critical of myself. It was a dark time. But what seemed like the worst thing was actually a shift in my life that made me curious about God. Did He like me? Was He aware that I was crowned under those Friday night lights? Slowly I became interested in knowing those answers. I wanted to become a Christian and know this God who made me. I discovered He does know every part of me—and He loves me.

Friend, do you ever wonder if you are enough? This verse assures us that He places His very own crown on our heads, a crown of love and mercy. This crown is more than a popularity crown—it's a crown hard won through His death in our place. We are His, we are enough, and we are loved. Wear the crown and live your best life because of Him!

Today I will remember:
• He redeems me from dark and brings light to my path.
• He crowns me with a victory crown.
• His crown is one of love and mercy, compassion and forgiveness.

*Lord, some days I live in the "not enough" space, forgetting all
You have done and the things You promised. You crown me with love.
May I wear it daily and never forget that You live in me by Your Spirit.*

HE HOLDS ME

In peace I will lie down and sleep,
for you alone, Lord, make me dwell in safety.
PSALM 4:8

I remember the night well. I was alone in our big house, hearing every noise and filled with fear. I knew I had lived too long like this. God offered me peace; it was up to me to receive it.

Since I was young, darkness and fear crept into my thoughts. I lived my entire childhood with unreasonable fears that I never outgrew. I struggled with feelings of not being safe, even in my own home—the opposite of peace. That night, in exhausted desperation, I exhaled the fear and prayed this verse out loud. Then I started doing it every single night. It was a declaration of trust, even when my heart felt afraid.

In this crazy world there are many things that can cause fear. It's no wonder we need to learn to dwell in the promise of being safe in Him. Praying a verse and declaring its truth over us is a powerful way to overcome fears and other limiting beliefs that hold us captive and keep us living afraid and small.

Today I will remember:
- Declaring and agreeing with the truth of God watching over me is powerful.
- The Lord alone is my safety, my peace, and my comfort.
- God is not upset with me for my fears—He just wants to give me His peace.

Father, I come to You with all my fears, thanking You that You are
my safety. May I dwell in peace because You are with me always.

IMPERFECT AND LOVED

But God demonstrates his own love for us in this:
While we were still sinners, Christ died for us.
ROMANS 5:8

Growing up a not-good-enough girl resulted in me doing anything to be popular. Looking for love led me down some wrong roads. I was simply missing the mark and living apart from God. Living for self was my survival mode, and though we went to church, we never talked about God. I hadn't a clue how to live for God. The truth is, I probably felt not-good-enough for Him, too.

This wrong thinking can keep us from drawing close to the God who loves us— the imperfect us. In His love we can learn to live a different kind of life. It's a simpler path, and the enemy will try to keep us from entering in because He is a thief, a liar, and our accuser. He wants to steal good from us, and Jesus came to be good for us and in us.

Embracing God's love enables us to walk away from insecurity. We can rest. Some of the hardest things I have walked through turned out to be holy halls of transformation as His love met me in the depth of disappointment and heartache. His love is ever reaching for us—the imperfect, sin-bent people that He died for and will forever love.

Today I will remember:
- All of us miss the mark and are by nature bent toward sin.
- Jesus died for me, covering my sin and all my brokenness.
- He is not looking for perfection, only for my honest surrender.

Lord, thank You for the way You pull us from the dark hole of
a dead-end life. May I relinquish myself to You, one day at a time.

BRINGING BEAUTY TO LIFE AGAIN

I have loved you with an everlasting love; I have drawn you with unfailing kindness. I will build you up again, and you...will be rebuilt.

JEREMIAH 31:3-4

The day I heard the words "I have never loved you" confirmed my deepest belief about myself—I was not lovable. Try as I might, nothing would be enough. My life crumbled with those words, and I never thought I could come back from the trauma of that time. With nothing solid to stand on, I was living for the love of people— good people and good things. Rather than being built up, I was broken down. I knew Jesus and was a Christian during those days—I was even a pastor's wife—but I was still chasing love from people and a good outward performance. It's all I knew. Now, with a divorce looming, everything I ever dreamed of or hoped for was gone.

Then Jesus called me to His side—to a place where He could rebuild all that was devastated and repair the broken and faulty messages that had filled me since I was young. It was time for renewal, for a life where I could live like a loved woman even if people didn't love me much. Could He be calling you to His side today too? Perhaps you know Him but never learned to live in the truth of His love. It's time to get off the spinning wheel and run straight into His arms. He is the God who loves you and will rebuild every fractured part of you.

Today I will remember:
- God's love is everlasting and unconditional.
- His love calls to us daily.
- We may be broken by life and relationships, but in His love He rebuilds us.

Lord, it took me a while to embrace the reality of love,
but once I started, it began changing me. I don't want to forget;
remind me daily and give me the grace to stand in love.

LEAN INTO LOVE

And so we know and rely on the love God has for us. God is love.
1 JOHN 4:16

Years ago, I worked for a national weight-loss organization. I taught clients about calories, carbohydrates, and weight-loss strategies. But during that time, I gained twenty pounds! Obviously, you have to practice what you know. This is true in our spiritual walks too. Some of us have lots of head information but very little life transformation.

We can google anything, including God's love, and learn the facts. But it's the second part of this verse that turns the key and changes lives. Often we think of knowing as just head knowledge, but the word *rely* reminds us that we should be leaning into what we know with all of our being.

We can memorize the words, but it's when our hearts sing the song that things change—that is how we lose our insecurities, fears, and all that keeps us stuck in our heads. We need to pour God's love into the learning center of our minds so it can make its way into our hearts because it's not natural to believe in a love you can't see or touch. We learn the truth one verse of love at a time. As we do so, the truth replaces the lies we believe about ourselves one lie at a time. God is love—this is who He is and the most important truth we can ever learn to lean into.

Today I will remember:
- To know the facts about God's love is head knowledge—an important step.
- To rely on God's love is the heart leaning into what the head knows.
- When we rely on the truth, our life changes.

Lord, teach me the steps of relying on truth and
move my heart to the melody of Your love for me.

THE LITMUS TEST

There is no fear in love. But perfect love drives out fear, because fear has to do with punishment. The one who fears is not made perfect in love.
1 JOHN 4:18

I grew up with unreasonable fears. I would not take a shower and lived on alert even though I hadn't seen the thriller movie of the day, Psycho. Had I seen that movie I'd probably still be locked up! After years of living in secret fear but claiming deep spirituality, this verse began teaching me something important: I am not living maturely in Christ's love when I am living in fear.

When I began speaking to women about God's love, they were not impressed. They said they already knew God loved them and wanted messages on something deeper. Being convinced that love was the deepest truth, I'd ask if any of them dealt with insecurity, fears, or the feelings of being unseen or not enough. Hands went up.

Friend, fear is the litmus test for us to evaluate if we are leaning into God's love at any given moment. When I am afraid, I am not living in the truth of His love for me. I am still loved completely by God, but on my side of things, I am forgetting that His love covers me and will carry me. I still forget, get caught up in unreasonable fear, and have to turn back again. He keeps loving me to freedom.

Today I will remember:
• When I am living in fear, I may have forgotten God's love.
• God's love drives out fear as I believe the truth of His love.
• Fear torments and punishes; God's love calms and strengthens.

Lord, give me signals when fear is creeping in to
oppose the truth of Your love. May I live in Your love
and be strengthened by the truth that You are for me.

TRUE IDENTITY

*See what great love the Father has lavished on us, that we
should be called children of God! And that is what we are!*

1 JOHN 3:1

God has lavished His love on us. *Lavished,* according to the dictionary, is an extravagant display of something—it is linked to the word *shower.* Think of that. God showers us with His love even when we don't see it or feel the touch of it. This extravagant covering, when realized through faith, can calm us, center us, and build confidence in us.

We know who our parents are—for better or worse. But we don't often think of God being our parent. As simple as it sounds, we are His children. Do you live as a daughter of God? We need to challenge ourselves to not overlook this basic yet profound truth. When we live as one who is loved, we live differently. Life is no longer a set of unfortunate circumstances, but instead a journey with the Father. When living loved, we have a changed viewpoint. Our focus is the bigger picture of God's unseen plan.

Think of what it means to be a child—dependent, trusting, longing for acceptance. Ask God to help you with any area of unbelief regarding your true identity as His. Set a timer on your phone and thank God every few hours that you are His child and God covers you with loving kindness.

Today I will remember:
• God showers me with His love every day.
• When I don't see or feel love, it is still operating in my life.
• I am God's child—loved, protected, and created with purpose.

*Lord, help my heart to always know
who I am and how I am led and loved.*

SCARS

But you, the Lord God, are kind and merciful.
You don't easily get angry, and your love can always be trusted.
PSALM 86:15, CEV

My four-year-old grandson was swimming with me when he noticed a large scar that wrapped around my leg. "Grammy, what is that?"

Feeling like having some fun, I answered, "Oh, that was when Grammy was a shark wrestler."

His eyes lit up. "A shark wrestler?" I soon realized he believed me—he went to school and told his teacher about it. The story got bigger, and soon I was a famous shark wrestler. I went along with it, buying him shark T-shirts and things. But eventually he caught on and realized the scar was something else. "What really happened, Grammy?"

It was then that I told him about a very bad car accident I had in my twenties. Talking about it reminds me of God's mercy. I was hurt badly and could have lost my leg, but God spared me. I thought about the drunk driver who parked in the fast lane on a dark freeway with no lights. We hit him. Then he drove down the freeway and did it again, causing a multiple car pileup.

I was bleeding badly, and my husband was trying to wave down help. The ambulances almost missed us because they didn't know there was another car involved. Had they not seen our car, I may have bled to death or lost my leg. As it was, the doctor made no promises. I left the hospital with drain tubes and too many stitches to count. Now I have a big enough scar to pass for a famous shark wrestler—though I'm pretty sure there's no such thing.

Today I will remember:
- God moves in our lives with compassion.
- He is patient and faithful.
- His love and mercy follow us and watch over us.

Lord, I remember Your kindness and praise
You for loving me faithfully and compassionately.

—❧ ❖ ❧—

HE PAID THE PRICE

For God so loved the world that he gave his one and only Son,
that whoever believes in him shall not perish but have eternal life.

JOHN 3:16

When I was a child, we went to Mass on Sundays but never talked about God on ordinary days. I remember hearing that God loved me, but love was conditional and seemed hard to attain. Besides that, God loved the whole world, and in light of my little life, that seemed out of reach.

Later in life this verse began to meet me where I was. God just didn't just love the entire world, He loved me personally. I was part of His plan and important to Him. Out of love, He wanted me to be with Him for eternity. Things started shifting. God didn't change, but I did. My eyes were opened. God sacrificed His only Son to bring me into a relationship with Himself through the saving grace of Jesus. This is not just true for me, but for you too.

My love relationship with Jesus began 50 years ago when I received Him and committed my life to Him. There were no hoops to jump through, just a simple prayer—Jesus, I want to know You, please forgive me for the years I have not believed in You and teach me Your ways. I didn't know what I was doing, I just began to understand that God loving the whole world included me.

Today I will remember:
- God is love.
- God loves me and wants to spend eternity with me.
- God isn't interested in the rules I follow, but that I believe in Him.

Lord, thank You for loving me and drawing me out of religion
and into relationship. May I live to tell the good news to others—
that You love us all, big and small, rich and poor, young and old.

LOVE AND DISCIPLINE

The Lord disciplines the one he loves,
and he chastens everyone he accepts as his son.
HEBREWS 12:6

How many of you parents have used the "count to three" method? Is there some magic in three? I'm not sure, but I do know that when someone loves you, they care enough to discipline you. As a parent, I found no joy in disciplining my children but even less joy in the idea of allowing them to become monsters because I was not willing to hold them to certain standards. Have you ever sensed the "count to three" coming at you from God? I know that I have. God doesn't discipline us because He's mean, but because He loves.

Love is not just warm feeling stuff. God's love for us goes much deeper. He calls us His children, and as such He is responsibly taking care of us in each season of life. Some of those seasons might be pruning seasons as He cuts away things that keep us from being all He's created us to be. Jesus said, "every branch that does bear fruit he prunes so that it will be even more fruitful."[4] Let that sink in. Imagine that you are growing and bearing fruit. Life is good. Then the good gardener comes and snips at the branch. It hurts, but it's necessary. Why? Because only when pruned will you bear more fruit. Only when disciplined will you be your best.

Today I will remember:
• God is committed to seeing me become the best version of me.
• God loves me through disciplining me; it hurts but brings holy results.
• Every child of God is chastened when needed, to bear more fruit.

Lord, thank You that the hard discipline stuff is necessary and something that
I can endure for a season—because I am Yours and You love me as a daughter.

---

4 John 15:2.

LOVE CHASES AFTER ME

Surely your goodness and love will follow me all the days
of my life, and I will dwell in the hose of the Lord forever.

PSALM 23:6

"Mom, I want you!" In the rearview mirror I saw the heartbreaking image of my youngest running after my car because he didn't want me to leave. Sometimes that's how it is with us and God. His love is chasing us down. He is calling after us, saying, "I want you and I want to bless you!" We put the pedal to the metal and keep going our way.

Why is it so hard for us to be convinced of the goodness of God? Life can be hard, but there is plenty of good waiting for us. I have gone through disappointing things in life. But if I had to look back upon the greatest joy it would be that God has always been faithful. I can now look at each day as it comes, with the challenges before me, and exclaim that for sure there are three things I can count on—goodness follows me, love chases me, and I will be with God forever when this life is done.

The New Living Translation says, "My cup overflows with blessings. Surely your goodness and unfailing love will pursue me all the days of my life." And The Message says, "Your beauty and love chase after me every day of my life."

Today I will remember:
- The beauty of God's goodness is chasing me.
- The love of God is running after me.
- All the days of my life, I am pursued by a loving God.

Lord, today I thank You for the indescribable gift of
Your love. Help me to live loved in all the daily things.

THE OFFERING OF MYSELF

I urge you...sisters, in view of God's mercy, to offer your bodies as a living sacrifice, holy and pleasing to God—this is your true and proper worship.

ROMANS 12:1

Living loved is more than internalizing truth. Living loved leads us to act like we are loved by the choices we make. Here Paul exhorted the early church to remember God's mercy and live differently as a result. In view of God's love, he urged them to live out God's love by offering their bodies as living sacrifices. These people were accustomed to animal sacrifice, but now Paul held out the new idea of them being a living sacrifice.

To *offer* simply means to present or yield. Think of this practically. We are being called to present our bodies to God. They are His because all that we are and have is His. Yet we treat our bodies as if they were ours and excluded from our spiritual journey. How we treat our bodies is a direct reflection of whether we are living loved. This is not a body shaming or diet culture statement, it is about yielding who we are to God, all the way down to how we care for our health. Maybe today is the day that God is urging you to present all of yourself to Him—not just your works, but even what you eat, how you sleep, how you move, how you hold stress—all things should be surrendered to Him.

Today I will remember:
- My viewpoint must be lined up with God's love for me.
- I am to present myself—all of me—to God.
- This sacrifice might cost me, but it pleases God.

Lord, I want to align with Your will for me in yielding every part of myself to You. Teach me what that means for me personally.

BE CHANGED

Do not conform to the pattern of this world,
but be transformed by the renewing of your mind.

ROMANS 12:2

California newspaper article stated that an American teen will process over 3000 advertisements in a single day, and 10 million by the time they reach 18.[5] Can you imagine how much we have processed by 30, 40, or 50? Advertising has always sold anxiety. We grow up thinking we are not thin enough, not pretty enough, not smart enough, not wealthy enough. Nothing is enough.

The patterns start young. The rules for acceptance are unspoken chains. Our minds have much to do with whether we will be able to live loved or not. If we do not have a strong foundation, mentally and emotionally, of God's love for us, we will be looking for love in all the wrong places, trying to fill our thirst with acceptance.

The cultural norm goes against the truth of Scripture. Jesus wasn't of this world, so why do we try to fit into this world? To be transformed means to be fully changed, and that happens when we internalize one truth at a time. We don't have to memorize the whole Bible to align our mind with Christ. Start with one verse. Read it, pray it, recite it—commit to whatever it takes to remember it. This will change your life and help you live loved because you will begin to realize more and more that the story of the Bible is centered around God's love for His people.

Today I will remember:
- The world has a pattern that is opposite of God's will for me.
- I am invited into real-life transformation through yielding to Jesus.
- My life changes as I lean into the truth and change my perspective.

Lord, I want to have a mind aligned with Your thoughts about Your love
for me. I want to be transformed by truth. Lead me in that direction.

---

5 Susan Young, "Trends," *ANG Newspaper: Inside Bay Area,* February 27, 2001.

HE COMPLETES ME

You also are complete through your union with Christ.
COLOSSIANS 2:10, NLT

From the time we were little girls, we learned the prince is looking for the one whose dainty foot fits the glass slipper. If the sparkly slipper fits, we will be made whole. But, though it worked in fairy tales, in real life you are complete without another person. At the moment of salvation, you received the indwelling Christ. It is a Savior, not a prince, who completes you. When you learn to see yourself through God's eyes, you realize that one is a whole number. You are complete in Him. You are loved by Him. He lives in you daily and works through you even when you are unaware of it.

Our belief system starts forming in our earliest days and continues forming throughout life. We need our minds renewed daily so that we can keep turning away from old thought patterns, self-rejection, and the ever-changing principles of the world we live in. But for some reason we stay stuck in old beliefs that we are not enough or our life is not enough without that one missing piece. Friend, lets agree that in Christ we are not waiting on missing pieces for fulfillment, but we are enough today for His purposes.

Today I will remember:
- I am a child of God through my union with Christ.
- He completes me—not a spouse, friend, or prince on a white horse.
- I am deeply loved and can learn to live out of that love rather than insecurity.

Lord, teach me to live out of the secure
place of being loved and connected to You.

ADOPTED INTO GOD'S FAMILY

He predestined us for adoption to sonship through
Jesus Christ, in accordance with his pleasure and will.
EPHESIANS 1:5

The morning was filled with joy as our family gathered at the courthouse. Two years of waiting culminated in this moment. Just a couple years earlier, our kids picked up a baby boy from the hospital, and though it began as fostering, they knew he was the answer to their prayers. They couldn't love him more, and as we all gathered with laughter and tears, he officially became our grandson and irrevocably our family.

Adoption is a beautiful thing. The adopted child is wanted and has been loved long before any documents are signed and sealed. This is true for us, too. We have been adopted by God. As daughters, He loved us while we were forming in our mother's womb and through every day of our story since. When we were unaware of His presence, He was caring for us. He couldn't love us more. It's important to remember that we are officially and irrevocably His.

Being His child is not dependent on your goodness—it all rests on His love. Just like no one can remove our grandson from the family, no one can remove you from the family of God. You might stray or walk away, but because you are His, He will find you and lead you home. It pleases Him to love you and He delights for you to live in that love.

Today I will remember:
- It was always God's plan that I would be His.
- I have been adopted as His much-loved daughter.
- I may have parents who love me, but my heavenly Father loves me most.

Lord, thank You that it pleases You to love me as Your own.
I want to live in the assurance of Your love daily.

HE IS ALWAYS WORKING IN MY LIFE

*In him we were also chosen, having been predestined
according to the plan of him who works out
everything in conformity with the purpose of his will.*
EPHESIANS 1:11

I never got picked for the teams. I was not athletic, so by default I was the last to be chosen. In those younger days, it was devastating when teams were forming and I was left behind. And, though I have been picked for many things over my lifetime, I still know the deep longing to be chosen. Since I was a little girl, my heart has longed to be special and important.

Enter the truth of God's Word—we have been chosen. We don't have to hold special abilities for God to pick us. We may think we chose Him, but He worked in our hearts, and that led to us saying yes to the adventure of knowing Him. Part of living loved is to stand strong in the reality that our lives are not a mistake. You and I were chosen for the team—we were His pick! And He is always at work in those whom He has picked. He knows where we will be positioned and how the story will go. We show up and follow the coach. He leads us play by play because He is for us and loves having us as one of His own.

Today I will remember:
- I have been chosen by God to be His.
- My life has purpose because it's part of His plan.
- I can live loved because I was His pick, and He knows exactly where to position me.

*Lord, may I live as one loved, chosen,
and handpicked by You—even if no one else picks me.*

A NEW HEART

I will give you a new heart and put a new spirit in you.
EZEKIEL 36:26

I grew up in the beach cities of Los Angeles, where appearances are everything. If you need a nip or a tuck, the options abound. Many people are living with hearts that have been broken by life—rejection, unfaithfulness, and shattered dreams. There is no heart procedure that takes away the pain of a heart darkened by hurt. Hurting hearts become hard. But God came to change all that.

People will hurt us, but we aren't left alone to deal with our pain. This verse goes on to say, "I will remove from you your heart of stone and give you a heart of flesh." What a contrast—a heart of stone is a heart that is cold, dead, and no longer beating to a proper rhythm. A heart of flesh is warm, alive, and in sync. God doesn't gloss over our stony heart—He says He will remove it. He is not offering to patch you up, He is offering spiritual heart surgery. If that's not enough, He replaces it with something better.

I have experienced the need for a new heart and been in such a hopeless state I didn't think such a transaction would be possible. But it was, and though my heart was hard, it became warm and pliable again because Jesus met me at the crossroads of love and hate, and gave me Himself—His heart.

Today I will remember:
- God offers me a new heart.
- God removes the dead stuff so I can be healthy enough to live and love again.
- To live loved is to live from this new heart that God so generously offers.

Lord, may my heart remain alive in
You and beat to the new rhythm of grace.

NEW LOVE EVERY MORNING

Because of the Lord's great love we are not consumed, for his compassions never fail. They are new every morning; great is your faithfulness.
LAMENTATIONS 3:22-23

Just when you think God is disappointed in you, He is actually filled with compassion for the things you struggle with. He sees the anxiety, frustration, and fears. Though we often want to give up on ourselves, God never gives up on us. He works patiently and is not expecting perfection.

Nature mimics this patience and care too. Some plants seem to have no fruitfulness or forward movement for a very long time. We care for the plant—watering, weeding, fertilizing—but not much seems to happen. In the same way, as God is faithfully tending to our souls—watering, weeding, and fertilizing—something is happening that we can't yet see.

In our lives there are many days where nothing fruitful happens. Yet God's love and faithfulness never ceases. Despite our faithlessness, He remains faithful. His compassion is far-reaching, and He will never fail us. Created in God's image and re-created in Christ, we are empowered by the Holy Spirit to live fruitful lives in this world of chaos, confusion, and brokenness. Nothing is ever perfect except Jesus. And His perfect love is a blanket over us, giving us all that we need to live today.

Today I will remember:
- The Lord's love for me is great.
- God's love holds me together because He is faithful.
- His compassions are new every single morning.

Lord, may I live in Your love that is new every morning. Thank You for Your faithfulness.

I SET MY HOPE ON HIS LOVE

*Because the Sovereign Lord helps me, I will not be disgraced. Therefore
have I set my face like flint, and I know I will not be put to shame.*

ISAIAH 50:7

Her name was Jinny, and she was one of my early spiritual mentors. She was both strong and fragile, and her reliance on God moved me. During one particularly hard emotional season in her life, she held tightly to God's sovereignty and this verse. She was using all her energy to set her face like flint—meaning she was not going to allow her circumstances or emotions to move her. She was steadfast in one thing and one thing only—the knowledge that her Sovereign Lord loved her deeply and would not fail her.

We never know how God will use someone in our life, but let's be clear: life is filled with divine appointments and God-sized connections. My friendship with Jinny was both of those things. Her fierce determination challenged my young faith. She was already a wealthy woman, so she didn't need things. And she was a true beauty, so she wasn't focused on being more beautiful. The beat of her heart was a determination to know Jesus more. And her life changed mine forever.

Whom might you encourage by your life with Christ and your example of living loved today?

Today I will remember:
- God is sovereign, and He always helps me.
- I will not be disgraced or put to shame, because God is for me.
- I will set my face and faith forward, unmoved by problems.

*Lord, may I stand in your love for me as I set
my face upward and move my feet forward.*

INVITED INTO GOD'S LOVE

Love...always protects, always trusts,
always hopes, always perseveres. Love never fails.
1 CORINTHIANS 13:6-8

Embracing God's love for me was hard because I was stuck in perfection and performance. This created a problem because it became about me earning love rather than receiving it unconditionally from God. I was set me on an endless cycle of trying harder—falling flat—then trying again. I felt like I was never enough.

The word for love in this passage is the word *agape*, which is the noun that identifies who God is. The word for love in this passage is the word *agape* which identifies both what love is and who God is. *Agape* love is an expression of God's own character. This passage is not a to-do list but an invitation to experience and extend the love of God.

Love is patient, love is kind. It does not envy, it does not boast,
it is not proud. It does not dishonor others, it is not
self-seeking, it is not easily angered, it keeps no record of wrongs.
Love does not delight in evil but rejoices with the truth.
1 Corinthians 13:4-7

To live loved is to step into the promise of who God is. We can read the passage as: God's love for me is patient, kind, humble, keeps no record of wrongs—and on through the verse.

It is not dependent on us being good, checking off our list, or behaving perfectly. God is inviting us into a love story. You and I can live better lives by believing His love and walking in it.

Today I will remember:
• God's love is inviting me into a relationship of security.
• God is patient and kind toward me.
• God always acts out of love toward me—it is who He is.

Lord, may Your love be my daily reality, and may I be someone who dares
to live in the truth of being loved despite my weaknesses and failings.

BECAUSE OF WHO HE IS

God is love.

1 JOHN 4:8

I led an Elvis impersonator to Jesus. It's a whole story, but let me just say he had been searching through religions, nature, and occult practices to find God. Through a series of events he prayed with me in Vegas to know Jesus personally.

Like my Elvis friend, we might try to understand God through the people He made or the nature around us. On a good day, these make God look good. But when people fail us or tornadoes twist the life out of a city, not so much. To have a relationship with someone requires knowing them in experience, not just through secondhand stories of others.

It's important that we understand who God is as Creator and who He is by character. This three-word statement in Scripture is not telling us what God is capable of doing—loving us. It is describing who He is. God is love. These words are to be imprinted on our hearts and kept in the forefront of our minds because God will not go against His character, and He always works out of His love for us. Even in hard times or when we don't fully understand, His character never changes. He is a God of unconditional love who invites us to live in His love today and every day.

Today I will remember:
- God is love—this is the character of who He is.
- God calls me into love—this is the relationship He invites me into.
- God hears my cries for help and cares—He can't go against who He is.

Lord, help me to remember that love is who You are.

TURNING BACK TO LOVE

Yet I hold this against you: You have forsaken the love you had at first.
REVELATION 2:4

Do you remember when your love story with Jesus began? I remember. Over time life got busy—marriage, full-time ministry, and then babies. My family and the ministry became the center of my world—a good center, but not a first-love-for-Jesus center. It looked like Jesus was first, but that's how it looked for the church of Ephesus too. They had good works. Good works don't make up for deep connection with Jesus.

Over time our lives can be filled with so much that our relationship with Jesus gets watered down to mediocre at best. When we find ourselves in that place, we need to remember that Jesus didn't move, we moved. We move through good things that keep us distracted from the God. You can be spiritual, lead ministries, do good things...and have left your first love.

"Keep yourselves in God's love as you wait for the mercy of our Lord Jesus Christ to bring you to eternal life."[6] We are to keep ourselves in the love of God every season of our lives. If Jesus feels long-distance today, turn back to Him. To live loved, we must keep ourselves walking in His love. It is a daily walk that isn't perfect but is connected to a God who will carry us through life—guiding our way and ultimately leading us home.

Today I will remember:
- I have been called, loved, and kept for Christ.[7]
- I am to stay connected to Christ each day.
- When I am spiritually lukewarm, I am to turn back to Him.

Father, it is so easy to put everything before You. Forgive
me for the things I put before You, and draw me close again.

---

6 Jude 1:21.
7 Jude 1:1.

February

LOVING OTHERS

"Go a little deeper with your love. Engage the people
you've avoided. Delight in how different they are.
Will they be hard to love? You bet. Do it anyway."
Bob Goff[8]

---

8 Bob Goff, *Live in Grace, Walk in Love* (Thomas Nelson: 2019), 141.

THE CHALLENGE OF LOVE

*"Love the Lord your God with all your heart and with all your soul
and with all your mind." This is the first and greatest commandment.
And the second is like it: "Love your neighbor as yourself."*

MATTHEW 22:37-39

Love is tricky. I could learn to live in God's love if I were tucked away in a cave. There in the peace of not having to deal with other people, I could come up with a great plan. There would be nothing to stop me from loving—no disappointments, no disagreements, and no conflict. Can you relate?

We have been created for relationship with God and one another. We often don't take this seriously, instead living like we have a menu of different options. We pick and choose whom to love, whom to forgive, and whom to reach out to. Our choices are often based on the past baggage we bring into our Christian walk. Unfortunately, even though we love God, our relationships and actions often don't line up with His will.

My personal mission statement is taken from these words of Jesus and Colossians 1:16. I have been created by God and for God to love God and love others. This is the filter everything must pass through. I am not perfect at this, but I do try to pay attention and live on mission. If nothing else, my mission statement has given me direction and peace.

Today I will remember:
• Jesus said the greatest commandment is to fully love Him.
• The second greatest commandment is to love others.
• I am created by God and for God to love God and love others.

*Lord, may I live on mission to love You and love others.
Remind me when I am straying off this one centered goal and focus.*

LIVING LOVED TO LOVE OTHERS

Love your neighbor as yourself.
MATTHEW 22:39

Penny was stuck in her relationships because she reasoned that Jesus said to "love others as yourself," and she didn't love herself. The truth is, coming from a background of shame and rejection, she didn't like herself. But Jesus came to give all of us a full life rather than one imprisoned in our own walls of insecurity or self-loathing.

Jesus wasn't saying to love others with our own store of love, but His. The Greek word for love used here, *agapao*, is the same word used to describe God's love for us. Jesus doesn't tell us to rely on the strength of our love, but on God's love.

We have never been asked to pour out of ourselves, but to receive the love of Jesus into ourselves, and then move about in the love of Jesus rather than depending on self-love. All of us have a natural instinct to protect ourselves and make sure we have what we need. Care about others in the same way. According to Jesus, we all can love others when we are first loving Him with all of ourselves—heart, soul, and mind.

How do you want people to treat you? Try that on them. Do you want to be forgiven when you make a mistake? Then forgive others. Would you like a helping hand when you are in need? Then help others. As cliché as it sounds, "What would Jesus do?" We know the answer—He would love because that is who He is.

Today I will remember:
- God has called me to walk in love.
- First, I receive His love daily into my own soul.
- Second, as a vessel of love, I freely pour His love out to others.

Jesus, flow through my life with Your love. May unconditional kindness be something that guides me. May humility cause me to rely on You and remember others.

REAFFIRM YOUR LOVE

You ought to forgive and comfort him, so that he will not be overwhelmed by excessive sorrow. I urge you, therefore, to reaffirm your love for him.
2 CORINTHIANS 2:7-8

We all wish we had no-hassle, drama-free, love-filled relationships. In some seasons this is our reality, but many times it's not. Life is filled with imperfect relationships. People hurt, disappoint, or even betray us. When this happens, walls can go up and our stubborn, hurting heart can keep others at a distance. Is this the best way?

While there are times when healthy boundaries are important, they are not meant to be walls but rather parameters that help us back into healthy relationships again. The goal is love. Biblical wisdom encourages us to consider the other person. Sadly, it is more common to make excuses, hold on to hurt, and repay those who hurt us with distance. Biblical wisdom also speaks to softening our hearts and laying down the hurt because our unkind actions might be the thing that pushes someone else into a place of complete discouragement.

Forgiving does not always mean reconciling. God allows some people to be out of our lives for a reason. But kindness requires that we love them as a human created by God—even if the relationship is no longer healthy. To know we could be used to alleviate discouragement by being kind is a powerful game changer.

Today I will remember:
- There is a time to forgive others.
- Comforting others is a sign of strength, not weakness.
- Reaffirming love is an important step in relationships that have been broken.

Lord, You know my heart, hurts, and hang-ups. I give You all three and lay the hurting part of myself at Your feet today. I want to hold on to anger and ugliness. Change me, Jesus, as I step out in faith to be kind even when I don't want to.

FAITH IT UNTIL YOU MAKE IT

Love must be sincere. Hate what is evil; cling to what is good.
Be devoted to one another in love. Honor one another above yourselves.

ROMANS 12:9-10

As Christian women, being unloving or unkind is not an option. Though we might be treated unkindly, we are still taught to honor others. We can do this even at a distance with a sincere compliment or a kind hello. It's not easy, but faith steps are rarely easy. We tend to think of faith steps about bigger things, but in the practical world of relationships we often go with the flow of our emotions. It takes faith to continue honoring others even if they aren't honoring us. This is going against the flow of our emotions and moving in the love of God's Spirit.

How we treat others is a reflection of who we are, not a behavioral report on them. It's hard when we feel we are putting on a fake front. But God has called us to higher things than being unkind toward others. Sometimes we "faith it"—not fake it—until we make it. We choose to walk by faith that it is God's will for us to hold on to the good in others because Jesus loves them fiercely. To do this we will have to put ourselves aside many times over. Walking in love by faith, not feelings, is a true sign of a Jesus-transformed life.

Today I will remember:
- How I treat others is a reflection of me, not them.
- It is evil to treat others badly, purposely hurting those God loves.
- I must put myself aside when my feelings are not aligned with love, faithing it—not faking it—until I make it.

Lord, it is hard to love because sometimes people are prickly
and unloving. May I trust You for the higher walk of faith
that includes putting my interests aside to live for Yours.

PUTTING DOWN THE STONES

Let any one of you who is without sin be the first to throw a stone at her.

JOHN 8:7

You might know the story. The Pharisees, who were the religious leaders of that day, brought a woman caught in adultery to Jesus to see what He would do. Jesus spoke directly to them. Instead of accusing the woman of her sin, He corrected those who were accusing her. He clearly pointed back at them, telling whoever was sinless to throw the first stone. None of them were without sin, and they knew it. Jesus knew it too. When it comes to Jesus, we are all on a level playing field—Scripture says we are all sinners.

Others might not see our sin, but God sees our hearts, minds, and attitudes. For me, an ugly attitude has to be wrestled to the ground when it pops up. And even then, I often still blow it and do something stupid or sinful that hurts others.

Though we know we aren't perfect, we still have a propensity for stone throwing, don't we? But what if we challenged ourselves the next time we were caught in the cycle of judging someone else? Instead of being negative, what if we turned our energies toward being kind and praying for them? What if we dropped the stone?

Today I will remember:
- We are all sinners in need of God's grace.
- There is no perfect person, only people who need Jesus.
- Jesus was not in favor of stone-throwing religious or judgmental people.

Father, help me to remember that Your love covers a multitude of sins in my own life. Make my heart toward others more in line with Yours.

GOSSIP HURTS

A gossip betrays a confidence, so avoid anyone who talks too much.
PROVERBS 20:19

Everyone dislikes a gossip, but most of us know how to gossip eloquently. Words about another may be hidden behind the veil of prayer and concern. The concern becomes conversation that goes on and on—revealing more than anyone should know, but we just can't stop.

I learned the art of gossip and girl talk on the playground. Girls huddle and talk about everything and anything. Mostly they talk about the other girls. No one stops us; it's the way girls roll. And thus begins the pattern of being loose with our lips and careless with the secrets of others. As we get older, many sweet relationships turn sour because "The mouths of fools are their undoing."[9]

Gossip is far from innocent; Proverbs 18:8 says it's like a tasty morsel that goes down to the innermost part of a person. Gossip doesn't just betray a confidence, it builds toxic waste in the heart of the person listening, while damaging the one delivering the goods. When we betray a confidence, we also betray our own heart.

Today I will remember:
• When I tell someone else's story, I am gossiping.
• When I guard my tongue, I am also guarding my heart and friendships.
• It is wise to avoid conversations that turn to gossip.

Lord, help me to pay attention to my words about others.
May I be wise with words and love others by being a safe friend.

---

9 Proverbs 18:7.

BE INTERESTED IN OTHERS

Value others above yourselves, not looking to your own
interests but each of you to the interests of the others.
PHILIPPIANS 2:3-4

I suggested a lunch spot, but my friend really wanted to try a different place. From the moment we walked into the shabby building, I had an attitude. I was frustrated, tempted to do the eye-roll thing, making it even more uncomfortable. Just as I was tempted to complain, the Holy Spirit stopped me in my tracks. Why was what I wanted more important? Why was my plan the better one? Why couldn't I go with the flow and just be happy we were getting together? Simply because far too often, without words, I place myself and my wants above what someone else wants. I hate to admit that, but maybe you can relate.

The call to regard others above ourselves comes on the heels of Paul speaking about humility in the verse before. And that is the bottom line, isn't it? Pride gets in the way of us walking the best life that Jesus has for us. There is joy in learning to walk humbly instead of selfishly. But to do this is a hard-fought relational habit because our culture trains us to look out for ourselves first. When we live like that we can become entitled, controlling, ungrateful, and self-focused. Jesus has more for us than thinking about ourselves.

Today I will remember:
• I am to value others.
• I am to consider them even before myself.
• I am to regard others by being interested in what interests them.

Lord, I want to walk humbly before You and kindly toward others.
May Your Spirit break through any ugliness of pride and selfishness.

FORGIVING OTHERS

*Bear with each other and forgive one another if any of you has
a grievance against someone. Forgive as the Lord forgave you.*

COLOSSIANS 3:13

To bear with someone is to patiently put up with them. Most of us don't want to put up with people or accept their differences. But Scripture teaches both things. We have all been hurt and find it hard, if not sometimes impossible, to extend the same kind of grace that God gives to us.

Anyone can be bitter when someone hurts them. But what if God is inviting you to a higher place? We all go through hurt and betrayal in this life, and the enemy wants to bait us into having bitter hearts. But God wants to set us free from having an ugly hurt. Forgiving others is living in a different maturity than continuing with anger, resentment, and pettiness.

I've been hurt many times. I cried, pleaded, and tried to change the situations. It seemed like I was destined to a life of hurt and hard-hearted bitterness. Then God called me to a different place—a place of forgiveness. Did I magically forget the offenses? No. There are some memories I will probably never forget. But they no longer have any power over me. Taking small steps that line us up with biblical truth changes us. We do this one hurt at a time.

Today I will remember:
- Bearing with someone is being patient toward them.
- Forgiving grievances doesn't remove the offense, just the power of it.
- Forgiveness is a choice of my will that I can make because God keeps forgiving me.

*Lord, work in me a heart that is patient with other people.
Enable me to accept differences without withholding love or forgiveness.*

LIKE-MINDED

Make my joy complete by being like-minded,
having the same love, being one in spirit and of one mind.
PHILIPPIANS 2:2

Division erupted as the world shut down, the pandemic loomed large, and people had differing thoughts about politics, masks, and religious freedoms. Sadly, many Christians parted ways in friendship and family due to pride-fueled differences. What if we could be people who loved regardless of whether or not we agreed on everything? Paul was used to people fighting to be right and to be heard. Yet, he said his joy would be complete if they became like-minded. He didn't say if they agreed on all things. No, he said being like-minded because they were of the same love, spirit, and purpose.

Imagine a world where we were like-minded based on being loved by God. Like-minded because we are all called to His glorious purposes. Instead, we are divided because we stand in our opinions more than we stand in love. We don't have to agree, but we can accept people where they are, knowing this one thing we do have in common: the love of Jesus. This is the kind of like-mindedness we need and the very thing we need to focus on when we don't agree.

Today I will remember:
- The same love that rescued me loves my neighbor who thinks differently than me.
- Being like-minded does not mean I agree on the issues, but rather than I agree to love anyway.
- The same God who has called me to a purpose has called those whom I don't understand.

Lord, when I disagree, give me the grace to focus on being
called to the same purpose, not the same opinions.

OVERCOMING OFFENSE

A person's wisdom yields patience;
it is to one's glory to overlook an offense.
PROVERBS 19:11

Most women know about being offended. Some of us are more prone to this than others, but as people pleasers and love seekers, women get their feelings hurt easily. Years of working alongside women informed me that I am not alone in this. What if we could learn to overlook that thing that gets on our very last nerve? The definition of *overlook* is to fail to notice or consider. Since most of us notice when we have been slighted or wronged, let's hold on to the second part of that definition—fail to consider. When someone does something that would usually send us to an ugly place, let's practice not considering it. Let it go, brush it off, say a silent prayer to God for grace to overlook it.

Our culture says stand up for yourself, own your rights, and speak up. There is a time for those things. But not every time. A wise woman is one who lets go of the things that offend her. And it is to her glory to honor and trust God this way, not taking offense at every little thing said in the wrong way or at the wrong time. We can do this as we look to God and become patient with others.

Today I will remember:
- A wise woman leans into patience.
- A wise woman is honored by overlooking being wronged.
- A wise woman does not think the things said to her are worth losing her peace over.

Lord, You know how easily I can get offended. I ask You to
make me a wise woman who notices the offense, and instead
of rising up against it, let it roll off of me and onto You.

LET IT GO

Forgive, and you will be forgiven.
LUKE 6:37

My littlest granddaughter is talking and singing. It's so funny to hear her toddler voice busting out, "Let it go, let it go." Every time, it reminds me of Jesus telling me to let things go. Jesus didn't teach, *Forgive when someone takes full responsibility or when you can finally forget the hurt.* No, forgiveness has more to do with us than the other person—it's a choice of our will. He is calling us to be brave and obedient enough to make that choice.

The Greek word behind "forgive" in this verse, is the word *apoluo*, meaning to release, send away, or let go. We have all had Jesus lay aside our offenses toward Him. When we yield to God the hurts caused by others, we also receive forgiveness for the things we've done. It's a win-win and the way of life that Jesus taught.

Too often we can stay stuck in overthinking the hurt or waiting for an apology while pointing the finger at someone else. But forgiveness isn't about an apology or forgetting—forgiveness is laying aside what happened. We all know it's not easy. But out of obedience to God, you and I can learn to let things go. This does not require continuing in relationship with the offender, but it does require making peace and yielding the hurt to God. There is a peace that comes with knowing we are following the ways that Jesus taught.

Today I will remember:
- Forgiveness is a choice of my will, not a response to an apology.
- Forgiveness doesn't mean I will forget the hurt, just that I am giving it to God.
- Forgiveness might not give someone access to me, but it always gives my heart access to God.

Lord, Your ways are different and better than mine. May I learn the practice of laying aside offenses for the sake of following hard after You.

⊸౿⟨⟩౩⊶

PEOPLE MATTER TO GOD

"Comfort, comfort my people," says your God. Speak tenderly to Jerusalem.
Tell her that her sad days are gone and her sins are pardoned.

ISAIAH 40:1-2, NLT

I have had my feelings swept aside more than once. Even within the church, the presence of criticism and the lack of care for one another can be alarming. Maybe it's not an obvious dismissal, but receiving the brunt of someone's aloofness or arrogance doesn't feel great. On the other hand, when someone takes the time to care and speak tenderly, it feels great and gives us courage.

People matter to God, so it's no wonder we are instructed to put others before ourselves. Comforting others includes caring about where they are and what they are going through. We aren't called to fix others, but we are called to care. This kind of humbling of self is not natural, and many people will never try to practice it. In our me-first world, putting others first is not the norm. But God has a better way.

We are invited into a life where we are becoming more like Jesus. The Bible calls Jesus the God of all comfort and the Father of compassion.[10] He is a God who cares about the troubles people face. He cares about ours. And, with the same comfort we receive from Him, we are called to comfort others. This requires a humility that desires to shadow the life and nature of Christ. We need a humble heart if we are going to live in love toward others.

Today I will remember:
• Jesus is the God of all comfort.
• Jesus is the Father of compassion.
• Jesus comforts me, and I am to comfort others.

Lord, I humble myself before You and ask You to make
me more like You—comforting, caring, and compassionate.

---

10 2 Corinthians 1:3.

MEASURE OUT PRACTICAL KINDNESS

Give, and it will be given to you. A good measure, pressed down,
shaken together and running over, will be poured into your lap.
For with the measure you use, it will be measured to you.

LUKE 6:38

It started with offering me her ice pack. I didn't know her personally, but she knew I was suffering with neck pain, and she'd been down that road. Moved with compassion, she stepped out of herself and into my life to help. We ended up becoming friends. Little did she know that my heart needed a friend. I was in a new state, far away from those I loved. Since that time, I've watched her measure out kindness to many. She looks past herself for ways to help others. I marvel at how she persistently measures out goodness. She gives of herself the way that Jesus taught us to—sacrificially.

These words, "give, and it will be given to you," are the words of Jesus inviting His followers into a better way. It's easy to be caught up in our own lives without a care for others. Giving is a biblical principle, and every opportunity to do good to others is a God-sized opportunity.

Make a list of people God has placed in your life, and pray about how you can give them love, kindness, or a helping hand. Focus on giving and the dividends will be received from God Himself.

Today I will remember:
- Jesus calls us to practical giving.
- God calls us to live by a Kingdom-of-love measurement.
- God promises to give to us—it's the principle of reaping and sowing.

Lord, may my attitude be that of kindness, goodness, and measuring out
to others the way You so generously have measured Your love to me.

LOVE IS...

Love is patient, love is kind. It does not envy, it does not boast,
it is not proud. It does not dishonor others, it is not self-seeking,
it is not easily angered, it keeps no records of wrongs.

1 CORINTHIANS 13:4-5

Red hearts fill stores, chocolates line the shelves, and flowers are marked up for the grand-slam day of love—Valentine's Day. This is a day that can exceed our expectations or bring us down in disappointment. Expectations are powerful, so an exercise in aligning our minds with Scripture will help us navigate our emotions and the unrealistic fluff that we've picked up in childhood fairy tales.

God did not create us to be swept off our feet, carried away on a white horse, or to magically fit into Cinderella's glass slipper. Love is sacrifice and hard work. Love is meant not to fill us up, but to teach us to pour out.

Don't wait for the card; buy one for someone else. Instead of expecting gifts or flowers, give them. Surprise your significant other with something they love rather than demanding they prove their love for you on Valentine's Day. Tomorrow will come and the Hallmark celebration will be over. But God's love is something that is available to give and receive 365 days a year.

Today I will remember:
- Love is more than a holiday—I will make a goal to look for ways I can love others.
- Love is shown in patience and kindness and is not self-focused.
- Love is not easily offended or angered; I will be kind and not be offended today.

Lord, teach me how to love and to guard my heart from
unrealistic expectations on holidays and special occasions.

BLESS THOSE WHO MISTREAT YOU

*But to you who are listening I say: love your enemies, do good to those
who hate you, bless those who curse you, pray for those who mistreat you.*

LUKE 6:27-28

Love my enemies? Why on earth would I love those who hate me, curse me, and mistreat me? That sounds like insanity. But God knows the best way, and it's not living according to feelings but rather the path that leads me to walk in his love no matter how I have been treated.

Loving others is a challenge. It means listening to the words of Christ—with the intent to follow Him by paying attention to what He said and acting on those things. Why is it hard? Because the way of the cross and following after Jesus is countercultural. It runs opposite of our flesh nature and is often the very last thing we would naturally do when presented with a situation.

Our feelings inform us of our hurt, while faith leads us higher than ourselves and our limited perspective. *Love* here is the Greek verb *agapao*, which requires living in God's love toward our enemies. We are not asked to live in feeling-based love, but to live beyond that. With Christ in us, we can lean into the love of God toward others.

Today I will remember:
- Jesus speaks, and I am to listen.
- I am called to live by faith, not only feelings.
- I am called to do good, bless, and pray for those who mistreat me.

*Lord, the practical places of Scripture are hard because my
flesh wants to repay or retaliate when I am mistreated.
Help me to learn the rhythm of living in the way of agape love.*

REMAIN IN GOD'S LOVE

As the Father has loved me, so have I loved you. Now remain in my love.
JOHN 15:9

Jesus holds out a completely new way to live. It doesn't depend on our emotions. It is not dependent on receiving from others. Rather, it is solely dependent on the love of the Father, which is unchanging. God's love is not about us, but all about the nature of who God is. Scripture tells us God is love. Why, then, do we stay bent on living in unloving patterns of being easily offended, gossiping, and withholding kindness? If we are honest with ourselves, that kind of living is ugly. It is not in line with the beautiful heart that God desires to create within us.

God's love is the new paradigm. But it's not easy, is it? We naturally live a life apart from the path of agape love and develop patterns of relating to people that are not biblical but carnal. We don't like to admit this or look it squarely in the eye, but it is the truth, and Jesus calls us to a better way.

What would it mean to remain in God's love today? How would you treat those who are prickly, unkind, or have offended you? What is more fruitful—living in your emotions or living toward eternity?

Today I will remember:
- God has loved me fully, even though I do not deserve it.
- I am to remain in His love—to be present in the love of God.
- As I remain in God's love, I am to extend love to others.

> *Lord, take the natural part of me that is bent on my own way*
> *and change me. May the love of God in me transform my*
> *life and my way of relating to the world around me.*

ENTER INTO THEIR STORY

Rejoice with those who rejoice; mourn with those who mourn.
ROMANS 12:15

While I may be tempted to make life about myself, Scripture teaches that my life is to be about others. Stop and read today's verse out loud with that in mind. It says nothing about how we are feeling or the lens through which we are viewing the day. It is all about paying attention to the needs, feelings, and experiences of others. Too often we are caught up in self and can be oblivious to others and their needs.

To *rejoice* is to find joy in something. When your friend is happy, find the joy in that moment with them. Celebrate with a friend who has achieved success even when you are still waiting for your own. Find creative ways to let them know you are proud of them, are with them in their joy, and are not competing with them. There are enough jealous and competitive people in this world; don't be one of them.

When a friend mourns loss or change, don't brush it off because you don't understand it. Enter into that space with them by offering comfort rather than answers, help rather than staying away. All of us will go through loss at some point in our lives, and it's good to experience God's love through other people when our tears are plentiful and the future looks hard.

Today I will remember:
• Life is filled with both joy and sadness.
• Walking with Jesus changes my focus to look outside of myself.
• I am to meet people where they are, asking God to use me to help them.

Lord, help me to extend care to others in both their joy and sorrow.
Teach me to love, care for, and celebrate with others.

LAY DOWN THE CRITICISM

Each of us will give an account of ourselves to God. Therefore let us stop passing judgment on one another. Instead, make up your mind not to put any stumbling block or obstacle in the way of a brother or sister.

ROMANS 14:12-13

It's easy to be critical. But this puts an obstacle in the way of peaceful living. Dale Carnegie said, "Any fool can criticize, condemn or complain...But it takes character and self-control to be understanding and forgiving."[11] Daring to walk away from being critical is a big step toward spiritual maturity.

Because we will all be held accountable for how we treat others, it's probably important to take a cue from Romans, where Paul teaches us to love from the center of who we are, run from evil, bless our enemies, get along, discover the good in everyone, not insist on getting even, and not let a critical spirit get the best of us but combat it by doing good toward all people.[12]

When was the last time you were actively critical of someone? How did it affect you? How did it change how you treated them? Perhaps today is the day to turn away from a judgmental, critical slump. Rise up and be all God has planned for you to be by loving God and loving others.

Today I will remember:
- I will give account to God for how I handle other people.
- I am to stop passing judgment on others.
- I am to uphold others, not throw challenges in their path.

Lord, I know You love me, but I also am aware that You hold me accountable for how I treat others. Teach me Your way, Lord.

---

11 Dale Carnegie, *How to Win Friends and Influence People*, revised edition (New York: Simon & Schuster, 2009), 37.

12 Romans 12:9-18.

FAITHFUL TO GOD AND OTHERS

A friend loves at all times.
PROVERBS 17:17

Relationships are easy when there is no betrayal. But when a friend breaches our trust, loving becomes an issue of faith. Will I react according to my feelings only, or will I choose to respond in faith—addressing the problem honestly and allowing room for grace and forgiveness?

A few years back, a good friend heard something untrue about me. But rather than asking me, she believed the gossip and passed it on to other friends. I was devastated. I could choose to forgive my friend or I could hold on to this justified hurt and walk in unforgiveness, allowing a breach in our relationship. I held on to hurt far too long.

Scripture teaches that we can choose to move toward whatever would promote healing in our relationships. At first it will be a non-feeling faith choice. When we do this, God in His timing aligns our feelings with the faith choice we've made.

It's impossible to love at all times, especially if I expect my feelings to comply. But when I walk by faith, I can move in directions contrary to my feelings and see God work in mighty ways.

It might be easier to stick our heads in the sand or hold on to hurt. But when we do so, we are not the friend who loves at all times.

Today I will remember:
• To be a friend is to love in good times and bad times.
• Love must be sincere and not moved by others' opinions.
• Love stands guard to protect our friend from harm.

Lord, help me to be a friend who loves at all times. Teach me how to do this as I continually learn to walk in the Spirit instead of my feelings and flesh.

CLEAN BEFORE GOD

Forgive us our debts, as we also have forgiven our debtors.
MATTHEW 6:12

Each time I make mistakes, I ask for God's forgiveness. But when someone offends me, I'm not as quick to forgive them. Can you relate? Forgiveness, both from God and toward others, is to be a daily part of our lives. Jesus taught the disciples to address this regularly.

Confession and forgiveness are about keeping our hearts clean before God and our accounts balanced with others. There are two parts to forgiveness—the first is our relationship with God and the second is our relationship with man. We are to confess our sins to God and forgive any offense toward us. Forgiveness is an act of dealing with our own heart and hurt. It has little to do with the other person but everything to do with our heart before God.

I wasn't raised to deal daily with the conflicts in my heart. I reacted to conflict by hiding the pain, holding the anger, or treating others unkindly. I knew how to fall apart but didn't know how to fall upon God. The two are very different. One is a natural response to life and the other is a supernatural reaction to life based on Christ's life within me. This is where life change starts getting real.

Today I will remember:
- To pray to my Father in heaven.
- To ask for His Kingdom to come in my life daily.
- To receive forgiveness and to forgive others by faith.

Lord, may I be quick to ask for forgiveness and quick to forgive others.

A LIFE THAT MATCHES THE CALLING

I urge you to live a life worthy of the calling you have received. Be completely humble and gentle; be patient, bearing with one another in love. Make every effort to keep the unity of the Spirit through the bond of peace.
EPHESIANS 4:1-3

All of us have relational patterns that go with the flow of our emotions. The apostle Paul was giving a strong recommendation to live differently, as one who has been called and set apart by God. This calling requires treating others in a way that reflects Christ. The call requires not just a humble heart, but to show up fully humble, gentle, and patient when dealing with others.

Are these things you consider in dealing with family, friends, and coworkers? What about when someone's personality annoys you? Rather than focusing on weaknesses or quirks, try yielding to God and silently praying for the person. Practice the things mentioned here, but remember this love is not human, selfish love. It is *agape*, which is drawn from God's unconditional love. This is important to remember because we must seek to be filled with God's love and live out His love toward others.

This is more than behavioral change. It is a transformation of the heart, being filled with God Himself. The key here is a daily yielding to God and a daily indwelling of God's love and God's Spirit.

Today I will remember:
• I have been called to more than living just for myself.
• I can walk fully present and fully humble because of Christ in me.
• God's love changes me, and that can change my interactions with others.

Lord, remind me daily of the calling on my life to live according to Christ in me.

TAKE OFF YOUR OLD SELF

But now you must also rid yourselves of all such things as these:
anger, rage, malice, slander... Do not lie each other,
since you have taken off your old self with its practices.
COLOSSIANS 3:8-9

I have been known to try on many outfits before deciding what to wear. Sometimes I change my mind because things aren't comfortable or don't fit right anymore. Sometimes this is also true with the attitudes toward others that we put on daily. Walking with Christ is about wearing the new outfit or attitude of the Spirit.

Have we taken off our old self? Or are we still wearing attitudes that no longer fit—things like anger, malice, and slander? In Christ, we see clearly that those bad attitudes are no longer in style for those who love Jesus. Some things clearly need to be tossed into the trash.

For many of us, the ugly outfit comes out when we think we need to be heard, be right, or prove ourselves. Regrouping and healing our bruised relationships is important. Scripture places a high value on how we treat others. Let's take off the jacket of unkindness and put on something new that has been created to love and protect—not tear down and expose.

Today I will remember:
- I am to take off the old self—characterized by anger, malice, and slander.
- I am to put on the new self—created to encourage and uplift.
- I am to speak truth in love and stand firm against lying or exaggerating.

Lord, forgive me for the many times I live according to my
flesh and its selfish, ugly ways. Give me the courage to take
off the ugliness and put on the newness of life and love.

NO MORE PAYBACK

Do not repay anyone evil for evil…
Do not take revenge…If your enemy is hungry, feed him.
ROMANS 12:17, 19-20

Maybe it's too much Netflix, or perhaps it's being hurt one too many times, but I can easily craft a good plan to get even with someone who has done me wrong. In my place of pain, I want them to hurt as much as I do. Childish? Probably. But it is a typical response for most people. God has called us to more than typical revenge and spiraling into plans of payback.

Rather than revenge, we are to meet our enemies at their need. Feed them. Care for them. Do good to them. Let's face it, anyone can be mean, but it's going to take a changed woman to walk away from her right to revenge and bless her enemy instead of hurting them. Remember, we don't treat people according to who they are, but according to who we are.

Who are we? God's daughters, Christ's ambassadors, women filled with the Holy Spirit of love. We treat others based on the position of being His—and leave the outcomes in God's hand.

Today I will remember:
- I am not to repay people who hurt me.
- I am not to take revenge or plot a plan of evil.
- I am to meet people at their need and provide for them as Christ would.

Lord, help me to walk in Your best and live a story of victory
and redemption in the midst of difficult relationships.

JEALOUSY AND OTHER UGLY THINGS

*If you harbor bitter envy and selfish ambition in your
hearts, do not boast about it or deny the truth.*

JAMES 3:14

I was secretly jealous. "Such 'wisdom' *[jealousy]* does not come down from heaven but is earthly, unspiritual, demonic." Unspiritual and demonic? What the heck! There is more: "For where you have envy and selfish ambition, there you find disorder and every evil practice."[13] Every. Evil. Practice.

I wanted what she had. Focusing on what I didn't have and staying in that jealous place gave the enemy a foothold. Now, I didn't tell anyone I was jealous, but God knew my heart and the enemy was having his way with my thoughts. I was opening the door to the enemy while smiling and saying, "Bless your heart." Though I was walking with Jesus and thought myself spiritual, there was unspiritual stuff brewing in me.

"The wisdom that comes from heaven is first of all pure; then peace-loving, considerate, submissive, full of mercy and good fruit, impartial and sincere. Peacemakers who sow in peace reap a harvest of righteousness."[14]

The bottom line is that jealousy is actually evil—and certainly not peaceful. If you are secretly harboring envy or jealousy, catch yourself and don't deny the evil that it is or the damage it does. Most of us want to be peace-loving people. And Scripture tells us how to get there—by avoiding jealousy.

Today I will remember:
- Jealousy, bitterness, and envy have evil at the core.
- If I deny the truth, I allow the enemy a place in my life.
- Where there is disorder, back up and look for the seed of jealousy that started it.

Lord, forgive me for focusing on others rather than being grateful for what You are doing in me. Help me to turn from envy or jealousy each time it raises its ugly head.

---

13 James 3:15-16.
14 James 3:17-18.

WANTING OUR OWN WAY

What causes fights and quarrels among you?
Don't they come from your desires that battle within you?
You cannot get what you want, so you quarrel and fight.
JAMES 4:1-2

A peaceful coffee date was disrupted by a power struggle between two young kids at the next table. They pushed and pulled until a toy broke. I remember those days, and some things haven't changed. Kids fight to get what they want, and we still do it too.

In learning to love others well, it's important to pay attention to the battle within. Think back on a recent argument. Did you need to be right and have your own way? Half the battle is understanding what makes us react the way we do. The selfish desires within can cause a lot of problems, quarrels, and fights. If it weren't true, it wouldn't be in God's Word.

The passage goes on to say, "You do not have because you do not ask God."[15] When was the last time you asked God to meet your needs rather than expecting others to fulfill them? We can learn to trust God with every need and desire. And we can count on Jesus to soften the stubbornness and selfishness within.

What if we began practicing putting others first even when we didn't feel like it? What if we didn't have to be right? What if we truly trusted God?

Today I will remember:
• Fighting is caused by a need to have my own way.
• There is an internal battle, and it is at the core of me acting out.
• God quiets the battle within as I come to Him with my desires.

Lord, work in me more of You and
change the selfishness at the core of who I am.

---

15 James 4:2.

BE TRUSTWORTHY

A gossip betrays a confidence, but a trustworthy person keeps a secret.
PROVERBS 11:13

No one wants to be known as a gossip, but keeping a secret is hard. Some female friendships are grown by the telling of deep secrets—ours and those of people connected to us. This is not a good foundation to build on, but it's what we have learned from the time we were huddled in corners on the school playground. We've all been there. Gossip starts innocently, but little by little we are saying too much. "Bless her heart" becomes a covering that we hope will justify a multitude of tales told. Excuse the tongue all you want, Scripture is very clear that using our mouth to betray others is not the way to live.

"With their mouths the godless destroy their neighbors."[16]

"Whoever derides their neighbor has no sense, but of the one who has understanding holds their tongue."[17]

We reap what we sow. If you want to be trusted, you will have to keep your mouth closed when you want to blab and your words few when it's not your story to tell. We show a complete lack of judgment when we spread stories that aren't our business. God cares about our conversations about others, and we should too.

Today I will remember:
- Loving others involves watching my words.
- Loving others requires me to keep secret the things they entrust me with.
- A wise woman practices holding her tongue.

Lord, please convict me when I am tempted to go down the path
that lacks judgment. I want to be a trustworthy woman.

---

16 Proverbs 11:9.
17 Proverbs 11:12.

KIND WORDS HEAL

Anxiety weighs down the heart, but a kind word cheers it up.
PROVERBS 12:25

She walked toward me smiling and looking more beautiful than ever. We chatted—mostly small talk—and I was tempted to want her life, one with the time and money to live pampered and polished. Later I heard that she attempted suicide that evening. I had no idea that she dealt with extreme anxiety and depression. Her exterior didn't reveal her inner turmoil. It was her secret, and the weight of it almost killed her.

Life is hard. Every person is fighting battles that you know nothing about. Hearts are heavy with burdens that are buttoned up behind beautifully curated exteriors. Because of this, it is important to be kind. I recently saw a meme that said, "In a world where you can be anything—be kind." Kindness doesn't cost us anything, but it goes a long way in making the world a better place.

The next chance you get, be kind. Look for strangers to compliment or notice something nice about. Tip your servers and speak to them kindly. Give attention and grace in dealing with your in-laws and family members—they have burdens you most likely know nothing about. Kindness goes a long way. And remember, "whoever refreshes others will be refreshed."[18]

Today I will remember:
- People are hurting, anxious, and weighed down with problems.
- A kind word can add a light to their day and cheer them up.
- Living in kindness and caring about others refreshes me as well as them.

> *Lord, make me aware each day of other people and the fact that we all carry untold burdens. Help me find ways to be kind and lift others up.*

GIVE COURAGE TO OTHERS

Encourage one another and build each other up.
1 THESSALONIANS 5:11

Love is summed up with the word *others*. It's easy to dismiss this instruction and treat others according to our mood of the day. We can pick and choose verses that serve us rather than yielding to the truth in verses that will help us serve others. Life, according to Scripture, is to be about others. In a culture where we are encouraged to be about self, this is backwards, upside down, and unpopular.

To *encourage* someone is to give them courage, hope, support, or confidence. Isn't that beautiful? You and I have the ability to impart this kind of life-giving courage to others. To do so, we have to look for opportunities to encourage people. Imagine this mission statement: I live to submit my life to God and to encourage and build up others. This mission requires looking past ourselves.

In the original language, the root of the word *encourage* is to comfort, exhort, and pray for. The root for the word *build* is to edify, construct, or embolden. In both cases, when we live like this, we are imparting the gift of courage to others, and by doing so we are building them up. If we pay attention, God will give us the grace to see the need, meet the need, and build others up. Life isn't just about us—we are called to care about others.

Today I will remember:
- I am to live to encourage people—passing on comfort and hope.
- I am to use my words to build others up—to edify them, not tear them down.
- God cares about people, and how I treat others is an important part of my walk with God.

Lord, help me to be devoted to encouraging and building others up each day.

March

LIVING AS HIS

"Being the beloved constitutes the core truth of our existence."[19]
Henri Nouwen

19 Henry Nouwen, *Life of the Beloved* (New York: Crossroad, 1992), 21.

PART OF GOD'S DIVINE STORY

For from him and through him and for him are all things.
ROMANS 11:36

Every life change is etched into my memory. When my directional balance is off, any sense of security, identity, and belonging is challenged. This uncertainty has showed up many times over the years—graduation, marriage, career changes, raising kids, empty nesting, and growing older. Each new place and season presents the same questions: *Who am I? Why am I here? Do I still have value?* I have come to realize that I am not alone in this.

The doxology in this verse is a prayer and expression of praise to God for the wisdom of His plan. God is not arbitrary, but has made each human with a plan for us to depend on Him in this life. Though God's wisdom is beyond comprehension, we can be encouraged that we have come from the creative design of God, were born through His intentional plan for us to be part of His story, and live in the exact time we are living in for a purpose. There is nothing random here. Our lives have divine purpose stamped upon them.

In every season, we can come back to this as a core foundational part of our identity. And though life changes and some seasons are harder than others, our identity remains as women who are from Him, through Him, and for Him. Let the calling of that sink in today.

Today I will remember:
• My life is not random and without purpose.
• I am in God's heart and plan as part of His story.
• My one and only life is meant to be lived for an all-powerful God.

Lord, thank You for the seasons of life and the truth that my identity
as Yours never changes. May I move forward trusting You with
each change and each season until I meet You face-to-face.

THE GLUE THAT HOLDS US

He is before all things, and in him all things hold together.
COLOSSIANS 1:17

My granddaughter was holding a candleholder when it slipped, fell, and cracked. She was horrified because she knew it was one of my special pieces. Hugging her, I assured my sweet Jessa that she was far more important than Grammy's things. The candleholder was a thing with little value, but she was precious and beyond value. She smiled and hugged me tight, letting me know she was happy I wasn't angry. We got some glue and pieced it back together, placing it back on the shelf. She learned a few lessons that day—things break, she is more precious than things, and a little glue does miracles.

God is the superglue in our lives. He is not just the Creator of the world; He is the sustainer of all things. In Him we are held together and protected. God puts the pieces that have been broken back into place. He isn't angry when we make mistakes or if we have been broken a time or two. He tends to us graciously and with love. He holds us together—piece by piece, year by year, through heartaches and trials. I learned a few lessons that day too—things are not that important, value is always placed on what God created, and practical everyday life can teach us things about glue, God, and the miracle of being precious in His sight.

Today I will remember:
- God is before all things.
- I am His, and my life is in Him.
- As His, I am being held together by the superglue of His power and grace.

*Lord, thank You for sustaining me and fixing me when
I am broken and in need of repair. I am overcome with peace as
I hold on to the truth that in You, I am being held together.*

TRUE IDENTITY

As some of your own poets have said, "We are his offspring."
ACTS 17:28

I had a bracelet engraved with "His" on the front of the heart and the year I became a Christian on the back. The day I picked it up, the clerk was admiring and polishing it before laying it across black velvet for viewing. She smiled. "This must be when you met your husband."

I took a breath. "Actually, it's when I met Jesus as my Lord and Savior—" stopping me mid-sentence, she handed it over and shooed me out.

"Bye-bye now, have a nice day." The memory of it still makes me laugh. She was expecting to hear a romance story, and to her surprise the romance was about a woman and her God.

This reality is the truest thing about me: I am His. It was true for Christians in the early church and is true now. "In him we live and move and have our being."[20] Paul was speaking to educated religious men who did not know God. Today, God still remains unknown even by people who consider themselves religious or Christian. We are His, right down to every move we are able to make. It is the truest thing about us. He is up close and personal and calls us His own. We forget this and then live for ourselves—even as Christians. My bracelet was intentional. I wanted the reminder that I am His because what defines me—my true identity—will drive me. Remembering whose you are is how you discover who you are.

Today I will remember:
- I have been created by God.
- I am His.
- Being His changes everything and is the foundation of my identity.

Lord, it's easy to forget that I am Yours. I go through life doing things my way and in my time. Help me to remember my true identity and live in it confidently.

---

20 Acts 17:28.

DESIGNED BY GOD

For we are God's handiwork...
EPHESIANS 2:10

My grandson has gorgeous thick hair. One day while visiting I said, "Grammy sure wishes she had your hair."

He quietly said, "Well, I wish I could give it to you, Grammy. I hate it." My heart broke for this seven-year-old who already was exposed to the comments of peers—all because his hair was red. The word *handiwork* here in the original is *poiema*, which is a poem or a work of God. We are God's *handiwork*—His creative artwork or finely lined and well-thought-out poem. Sadly, we don't see it that way. Many of us have spent a lifetime not accepting ourselves. Perhaps it's because we compare ourselves with others, and if we are different then we aren't OK.

The psalmist said, "For you created my inmost being; you knit me together in my mother's womb. I praise you because I am fearfully and wonderfully made; your works are wonderful, I know that full well."[21] Who we are is wrapped up in who God created us to be. The insecurities start young and the search to fit in follows, but the truest thing about each of us is that we were formed by God—handcrafted, intentionally designed. He makes originals, so the next time the bully of insecurity or self-doubt tries to creep in, remember who you are and who made you.

Today I will remember:
- I have been created by God, uniquely me.
- I may be different than others, but I am exactly who God designed me to be.
- It is a privilege to be called God's *poiema*, His poem, masterpiece, design.

Lord, I am often insecure about parts of me that are different than others.
Help me to embrace who You created me to be. From body shape to the color
of my hair, may I live confidently in being Your design and Your work.

---

21 Psalm 139:13-14.

ON ASSIGNMENT

...created in Christ Jesus to do good works,
which God prepared in advance for us to do.

EPHESIANS 2:10

We are here to make a contribution. While many influencers tell us how to find success in life, that isn't what we are ultimately here for. God created us to add value in this life—to be givers, not takers. We were created to do good works—the very things that God prepared for us to do beforehand. This truth is loaded and rich with meaning. God has designed us with gifts, strengths, and talents. Our identity speaks to being a well-thought-out part of His plan and intricately made for His purposes in our life. This is empowering.

Years ago, I took a Strengths Finders test as part of a church staff assignment. I was astonished by my top five. Why? Because the test results outlined who I had always been. Ideation—my mother use to tell to quit dreaming and thinking so much about everything. Woo—I have always been a cheerleader. Learner—one of my favorite things about life is continual growth...I could go on. But what struck me the most is that who I am is not by accident. God has a plan. I am part of that plan. He has prepared me for His plan and goes before me to accomplish His plan. When I remember these things, I am filled with a holy and happy peace about who I am and why I am.

Today I will remember:
• I have been created to do good things in this life.
• God has filled me with all I need to accomplish His plan.
• I am not here to be a taker, but to live as a giver.

Lord, may I not forget that I have been created with purpose. I desire to use all
that You put in me to do good for others and bring You glory as long as I live.

MY BODY—HIS TEMPLE

Do you not know that your bodies are temples of the Holy Spirit,
who is in you, whom you have received from God?

1 CORINTHIANS 6:19

Over the years my body has changed—from tiny house to cathedral. This verse gives me pause. Paul was teaching that as Christians, our bodies belong to God. How would I treat my body if I truly believed it wasn't mine to use and abuse through excessive eating, drinking, or dieting? Would I be less critical and more grateful?

Recently, blood tests showed that I wasn't paying attention to the care of my body. I could make hard changes, which would require work and effort, or I could brush it off. This verse became key in my decision. I have a responsibility to care for what has been entrusted to me. I was convicted. I had treated my body terribly—not just physically, being irresponsible with my health, but emotionally, being critical of every imperfection. Would I do this to a temple set apart for God? No, I would honor the temple and care for it with love, respect, and gratefulness. It was a wake-up call. There is freedom in surrendering all of ourselves to God—even our bodies with how we treat them, how we use them, and what we allow to be done to them.

Today I will remember:
- I am His, and my body is a temple of His Holy Spirit.
- The Holy Spirit lives in me.
- I have received all things from God, and unto God I am to yield all of me.

Lord, I am convicted of the many times that I have disregarded
my body. Forgive me. Help me to view it as Yours, treat it as
Yours, and quit being critical but rather become grateful.

ALIGNING MYSELF WITH BIBLICAL TRUTH

You are not your own; you were bought at a price.
1 CORINTHIANS 6:19-20

The right to self is glorified in our culture. People are trying to find out who they are and why they are here. We all want to be seen and have value. The writer of Ecclesiastes said, "He has...set eternity in the human heart."[22] God's plan has always been for us to be seen and to do work that has meaning—not important in the eyes of others, but divinely prepared work that God has given us to do. We know this is fundamentally true, but culture fights against it so hard that it's easy to fall in step with the multitudes trying desperately to find themselves and be their best selves as owners and managers of themselves. This thinking does not align to Biblical truth.

The pathway to living better lives is found not by focusing on improving self, but aligning with the heart of God's love and the truth of His Word. This is very different than self-improvement. It's dying to the ways of self in favor of becoming fully alive to the Spirit within us. It's living in Him rather than living in us. This is a mind shift. Jesus paid the price for us to live a better story—a story of His power and life working in and through us. What a gift.

Today I will remember:
• I do not belong to myself.
• I can choose to live in myself or in the power of God within me.
• Living as His leads me to a better story of abundance and peace.

Lord, may I remember each day that You live in me and that I have been purchased by Your blood. I don't want to settle for being self-made when I can have the fullness of the Spirit shaping me.

---

22 Ecclesiastes 3:11.

CHOOSE LIFE AS HIS

For the Lord is your life.
DEUTERONOMY 30:20

Social media memories are fun and bittersweet. Time moves forward and the seasons of life clip by at record speed. As seasons change, we can find ourselves in places of uncertainty. I just recently told a friend, "I don't know how to be this age; I've never been here before." From college to retirement, life changes. But though time might affect some of our abilities, age doesn't alter identity. Our identity should impact our choices and how we live in each season. We can learn to stand in the truth that we are His and our life is secured.

"I have set before you life and death, blessings and curses. Now choose life, so that you and your children may live and that you may love the LORD your God, listen to his voice, and hold fast to him. For the LORD is your life, and he will give you many years in the land he swore to give to your fathers."[23]

The Lord is our life, but every day we choose whether to walk in that reality. Our way or God's way? When we choose life (His way) we also learn to listen to His voice and connect to Him. This choice ends with promised blessing. It's different and foreign at times, but the more days we choose to live tethered to Him, the more natural it becomes.

Today I will remember:
- The Lord is my everything—from beginning to end.
- I choose daily whether to live in this reality or go my own way.
- By choosing life, I am creating a spiritual legacy for my children and their children.

Lord, though my life is Yours, You still let me have the power
to choose Your way or my own. May I choose Your way so
often that it becomes my living reality to choose You daily.

---

23 Deuteronomy 30:19-20.

PART OF A BIGGER FAMILY

*See what great love the Father has lavished on us, that we
should be called children of God! And that is what we are!*

1 JOHN 3:1

When my kids were teens, I would remind them who they were before they went out with friends for the night. My hope was that they would think twice when tempted to do things that might not be the best for them. Sometimes it worked and got them out of some tricky situations. Other times, like all of us have done at times, they would forget they were part of a family bigger than themselves and would do whatever they felt like doing. Even when they made bad choices, their actions never changed the fact that they were our children or our love for them. The same is true with us and God. Our choices don't change His love for us but can change our outcomes. It's important to remember who we are—and more important to remember whose we are.

God created you to be part of His family—someone who would love Him, honor Him, and reign with Him forever. He treasures His relationship with us because as His, we are children of God. That is quite an identity. We are lavished with love and also given the responsibility to live out of that love. We are to live as people who belong to God and who honor Him. When we forget that we are His children, we live like orphans without any connection to anything greater than ourselves.

Today I will remember:
- God calls me His child.
- My Father lavishes His love on me.
- This new identity can change everything.

*Lord, before I go out into the day, remind me who I am. When I face
temptations or interact with others, may I live out the day as Your child rather
than an orphan without a secure foundation who lives based on emotions.*

A WOMAN BELONGING TO GOD

You are a chosen people, a royal priesthood, a holy nation, God's special possession, that you may declare the praises of him who called you out of darkness into his wonderful light...now you are the people of God.

1 PETER 2:9-10

From a young age, I learned to find a life outside of my family. I became a proficient overachiever. I was embarrassed by my home life—raised as an only child with an alcoholic father and a mean and distant mother. My daydreams consisted of wanting a different life, a home where daily stomachaches weren't the norm. I didn't want to be me, so I did all I could to become someone else. The trouble is, once twelve years of school were over, I had no idea who I was. Without teachers to impress or goals to achieve, my identity as a good student and popular girl came to a screeching halt.

The good news is, in Christ we have been not only adopted into a new family, but we have been given a new identity. It's an identity secured by Christ, not by us. It's an identity based on who we are as His—chosen, part of a royal priesthood, holy, belonging to God, light-bearers. This is who we are. What we do changes in every season. What never changes is who we are as His. We have been called to walk in the light of this new identity. Embrace that today.

Today I will remember:
- I have been chosen by God to be His.
- I am part of a royal priesthood.
- I have been called out of the dark into His marvelous light.

Lord, thank You that I no longer have to create myself, earn approval from people, or live with fake fronts. I am now free to live as Yours, walking in the light and bringing You glory instead of earning praises for myself.

TREASURED POSSESSION

For you are a people holy to the Lord your God.
The Lord your God has chosen you out of all the peoples on
the face of the earth to be his people, his treasured possession.
DEUTERONOMY 7:6

I used to collect things. I showcased them in a pretty cabinet with a light shining on them. They were my carefully acquired possessions and treasures. The word *possession* here is the Hebrew word *cegullah*, which refers to a private possession that was intentionally purchased and is carefully preserved. What a beautiful picture of who we are to Christ and in Christ. He personally acquired us, "while we were still sinners, Christ died for us,"[24] and then He carefully maintains us. Jesus said, "no one will snatch them out of my hand."[25] Why? Because God declared that we are His personal treasure!

Jesus Himself expressed our value when He told us we don't have to worry because He knows our needs. He even knows the number of hairs on our heads. He said we have the freedom to live one day at a time. I once heard someone say, "faith in God restores the missing sense of being somebody." Can you put your faith in the truth that you are His possession and personal treasure? *Treasure* means acquired wealth or something regarded as valuable. The Lord calls us His treasure. We are His wealth, and we are treasured and valued.

Today I will remember:
• The Lord has chosen me.
• I am holy to the Lord.
• I am His treasured possession—personally acquired and carefully maintained.

Lord, when I feel like trash, turn my thoughts to the
treasure that I am to You. May I know that I am a woman
who belongs to You, and may I daily live for You.

---

24 Romans 5:8.
25 John 10:28.

CURATED BY GOD

Before I formed you in the womb I knew you,
before you were born I set you apart.
JEREMIAH 1:5

Our identity started early—before anyone other than God thought of us. It isn't dependent on how we feel or what we do. We are each God's idea. We did not form ourselves—God shaped, formed, and assigned who we would be. Best of all, He knows us, even though often we don't know ourselves. Many of us are living a life processed through the lens of what other people think, following influencers who may not know who they are without the perfect curated photo or brand endorsement.

Who are you? You are a child of God. You have been created by Him and for Him. He has equipped you for every good work. He knows everything about you. He loves you enough to lay down His own life for your freedom. He declares you valuable. He is committed to providing for your needs. He has a design—a plan, intent, and purpose for your life.

Whose are you? *El Roi*— the God who sees. *El Elyon*—the God most high. *El Shadai*—the all-sufficient One. *Jehovah Jireh*—the provider. *Jehovah Rapha*—the healer. *Jehovah Shalom*—peace. *Jehovah Raah*—my shepherd.

We have two choices: 1. Create our own purpose and identity. 2. Accept the identity and purpose God has already given us.

What you choose to believe about yourself will impact how you live and relate to others.

Today I will remember:
- I am God's idea.
- God knew me before the womb.
- My life is set apart for His purposes—for His story in my generation.

Lord, in a world that says I can be anything I want, may I live as a woman
who wants to be everything You want me to be and all You created me for.
Remove any confusion so I may stand solidly on truth, living in freedom.

⚮

GOD'S VIEW OF US

People look at the outward appearance, but the Lord looks at the heart.
1 SAMUEL 16:7

Women have long found their identity in how they look. Barbie dolls aided in our early development of the mindset that women are to be pretty and perfect. But even Barbie gets old—you may have heard of hot-flash Barbie, which is not real, but is one of many funny versions found in a Google search.

As a cancer survivor, I am familiar with the "look good–feel better" organization. The idea is that when you look good, you feel better. When it comes to lost hair, eyebrows, and lashes, we know this to be true. What isn't true is that our outward appearance is the only thing that's important.

There are two views of us—the outside and the inside. While we care about the outward appearance, the part most important to God is often overlooked. "Do not consider his appearance or his height... The LORD does not look at the things people look at."[26]

Identity based on how we look is contrary to what Scripture teaches. Though there is certainly nothing wrong with looking good—the woman in Proverbs 31 was dressed like royalty[27]—the focus of our identity should remain where God is looking—our hearts. Rather than anxiously living in bodies that age over time, we can be consciously at peace because our hearts are right with God.

Today I will remember:
- People look at my outward appearance and form opinions.
- God looks at my heart and sees the beauty He created.
- Finding identity in my looks is fickle and changes with time.

Lord, as I do my best to represent You well here on earth, let me remain mindful of the truth that how You love me or use my life is not dependent on my appearance but rather on a heart that is placed daily before You.

---

26 1 Samuel 16:7.
27 Proverbs 31:22.

BEFORE AND AFTER

As for you, you were dead in your transgressions and sins,
in which you used to live when you followed the ways of this world.
EPHESIANS 2:1-2

Our belief system and perceived identities start forming in our earliest days. All of us lived differently before Christ. I drank too much and danced on tables. I am not proud of this, but it's my story. Though partying can be fun, it was empty, and I never had a solid or secure view of myself. I was one rejection away from collapse, so I kept on going with the crowd. Let me tell you, it's a dead end.

"So also, when we were underage, we were in slavery under the elemental spiritual forces of the world."28

Coming to Christ was exciting but also a bit uncomfortable, as old foundations had to come crumbling down. Before I met Christ, an identity based on self, pleasures, and doing anything I felt like doing became my template. When I stopped living for self, my personality wasn't robbed, but rather enhanced. My security wasn't blown away but made stronger. I have never missed the party scene because once I was in Christ, I realized that wasn't who I really was anyway. I still love to sing, dance, and have fun. It's part of me. What isn't part of me is hiding who I am in order to be liked, doing what others expect in order to fit in, and living in excess to fill the gaping hole when life is hard.

Today I will remember:
- I was once dead in my sins.
- I once lived in a place of spiritual death and followed others.
- Now that I am in Christ, my new identity shapes everything.

Lord, thank You for salvation and for giving me new life. May my
perceived identity align with who You say that I am, as Yours.

COMPARISON TRAP

Each one should test their own actions. Then they can take
pride in themselves alone, without comparing themselves
to someone else, for each one should carry their own load.

GALATIANS 6:4-5

For as long as I can remember, I have compared myself to the girl next to me. Or the one next to her. Or the one on the glossy cover of a magazine. This comparison thing starts young. No one tells us to compare; we come by it naturally. Grading ourselves against each other is a trap for women whom God has called as individuals, uniquely created for His purposes.

But if and when I remember that I am me, by God's design, I can exhale the worry that I need to match up to someone else. This trap of comparing ourselves to others is a bait that the enemy taunts us with until we learn to stand strong and secure in who we are. How do we do that? We start at the beginning:

God knew us before we ever came to be. God made us in His
image, intricately fashioning us in the womb.
Carrying us since our first breath, He created us for
Himself, for His story—which becomes our history.

No one else will ever be you. Embrace who you are in every possible way—doing your best when God leads you to a task and comparing yourself only with yourself. Align with biblical truth about the honor of being His vessel, His woman, His temple, His treasure, and His possession.

Today I will remember:
- I am not to compare myself against other people.
- I am to do my best and carry my own load.
- I wasn't created to be "her," but only created to be me.

Lord, help me to stop the insanity of comparison and the insecurity it breeds within me. May I live each day unto You, doing my best at what You've called me to do and be.

⟶ ⧉ ⬥⬥⬥ ⧉ ⟵

WHEN I DOUBT MYSELF

Not that I have already obtained all this, or have already arrived at my goal,
but I press on to take hold of that for which Christ Jesus took hold of me.
PHILIPPIANS 3:12

We expect ourselves to be better than we are. Self-focus robs us of moving forward. When we look around at others, it's easy to feel like we are falling short. In this place insecurity takes root once again. Author Holly Gerth says, "If we're doing better, then we're prideful. If someone else's life seems harder, then we don't feel entitled to our pain. God's answer? Focus on him and his plans for your life."[29]

The apostle Paul said, "I do not consider myself yet to have taken hold of it. But one thing I do: Forgetting what is behind and straining toward what is ahead, I press on toward the goal to win the prize for which God has called me heavenward in Christ Jesus."[30]

We can look around and be discouraged and dwell on the mistakes of our past and be defeated—or we can look to Jesus and press in and hold on while He continues to write our story. There is a prize that God has already won for us. He knows something that we often forget: We are His. Our true identity will lead us to confidence instead of discouragement and doubt.

Today I will remember:
• I am not perfect, but I press on, focusing on who I am in Christ.
• I am to focus on the price Christ has paid for me.
• I can find confidence in remembering I am His and He is at work in me.

Father, I spend too much time in self-doubt, discouragement, and even
low-grade depression. Help me to turn my focus to who I am, as Yours,
when the dark cloud of those doubts comes to threaten my confidence.

---

29 Holly Gerth, *You're Already Amazing* (Grand Rapids, MI: Revell, 2012), 48.
30 Philippians 3:13-14.

WELL-TIMED BEAUTY

He has made everything beautiful in its time.

ECCLESIASTES 3:11

Beauty is part of God's plan, but sometimes life and the messes we find ourselves in are anything but beautiful. So we wait for life to change, hoping that beauty will emerge out of the mess. Many of us stay stuck in limbo until circumstances change. But sometimes circumstances keep us waiting a long time because we usually can't make our problems obey our wishes. Do you ever find yourself stuck in the middle?

We move on to what we can change—us. We want to be beautiful, but insist that we are ugly, flawed, or in need of improvement. It's not surprising, because the culture we are in speaks of individuality but also encourages conformity. It's a mixed message. Which is it? Are we good? Or are we bad? Or do we find ourselves somewhere in the middle?

When we are in the middle of difficult circumstances or personal life changes, we can be assured of this: God is in the center of it all with us. He's not waiting for us to clean up or change. No, He's right in the muddy waters with us, assuring us that He has us and He will make our messes beautiful in His time. Hold on—stand on who you are and how He loves. You aren't lost. You may be in the mess, but beauty is coming.

Today I will remember:
- God is the author of all things.
- He isn't surprised by messy middles, but is in them with us.
- Beauty—all His doing—will come in time.

> *Lord, today I trust You with my life and its ugly and messier places. I am Yours, and beauty is Your idea. Thank You that You will make all the unlovely things beautiful in Your time.*

—≈ ❖ ३ ≈—

WOVEN TOGETHER BY GOD

For you created my inmost being; you knit me together in my mother's womb....
My frame was not hidden from you when I was made in the secret place, when
I was woven together in the depths of the earth. Your eyes saw my unformed body.
PSALM 139:13, 15-16

Each of us has been formed in miraculous ways. It's amazing to think that God was weaving the parts of us together when we were hidden from view. Even our parents couldn't direct our coloring, gifting, or the way we would show up in the world. Before our first wailing, welcome cry God knew us, planned for us, and put us together—exactly us—for His plan.

Each one of us has strengths and abilities that others might not have. We are uniquely God's masterpiece, even if we don't feel like we are. Researchers have said, regarding the miraculous making of us, "By the age of three, each of your hundred billion neurons have formed fifteen thousand synaptic connections with other neurons...Your pattern of threads, extensive, intricate and unique, is woven."[31]

The package of who we are is not only unique, but a mystery wrought by a miraculous, wonder-working God. All of our strengths are supported by our weaknesses, a balance that sometimes keeps us from focusing on the most important thing of all—we are His work.

Today I will remember:
- God created me from the inside out.
- I was hidden from people but being created by God.
- He wove me together—all of my abilities were woven in developing for later use.

Lord, what a miracle creation is, from the sky to the sea. Today I am thanking
You for the miracle of me. It is all Your work, and all surrendered
to You from this day until I meet You in eternity. Write the
story, Lord. I'm handing You the pen, once again.

---

31 Marcus Buckingham and Donald O. Clifton, *Now, Discover Your Strengths* (New York: Free Press, 2020), 37.

FREE TO BE ME

Do not be wise in your own eyes; fear the Lord and shun evil.
This will bring health to your body and nourishment to your bones.
PROVERBS 3:7-8

Kids are dreamers. We often say they could be anything they want—which used to mean a rock star, teacher, or astronaut. But now they are encouraged to choose on every level. No wonder we have an identity crisis. We should explore our gifts and talents, learn more about our strengths, weakness, and personality styles. But thinking we can be anything is not a biblical value. God made us unique for His plan. When we leave God out of the equation, we are no longer aligning ourselves to God's plan for us. We are learning to be wise in our own eyes rather than seeing through the eyes of faith and looking to God for direction.

We don't have to hold back from the talents and gifts God has given us, but we can hold out our heart to the God who promises to finish His work in us. We can be confident, yet not wise in our own eyes. We can have a confidence that is centered in the Lord, how He made us, and who we are becoming by following Him. We can be free to be all God has created us for.

Today I will remember:
- I am not to be wise in myself, dependent only on my ways.
- I am to fear and respect God as the One who holds my life and directs my steps.
- When I fear the Lord, my body and bones benefit with health and strength.

Lord, I grew up wanting to be many things. None of those things is
what played out in my life. You surprised me with Your ideas for me,
and I desire to gladly follow You, depending on You daily.

THE EVERYDAY VESSEL

But we have this treasure in jars of clay to show that this
all-surpassing power is from God and not from us.
2 CORINTHIANS 4:7

I have never liked emptying the dishwasher. One morning God spoke to my heart as I put away a well-used pitcher. The words "everyday vessel" came to mind. I looked at the container that I use every single day sitting next to a pretty little teapot. One is an everyday pot and the other a special occasion teapot that is much too fragile for everyday use.

I realized that I was living my life to be a special occasion pot, prepared to shine and be used only for special occasions—a solo at church, a song for a wedding, or a message at a conference. But God has created me to be an everyday vessel. He wants to use me every day in the most ordinary of ways—loving my family, bringing joy to others, and yes, even emptying the dishwasher. Real life and service happens in the everyday spaces of life. That's where God uses clay pots—cracked and imperfect but filled with the glory and power of God to be His hands and feet in the real world.

While we focus on imperfections, God focuses on His glory shining through the cracks. God has placed Himself within fragile, easily broken earthen pots. The focus was never meant to be on us, but on the priceless contents within.

Today I will remember:
• God is the treasure, I am the clay pot.
• Clay pots are imperfect, and God shines through the imperfections.
• An everyday pot is one that God uses every day as a display of His power and love.

Lord, thank You for creating me for a purpose and for letting me
know that cracked and fragile clay pots can be used by You every day.
May the power of God shine through my life and bring You glory.

STATUS AND IDENTITY

For by the grace given me I say to every one of you: Do not think of yourself more highly than you ought, but rather think of yourself with sober judgment, in accordance with the faith God has distributed to each of you.
ROMANS 12:3

Because of ministry travel, I have A-list status and free companion flights with the airlines. Initially I was giddy with excitement to be boarded early and get through the screening lines quickly. Then I got used to the special treatment. I felt a bit smug when whisking past others.

I began to realize my attitude was robbing me of the sweetness of spirit that puts others first, lowers expectations, and is not proud or haughty. It seemed like such a little thing because it was only an airport attitude, but it was bigger than I cared to admit because my identity got tangled up in status. Maybe you can relate. It might not be the airport, but perhaps it's your position at work, in the community, or at church. Anything that elevates us can begin to become an elevated identity. Identity is a tricky thing, because how you view yourself will determine how you act toward others. For instance, if you are self-critical, you will easily criticize others. On the other hand, if you view yourself as God's child, you will most likely want to live with the traits of the Father.

Paul taught the church to not think more highly of themselves than they ought to. Remember that next time you begin to attach who you are to something other than who He is.

Today I will remember:
- I am to pay attention to how I view myself.
- I am not to think too highly or too critically of myself.
- I am to identify myself according to the faith I have in God alone.

Lord, continue to teach me to view myself as You do and identify myself as Yours.

AGELESS TRUTH

Though riches increase, do not set your heart on them.

PSALM 62:10

For my husband's big birthday, his surprise was a sleek white convertible. Something happened when we slid into those low, ground-hugging seats. With music blaring and wind whipping around us, we felt free and young. In reality, we were getting old but identifying as young—if you know, you know! I'm all for staying youthful. It's a necessity to keep up with our ten grandkids. But who we are has been sealed and our identity is based on the foundational fact of being His treasured possession, regardless of age, status, or what we have. That car was fun for a bit, but we traded it in for something more practical. It's amazing what our minds can do and how they can trick us into thinking what we have, what we do, or what people think of us is who we are.

It's time we live as the spiritually rich people that God identifies us as, no longer assigning value on what we have. Riches come and go. One day your account is up and the next day it's down. If our heart is set on more things, we will always have a fickle view of our value. When our heart is set on God and who we are in Him, we are stable both emotionally and spiritually. Our identity is rooted in what God values rather than the values of the world around us.

Today I will remember:
• Where I set my heart is important because that drives my actions.
• Riches may come for a season, but I am to stay centered in my Provider.
• My heart will follow my lead; being foundationally secure will enhance my life.

Lord, thank You for all the seasons of life—the highs and the lows. In the high times, may I never point to money or possessions as my savior or value things as my identity. I am Yours, and I want to live like Yours in every season of life.

THE PROVERBS 31 WOMAN

She is clothed with strength and dignity;
she can laugh at the days to come.
PROVERBS 31:25

When most of us think of the Proverbs 31 woman, we are fixated on all the hats she wore and the many things she did. She was a wife, mother, seamstress, gardener, businesswoman, and dressed like royalty in fine linen and purple. A few verses later we are told how she dressed on the inside—clothed with strength and dignity. Years ago, there was a book titled, *Help, I'm Being Intimidated by the Proverbs Thirty-One Woman.*[32] Laughable, but relatable because Christian women have felt trapped by the expectation to be her.

What kind of woman can laugh or rejoice at the future? At days unknown to her? What we need to understand is that the many things she did weren't who she was. They were just descriptions of what she did. Who was she? She was a woman who trusted God. She knew who she was, and more importantly *whose* she was. This is important for women of today because we all do many things, and often those things become our identity. If those things are taken away, we no longer know who we are. Our identity is easily threatened when life or circumstances change. God assures us that who we are hasn't changed. "Know that the LORD is God. It is he who made us, and we are his; we are his people, the sheep of his pasture."[33]

Today I will remember:
• What I do and the things that define me aren't who I am—they are what I do.
• I can be clothed in strength and dignity as I trust God with my life.
• When I trust God, I can laugh at an unknown future.

Lord, may I be clothed in strength and wrapped in dignity as
I trust You with everything, knowing that I am fully Yours.

---

32 Nancy Kennedy, *Help, I'm Being Intimidated by the Proverbs Thirty-One Woman: My Battles with a Role Model Who's Larger than Life* (Portland, OR: Multnomah, 1995).
33 Psalm 100:3.

SELF-REJECTION

I have loved you with an everlasting love;
I have drawn you with unfailing kindness.

JEREMIAH 31:3

She sat in her room contemplating how to end it all. She was tired of the pain of hating herself. Tired of trying to measure up. Tired of all the negative messages she allowed in over the years—messages that now seemed like the truest thing about her. In the end, she decided that ending it all wasn't the answer, so instead she began the long journey toward healing.

"Over the years, I have come to realize that the greatest trap in our life is not success, popularity, or power, but self-rejection. When we have come to believe in the voices that call us worthless and unlovable, then success, popularity, and power are easily perceived as attractive solutions. The real trap, however, is self-rejection. Self-rejection is the greatest enemy of the spiritual life because it contradicts the sacred voice that calls us the beloved. Being the beloved constitutes the core truth of our existence. Self-rejection is the greatest trap of the enemy."[34]

When we are confused about who we are or why we are here, it's easy to reject ourselves. It might start with small thoughts, but soon the self-hatred and the internalized rejection go deep within our soul. Such negativity about our one and only life goes against the truth of God's love for us. "The LORD knows what is in everyone's mind. He understands everything you think. If you go to him for help, you will get an answer."[35]

Today I will remember:
- God knows me completely.
- He accepts me with unfailing kindness.
- He understands the way I have put myself down and will help me back up.

Lord, help me to walk away from self-rejection and run instead into Your
arms of love and kindness. I want to accept myself and the way You love me.

---

34 Henri Nowen, *Life of the Beloved* (New York: Crossroad, 1992), 21.
35 1 Chronicles 28:9, NCV.

DECEIVED BY SHAME

If anyone is in Christ, the new creation has come:
The old has gone, the new is here!
2 CORINTHIANS 5:17

Guilt is when you do something wrong and know it. *Shame* is when you think who you are is wrong. My entire life was built on shame. A child of an alcoholic, I felt something was wrong with me and our home. I lived trying to overcompensate for my father's inconsistencies and my mother's anger. I didn't know who I was outside of the dysfunction, and it took years for me to understand that in Christ I was made new.

The sins we commit and the sins committed against us are not our identity. They are not the sum total of who we are. Shame tries to convince us that we are damaged. The enemy wants us to believe this lie, but in Christ we have been made new. It's a fundamental truth that must be embraced if we are going to live in who we are in Christ. Today's verse refers to the previous verses: "And he died for all, that those who live should no longer live for themselves but for him who died for them and was raised again. So from now on we regard no one from a worldly point of view."[36]

If you are viewing yourself through eyes of shame, you are still looking through a worldly lens. Today is the day to embrace the truth of Christ's work in you. You are free to live for Him and not enslaved any longer to the shame of your past.

Today I will remember:
• I am a new creation in Christ.
• All the old things about me are now gone.
• I am to view myself as loved by God and not through the lens of shame.

Lord, thank You for bearing my shame and sin on the cross. May I live
honoring You by believing I am new and no longer who I once was.

HIS DELIGHT

*The Lord your God is with you, the Mighty Warrior
who saves. He will take great delight in you; In his love he
will no longer rebuke you, but rejoice over you with singing.*
ZEPHANIAH 3:17

I've always liked research. I especially enjoy the self-assessment tests that are so popular. I think I've done them all. Our culture is interested in the journey of discovering individual identity. Personality tests, assessments, and quizzes are everywhere. It seems like everyone is searching for someone to tell them who they are, where they belong, or how they fit into this world. The Bible says that we have been made in God's image. We have been created to reflect God's attributes. We can look for identity anywhere, but as followers of Jesus we are encouraged to find our identity in Him. It took me a while to realize the importance of looking to God first.

To understand your identity as a follower of Christ, you must understand how He sees you. It's important as you build your identity to understand that knowing God isn't just part of who you are—it's the whole of who you are becoming. Your identity can be defined by who God is making you to be in Christ. Jesus delights in you. You are not just put up with, but you have been welcomed into His family with great joy. He is a mighty warrior who saves you from all harm, including saving you from the carnal obsession of finding self. We find ourselves when we find ourselves in Him. It's then that He quiets our fears in His love.

Today I will remember:
• The Lord is with me.
• He is mighty to save and delights in me.
• He forgives me and sings over me with joy.

> *Lord, You have always known me, and nothing about me is a surprise
> to You. Thank You for delighting in me and for rejoicing over my life.*

SEALED IDENTITY

You see, at just the right time, when we were
still powerless, Christ died for the ungodly.

ROMANS 5:6

I wondered what impostor syndrome was—then I experienced it. Impostor syndrome is fear that you aren't authentically who you claim to be. You are part truth and part lie—a fake, a pretender, a fraud. It is the awful feeling of self-doubt. Oh, how the enemy loves to accuse us of being impostors.

His accusations keep our eyes on self, focused inward, so that we are living in fear and insecurity. He loves to tempt us to believe we are fraudulent Christians because we aren't perfect. We buy into it and are tempted to give up. It's too steep a climb, and so we hide behind facades so no one will know how we doubt ourselves and even secretly question who we are. It's not something we talk about, but the deep, insidious roots go into our soul, keeping us trapped in self-doubt.

There is a way out. Christ came for us though we are flawed and often weak. If we were meant to be perfect, Christ's death would be in vain. Our identity is sealed, and it's not an impostor identity, but rather blood-bought. Let's not take the death of Christ in vain by expecting perfection from ourselves. Let's readily admit we are sinners saved by amazing grace. Let's boast in that. Let's glory in the beauty of His power. Let's live in who we really are—His.

Today I will remember:
- Christ died for imperfect people like me.
- I wasn't created to be perfect in myself, but redeemed in Christ.
- I will stop the impostor taunts when they come, knowing they are a lie.

Lord, thank You for the blood You shed to save me from myself. I am not an impostor,
but a grateful, forgiven girl. I am Yours, and there is nothing fake about that.

CRISIS OF BELIEF

All Scripture is God-breathed and is useful for teaching...
so that the servant of God may be thoroughly equipped.
2 TIMOTHY 3:16-17

As we wonder who we are and why we are here, things can get muddled. It's important to stay in the basics of Scripture—who God is and what Scripture teaches. Going back to the very beginning, "God created mankind in his own image"[37] and "God saw all that he had made, and it was very good."[38] There are two truths that should help us in our search for significance: God made us in His image, and He said that what He made was good.

Oswald Chamber writes, "Before we choose to follow God's will, a crisis must develop in our lives."[39] For many the crisis of belief exists in chronic insecurities that affect our relationships and how we show up in this world. We can waste precious days doubting our significance and living with feelings of not being enough. This is when it's important to hold on to the truth that God made us in His image. To be made in His image has nothing to do with our physical bodies, because God has no physical form. Instead, we were created as reflections of God's glory, creativity, and character. We can continue to doubt ourselves and stay stuck in insecurity or rise up with the confidence that God made us and we are an important and valuable part of His story. We believe these things by faith in God's Word.

Today I will remember:
• All Scripture is God-breathed.
• All Scripture is valuable to teach and guide.
• Scripture informs me of my value.

Lord, may I stop doubting the truth that I have value and hold on
to the truth that You created me, in Your image, to reflect You in this world.

---

37 Genesis 1:27.

38 Genesis 1:31.

39 Oswald Chambers, *My Utmost for His Highest* (Grand Rapids, MI: Our Daily Bread
    Ministries, 1992), Jan 1.

UNPLANNED FOR

You created all things, and they exist because you created what you pleased.
REVELATION 4:11, NLT

I found out later in life that my mother didn't plan for me or want me. I have become convinced that it doesn't matter what she wanted at the time, because God wanted me and planned for me all along—I was born into this world on the exact day and time that God had written in His book. "All the days ordained for me were written in your book before one of them came to be."[40] Our birth isn't just the union of two lovestruck people, it's the miracle of life that takes place according to the will and plan of God. When I began to grasp that truth, my view of self, life, and purpose experienced a major upgrade.

When you were born, God was there as an unseen witness of your birth. He wanted you alive because your one and only life is part of His plan and greater story. When you fully understand the truth of your significance, your life will change as you realize that your value has been assigned by God. Your value has nothing to do with what you weigh, how you look, or how successful you are at managing life. Your value is wrapped up in the truth that God takes delight and pleasure in you. Yes, even when no one else is noticing, God is smiling.

"The LORD takes delight in his people."[41]

Today I will remember:
- My value has nothing to do with what others think of me.
- My value has been assigned by the God who wanted me and planned for me.
- My life is to be lived for God's pleasure.

Lord, when I am tempted to live life only for myself,
remind me that I was created for Your pleasure and purpose.

---

40 Psalm 139:16.
41 Psalm 149:4.

IDENTITY AND ATTITUDE

Good news makes for good health.
PROVERBS 15:30, NLT

Attitude is everything. When we know who we are, as His, our perspective changes. We see throughout Scripture how men and women chose to believe God had chosen them to be His. They framed the bad situations with the hope that God was with them. We can learn a lot about how a good outlook increases our joy and health.

The last few years have been hard. It's been easy to forget that we are His. I can have a hard time pushing past bad news, but even in light of a lung cancer diagnosis, my husband was not going to let the flames of circumstance cause him to forget who he belonged to. He developed the ability to focus on his faith in God, and his example taught me a lot about how daily attitude affects our health and well-being.

Have you ever been touched by someone's attitude? There is power in the way we engage with other people. Something as simple as remembering to smile, be pleasant, and respond kindly can add joy to someone's day. According to King Solomon, who wrote Proverbs, it can also contribute to good health. Perhaps we could develop a habit of smiling and paying attention to how we speak to others. It is proven that what we do repeatedly not only creates a habitual way of life, but it creates neural pathways in our brain. We give to others by the way we interact with them—while also creating positive energy in our brain that promotes personal joy and peace. It's a win-win.

Today I will remember:
- I might not be able to control my circumstances, but I can choose my attitude.
- The way I interact with people can change both me and them.
- My life can be a vessel of joy to other people.

Lord, today I choose gratitude. I choose to believe the good news that no matter what I go through, You are with me. Remind me to interact kindly with others.

THE MAKER'S MANUAL

Know that the Lord is God. It is he who made his us,
and we are his; we are his people, the sheep of his pasture.

PSALM 100:3

Imagine that for our anniversary my husband gives me a food processor and I give him a power tool. Then after the gifts are opened, he is reading my instruction manual for the food processor to figure out how to use his power tool. That would be crazy! But this is how we go about life. God made us, He has the instructions and knows what will be best, and yet we Google opinions on how to live. According to the Maker's plan, we are to approach life with the joy and confidence of being His.

Jesus said, "I am the good shepherd. The good shepherd lays down his life for the sheep...I am the good shepherd; I know my sheep and my sheep know me—just as the Father knows me and I know my Father."[42] It's good to be cared for by the shepherd. It's good to be loved by God and to be His. When it comes down to it, we can search forever for significance, meaning, and to figure out who we are, but all of those things are only found in relationship with Jesus. When you find Jesus and follow Him, you finally begin to start coming home to yourself. I can imagine Jesus smiling each day as He opens His arms to me, welcoming me home to the true me and the reason I exist—for Him.

Today I will remember:
- I am to know that the Lord is God.
- I am to know that He made me and I am His.
- I am to know that because I am His, He leads me as a shepherd.

Lord, I ramp up with overthinking my purpose, value,
and life. When I quiet myself before You, it's like
coming home. May I stay quieted by Your love and truth

---

42 John 10:11, 14-15.

April

LIVING WITH JOY

"Joy is the infallible sign of the presence of God."
—*unknown*

JOY—JESUS. OVER. YOU.

You will fill me with joy in your presence.
PSALM 16:11

We live in a culture that says if something doesn't bring you joy, toss it. But joy is deeper than an emotion and not dependent on circumstances or having a life filled with what we want. The dictionary describes joy as a source or cause of delight. As Christians, joy is more than a happy feeling; it's the assurance of God's care for us. Since joy is dependent on Christ's presence, we can experience joy regardless of what's going on in our lives.

I have often seen an acronym for Joy: Jesus, Others, Yourself. But as a recovering people pleaser, I easily get stuck on the "others" in the equation and end up emptied instead of filled—others focused rather than Christ centered. In a hard season, desperate for joy, I came up with this acronym:

J—Jesus
O—Over
Y—You

This positional commitment of God being with us and over us changes everything. Remembering this acronym of joy reminds me that joy isn't reliant on good times or happy feelings but rests on the assurance that I am covered and loved. Turning my thoughts to this is like exhaling. When I turn my thoughts in His direction, focused on being in His presence, believing He is with me and for me, my heart rate slows down and I have a settled peace that brings me joy in the good, the bad, and all the ordinary places of life.

Today I will remember:
• Joy is deeper than my happenings—it's found in knowing that God is over me.
• Joy infuses me with strength—I can learn to lean into its promise.
• Joy is for ordinary days—an invitation into faith in God's presence.

Lord, thank You that joy is much more than a fleeting feeling.
May I learn to live in the truth of Your presence over me.

GOD IS ALWAYS WITH US

Do not fear, for I have redeemed you... When you pass through the waters, I will be with you; and when you pass through the rivers, they will not sweep over you. When you walk through the fire, you will not be burned... For I am the Lord you God.

ISAIAH 43:1-3

Some of us are familiar with living overwhelmed. Stress becomes our norm until the storms of life pass. Hard circumstances and challenges plant fear and unsteadiness. We add worry to our overwhelmed thoughts, and before we realize it, we are no longer operating in faith. Our circumstances and feelings have stolen the joy and landed in the driver's seat of our life.

This portion of Scripture declares how surely God is with us. The next verse reads, "Since you are precious and honored in my sight, and because I love you...do not be afraid."[43] Powerful words from God to His people, and important for us to hold on to as well.

God promises to be with us in the circumstances and challenges of life—those things that cause us worry, fear, or be overwhelmed. It's a good practice to remember what He says, reminding ourselves who He is and praising God through it all because He is with us in it all.

Joy is experienced as—Jesus Over You—all of you, all of your circumstances.

Today I will remember:
- Jesus is with me.
- Because of His presence, my circumstances will not overwhelm me.
- Because I am precious to Him, the heat of my problems will not burn me.

Lord, today I lift my face and thank You that I am precious in Your sight and that You honor me with protection and Your presence. I can tell myself in weak moments, "do not be afraid—God is with you."

---

43 Isaiah 43:4-5.

FILLED WITH JOY

The Lord has done great things for us, and we are filled with joy.
PSALM 126:3

It's easy to forget how God has showed up in our lives. At the time of need, we are grateful for His provision. But then life goes on and we are prone to forget. We are not the first people who have been tempted to forget; the children of Israel were too. They were reminded, "Be careful that you do not forget the LORD, who brought you out of Egypt, out of the land of slavery."[44]

When we forget the goodness of God, we sink into grumpiness rather than rising up to gratefulness. Worse yet, forgetting God is one of the things the enemy uses to rob us of the very joy that gives us strength. But let's be clear—you have to hand over the joy; it doesn't get snatched out from under you. When we make our problems precious, they poison us and eventually paralyze us. How do we make our problems precious? By holding them close to our heart. In an attempt to protect ourselves, we might be handing over our joy by not handing things over to God.

Remembering the great things God has done fills us with joy. Don't hand the joy over to be stolen and buried. Inhale the joy and exhale the worries. Inhale the truth and let go of the enemy's lies.

Today I will remember:
- The Lord is great and always with me.
- I am filled with joy when I remember the goodness of God.
- Joy is something that I can hold on to despite my circumstances.

Lord, as I go throughout my day, remind me of Your goodness.
As gratefulness fills my heart, may I be filled with joy in
the middle of my everyday, ordinary circumstances.

THROUGH IT ALL

All the ways of the Lord are loving and faithful.

PSALM 25:10

I used to think that being a Christian meant my life would be wrapped up with the bow of abundance and blessing. But real life happens, and often it hits hard. When things don't go the way I've planned, it's important to frame my emotional response with spiritual truth. I tend to freak out in the middle of my mess, but if I reframe things with a Biblical perspective, my feelings calm down within me. My circumstances are not a surprise to God and can be the path to my spiritual growth. The frame around us is always His love and faithfulness—Scripture says His banner over us is love.[45]

What if we learned to frame the hardest thing we're facing with the hope of His love and faithfulness? The truth is clear: The Lord leads His people and is always at work in our lives. We can't see what's next, but He knows exactly what's needed to get us to the center of His plan for us. The fact of God's love is not a flimsy sentiment, but a powerful truth that we can hold on to when things make no sense. Through all the highs and lows of life, He is working out of love and faithfulness toward those who are His. Being His does not make life perfect, but it does give us indescribable joy in uncertain times.

Today I will remember:
- All God's ways are good.
- He works out of His love for me.
- He is faithful to bring out the best in me and for me.

> *Lord, what comfort it brings me to declare that all Your ways are loving and faithful! May I trust You in all things because in all things You are working out of two important motivations—love and faithfulness.*

THE BEAUTY OF JOY

Those who look to him for help will be radiant with joy;
no shadow of shame will darken their faces.

PSALM 34:5, NLT

I am drawn to lotions and potions that promise to bring back the glow to this well-worn face. In the effort to shine in a culture that shouts that youth is beauty, I can get sucked into the late-night advertisements and the promises of Instagram influencers.

Though we all probably care about looking our best, the Bible holds out a different path to beauty: "Your beauty should not come from outward adornment... It should be that of your inner self...This is the way the holy women of the past who put their hope in God adorned themselves."[46]

When we look to Him, we become radiant—we shine, glow, and emanate joy and health. We don't have to have perfect circumstances to be radiant. We don't have to use the latest or greatest goop to shine. What we do need is to put our hope in Jesus and look to Him to be our help. God helps us as we hope in Him, and we will shine with His joy, which is the most beautiful glow of all. Timeless and ageless, we can leave shame in the past and embrace hope for the future.

Today I will remember:
• Looking to God as my source is a pathway to joy.
• Light is beauty, and it comes from trusting God.
• Shame darkens us and drags us down.

Lord, may I radiate Your beauty and love to all I am in contact
with, regardless of their opinion of me or reaction to me.

THE JOY OF PLEASING GOD

To the person who pleases him,
God gives wisdom, knowledge and happiness.
ECCLESIASTES 2:26

As a mother, I really liked when my children did things that pleased me. Small acts from my little ones showed that they were paying attention and that they loved me. I can imagine how much it pleases God when I do the things that please Him. Our relationship with God isn't about the good things we do, but about the grace given to us in Christ. Does this mean that pleasing God no longer matters? No, living to please God is a worthy life goal for every believer and the measure by which we should choose our attitude and actions.

Living to please God in the here and now simply means putting faith in Him. But faith, as we know, is not so simple in lives with problems and heartaches, highs and lows. Faith requires trusting when we don't know the road ahead, believing when there isn't an answer to our problems, and following even though the road is dark. This kind of faith pleases God. It pleases God when we live in a way that says we know He has us, will take care of us, and has heard our prayers.

The benefit to pleasing God? He grants wisdom, knowledge, and happiness! Since joy and happiness intertwine, I can't think of a better exchange.

Today I will remember:
- Pleasing God is putting faith in who He is.
- God grants me wisdom when my faith is placed in Him.
- God gives happiness to those who rely upon Him for all they need.

Lord, may I have the kind of faith that pleases You. Take the small seed of faith that I have and increase it to a large, sturdy faith that trusts You in all things.

LIVING SET APART

The Joy of the Lord is your Strength.
NEHEMIAH 8:10

The day was going perfectly when I walked into a neighborhood store with a song in my heart. While scanning the aisle, I saw someone I knew, and she turned away to avoid me. I was hurt and confused, which quickly moved to an emotional spiral. Where was the joy I walked into the store with? Gone. I blamed Satan for stealing my joy until I realized that it was me who forfeited it. It was valid for me to be hurt, but if I give away the strength I have in Jesus each time I'm hurt or triggered, I will live discouraged and weak.

This verse has an opener: "This day is sacred to our Lord. Do not grieve..." *Sacred* simply means set apart. Because each day is sacred, I'm not to give my strength away so easily. The joy of Jesus is not dependent on circumstances, it's rooted in the strength of trusting God. When trusting God, even triggering events can be a window into our soul and a path to growth.

Each day is a gift. Maybe you'd like a gift receipt to return what you've been given in exchange for something better. Friend, God is inviting us to a place of joy where we deal with every hard thing in His strength.

Today I will remember:
- There is strength in joy.
- The joy of the Lord is not dependent on circumstances.
- Daily joy is a sacred path to lean into.

Lord, when I am triggered and emotionally upset, joy goes out the
window. Help me to realize that joy and strength go hand in hand.

COUNT IT ALL JOY

Consider it pure joy, my brothers and sisters, whenever you face trials of many kinds, because you know that the testing of your faith produces perseverance.
JAMES 1:2-3

This verse is a hard one to swallow. It doesn't seem natural to count my trials a pure joy, or as it says in one version, a sheer gift. Candidly, I dislike going through hard things. I am a conflict avoider. This verse seems to be saying I should press in with joy.

The single word *because* cues up the reason that the hard things we go through can be considered joy—*because* there is a promised outcome, and it's good. This points to the way we view the problem more than the situation itself. When we consider the reality that God is at work at all times and through all things, we will be able to hold on in the middle—in that space between a prayer and its answer. We can claim joy at the onset of hard things because something holy and beautiful will take place as our faith is tested. Friend, I don't know your place of hard today, but this I know—God is for you. When I stop and think of God being for me, I must admit it softens the blow and helps me see through a lens of joy.

Today I will remember:
- How I view my trials determines whether I can hold on to joy in the midst of them.
- Each trial is a testing of faith, and God plans for me to pass the test.
- I will remember what I know in the middle of the trial and hold on to God's promised outcome.

Father, help me to see my hardships differently. May I find joy by remaining in Your presence in the middle of trials.

JOURNEY INTO JOY

May the God of hope fill you with all joy and peace as you trust in him,
so that you may overflow with hope by the power of the Holy Spirit.

ROMANS 15:13

Recently a friend shared how God keeps assuring her that no matter how her situation turns out, it will be OK. Her circumstance would cause anxiety and fear for most. But the joy on her face was not only obvious, it was contagious. She was assured that because God is for her, always with her, and will never leave her—things, be as they might, will be OK.

Joy is something we journey into. It doesn't come with a snap of the finger. Real life requires more than that. God invites us into a relationship that is characterized by believing that we can trust Him in all things. Because I like to be in control, it's hard for me to let go and relinquish control—even to God. Jesus delights in filling us with the gifts of joy and peace as we put our hope in Him. There is a joy that comes from believing he's got you and that it's going to be OK because He will never leave you and goes before you.

Today I will remember:
- Jesus is the God of hope, not the God of rules or despair.
- When I believe in Him, I am filled with joy and peace.
- The Holy Spirit enables me to live not only in hope, but in true joy in believing God for every outcome.

Lord, some days it's hard to hand over my situations. They are complex,
and it seems in the moment like venting or worrying is my only option.
When I am in that headspace, I have no joy at all. Help me to remember that
whatever I am facing is going to be OK as I put my hope completely in You.

THE UNEXPECTED DARK

Light shines on the godly, and joy on those whose hearts are right.
PSALM 97:11, NLT

After a recent power outage, while I was grappling to find candles and flashlights, it became clear that the dark—especially the unexpected dark—makes life difficult. Maybe you have experienced the unexpected darkness of a relational hurt, a family misunderstanding, or turmoil in an area that is usually stable. When the darkness tries to come in, it's time for us to examine our hearts before God. While the dark seals things shut, the light opens up a window that brings the relief of being able to move about freely and with clarity. I much prefer the illuminating power of light over the instability of darkness.

How do we untangle ourselves from the things that keep light far from us? The psalmist said here that light shines on the just, those who are walking uprightly before God and men. It's not reserved for the perfect people who make no mistakes, but for those whose hearts are lined up to the heart of God despite their own brokenness and imperfections. Some days it will be easier to walk uprightly than others, but the truth is, when we love justice, God's way, and light over darkness, we begin to live in joy and gladness.

Today I will remember:
• Light is an option, and the opposite is darkness.
• The godly are those who have put their hope in God.
• Joy comes with examination of our hearts and a desire to line our hearts to His.

*Lord, set my heart right and fill me with
the joy that comes from living in Your light.*

GOD MEETS US WHERE WE ARE

When times are good, be happy; but when times are bad,
consider this: God has made the one as well as the other.
ECCLESIASTES 7:14

Today is one of those hard days full of relational turmoil and misunderstanding. A phone call left me devastated, and to think I can just choose joy is ridiculous. But God wants to meet me here in my hurt and frustration.

I don't know about you, but I don't need anyone to tell me to be joyful when life is easy. It's in the hardships that I need a gentle nudge or maybe even a push to remember that God is with me. Hardship doesn't necessarily mean you are doing something wrong; it just means you are experiencing real life. To be honest, as much as I don't like the hard times, I have grown much more in them than in the easy times. It's important to remember that both seasons—the good and the hard—have purpose. If we consider God in the middle of adverse situations, we will find an unexpected path to joy.

How do we get from point A to point B—out of the funk and into joy? It's all about redirecting our focus. When we are focused on our hurt, we hurt ourselves even more. When our focus is redirected to have faith in God through our hurt by praying over the details, we begin to live above instead of buried under the situation.

Today I will remember:
• Good days and bad days are both part of life.
• In the day of adversity, I must remember that even then God is with me.
• God is with me in all things, and I need to focus on that.

> *Father, when I don't know what to do, may I look to You and find a*
> *perspective of joy, remembering that in everything You are over me.*

CONNECTED TO THE SOURCE OF JOY

I have told you this so that my joy may be
in you and that your joy may be complete.

JOHN 15:11

Have you ever felt disconnected from God? Or have you felt your life was on hold, stuck in a pattern of unfruitfulness? There is much to learn from the words of Jesus. In John 15 He speaks about pruning, and though He used a plant as an illustration, He was teaching them about the cutting away of something in their hearts and lives. Jesus said that every branch will be pruned—either because there is no fruit or to make it even more fruitful. Pruning is good.

Everything comes down to remaining attached to the vine. It's easy for me to wake up to scrolling, emails, or texts. Coffee in hand, I can go down a rabbit hole or two before ever connecting with God. Did He say we must be connected to add one more thing and make life hard? No, the opposite. He told us these things so that we can live in joy. And He wasn't speaking of circumstance-based joy, but rather joy that comes from being tethered to Him.

Remaining in Him is not seasonal or a onetime decision. Remaining in Jesus is a daily connection that leads us to surrender and service. It begins when we open our eyes in the morning and ends when we close our eyes at night. It's this kind of life that finds joy even when being pruned, in pain, or in the middle of impossibilities.

Today I will remember:
- Jesus spoke of the importance of remaining in Him.
- Pruning is part of life, and though hard, is always for my good.
- Joy is complete when we are connected daily to Jesus.

Lord, when I wake, may I pray a simple prayer of surrender for
that day. And when I sleep, may I say a prayer of gratitude.

THE JOY OF LETTING GO

*I know that there is nothing better for people
than to be happy and to do good while they live.*
ECCLESIASTES 3:12

I have a plaque that reads, *Life doesn't have to be perfect for it to be wonderful.* I bought it at a time of unraveling. Seeing those words on my wall made me realize that I didn't have to be unhappy—I was choosing it.

The writer of Ecclesiastes penned profound words about living. Life would be different if we simplified and lived by these words: "He has made everything beautiful in its time...There is nothing better for people than to be happy and do good...eat and drink, and find satisfaction in all their toil—this is the gift of God."[47]

Living well is a gift from God. Life put into His hands is light, free, satisfying, and beautiful. When trusting His plan, we work hard, play hard, celebrate well, and declare our imperfect days beautiful. We quit waiting for things to be different before we live happy lives—we start today, right where we are at.

It's easy to joke, "Jesus take the wheel," but sadly it's hard for us to let go of the wheel of our lives. The need to control robs us of the joy we could experience by doing the next right thing and trusting God with the outcome. Letting go doesn't mean we quit showing up or trying—but it does mean we quit fighting happiness by controlling, complaining, and being ungrateful.

Today I will remember:
• God makes everything beautiful in His time.
• There is a time and season for everything in life.
• There is nothing better than to live well today and find joy in trusting God.

Lord, letting go is one of the hardest challenges. Help me to relinquish my life completely to You, for truly You want me to have joy and find satisfaction in my days.

EYES THAT SEE THE GOOD

A joyful heart is good medicine.
PROVERBS 17:22

Rather than thinking of joy as an emotional high, begin to view it as a spiritual practice that brings healing. Solomon said that having a heart filled with joy was like taking good medicine. God wired us for joy, and it is good for our body and soul. This healing practice of having a joyful heart can become a default or habit. When we do something repeatedly, we begin to build new and different pathways in our thinking. If negativity is on repeat in our thoughts, neural pathways will develop an unhappy groove in our thinking. But if we tune our mind in to positive things, we will have new pathways of joy and peace. Practicing the daily habit of joy is where we begin a healthier way of life.

The single most direct path to a joyful heart is gratitude. Looking for good and thanking God for everything changes us. When we approach life like a woman in search of a treasure, looking for any good we can find each day, we become women who are joy filled even when life is hard. But if we allow negative talk, overthinking, or obsessing over what we don't like or don't have to be our habit, we will be ungrateful and discouraged. We get to choose.

Today I will remember:
- I get to choose what I think about throughout each day.
- When I practice gratitude, the joyful mental pathways become stronger.
- Joy is like a good medicine, healing me from the inside out.

Father, forgive me for the times I am negative when there is so much to be thankful for. Help me to develop the spiritual practice of joy in my everyday, ordinary life.

HAPPY TO BE HIS

Joyful indeed are those whose God is the Lord.
PSALM 144:15, NLT

I have known people in enviable circumstances who are miserable, and people with miserable circumstances who are happy. Makes you think, doesn't it? When are you the happiest? Is it when you have what you want? Or can it also be when you have what you never wanted but you have assurance that God is with you?

Leaning into joy simply means pressing toward joy rather than settling for discouragement. This leaning into joy is not a flimsy, feeling-based thing; rather, it's a stance of confidence. There is nothing that can ultimately separate us from the love of God, and because of this, we can live in a place of being happy that we belong to Him. He is writing our story. Some chapters are harder than others, and some pages seem unbearable. And yet He is always working in us and for us.

The Amplified Bible says it like this: "how blessed (fortunate, prosperous, and favored) are the people whose God is the LORD!" Think about that. Today, practice telling yourself who you are and whose you are. Thank Him that you are favored and blessed—Jesus. Over. You.

Today I will remember:
- The Lord God has triumphed over all things in this life.
- I am His, and He leads me and cares for me.
- I will be happy and blessed when He is the blessed controller of my life.

Father, I want to live in my true identity, as a woman belonging to God,
having true joy, which is found by my surrender to You as Lord of my
life. This is not a onetime surrender, but a daily one. May I commit my
life, my heart, and my comings and goings to You once again today.

SHELTERED IN PLACE

But let all who take refuge in you be glad; let them ever sing for joy.
PSALM 5:11

I had never heard the term *shelter in place* until 2020. Rather than feeling sheltered, it caused a lot of fear. Problems can make us feel unsafe. Circumstances go sideways, and sometimes it seems it would be easier to run away. If we run, we will still be with ourselves wherever we go. As the worry over details increases, we can easily feel as if we are on shaky ground. Learning to lean into God and depend on Him is an inside job.

To take refuge means to find a place of shelter. Each of us can find the everlasting shelter we need in the Lord. Run to Him. Cry out to Him. Give Him your every detailed concern. Then step back and begin thanking Him that He is your hiding place and your shelter from every storm in this life.

When we do this, the problems we are facing begin turning around in joyful chorus because we begin to trust God with the practical, ordinary things that often make life complicated and heavy—things like relational struggles, financial hardships, and medical diagnoses. Even in—especially in—these things we can run to God for shelter and find joy in His presence.

Today I will remember:
- Taking refuge in Jesus is depending on Him to shelter me.
- Taking refuge in Jesus is outlining my requests before Him.
- Taking refuge in Jesus is proclaiming victory and joy over my life as an overcomer.

Lord, let me not settle for being out in the cold during the storms of life.
Remind me to run to You and find the shelter I need in every situation.

BLESS THE LORD, O MY SOUL

My heart leaps for joy, and with my song I praise him.
PSALM 28:7

I was waiting to go for my cancer treatments with a tear-stained face and discouraged heart. Cancer disrupted my life and placed my plans on hold. My eyes settled on the baby grand piano that I hadn't played for years. I was drawn to those black and white keys. As I pulled out the leather bench, I noticed a song sheet from the men's group that had met at our house the night before—"Ten Thousand Reasons" by Matt Redman. The chords were familiar, and my heart needed every lyric on that sheet. Slowly I began to play while saying the words—*whatever may pass and whatever lies before me, let me be singing when the evening comes.* As my speed and confidence picked up, I was playing and singing in real time. With each new lyric, my heart began to fill with joy. At first it was a trickling joy, but by the time I tucked that bench back in, I was filled to overflowing and ready to face the day—even with my treatments.

You don't have to play an instrument to bless the Lord in song. Turn up your car radio, sing with your home stereo, or sing in the warmth of a long shower. Praise Him in song, with your regular voice on all those regular days that make up your ordinary life.

Today I will remember:
• Praising God takes my mind off my problems.
• Singing ushers in joy.
• When we sing, our inner being leaps with gladness.

Lord, let me remember to praise You in the storms as well as on the regular days. Thank You for being the author of simple joys like singing.

THE EXCHANGED LIFE

You turned my wailing into dancing;
You removed my sackcloth and clothed me with joy.

PSALM 30:11

Julia walked though rejection and disappointment most of her life. Sad and afraid for her future, she settled into the rut of negative thoughts and daily depression. She couldn't pull herself out.

Though she was a Christian, she had never been given the tools to handle negative emotions. Nor had she been taught how to walk in the Spirit and push back the old habits of the flesh—habits as simple as negativity and discouragement, two traits she carried from childhood. She had made her problems precious, not looking to God with them, and they poisoned her. One day she declared—no more!

Julia dared to hand over her sadness to the God who loved her. When we come to God with something to exchange, He gladly makes the exchange for us. Today, try trading in your discouragement for a dance of joy. Hand it over; don't make it precious. You are precious to the God who loves you, but obsession over sadness and problems disrupt the joy and strength you can have in Jesus. Let go today. You will be glad you did as you find yourself clothed with new strength and a happier heart.

Today I will remember:
- God invites me to exchange my sorrow for His joy.
- He often takes the biggest disappointment and turns it to a trust experience.
- I will dance before Him and declare Him good and worthy of my praise.

Lord, help me not to gravitate to sadness when
I can exchange the sadness for joy in You.

THE BATTLE IS WON IN PRAISING GOD

Sing joyfully to the Lord, you righteous;
it is fitting for the upright to praise him.
PSALM 33:1

There is much to be said about resisting the enemy and standing firm in faith. Both are easier said than done. In the heat of the battle, it's usually hard to stop the negative spiral. But did you know that when we sing songs of worship, it puts up an ambush against the enemy?

The account of King Jehoshaphat and his people in battle tells us, "As they began to sing and praise, the LORD set ambushes against the men of Ammon and Moab and Mount Sier who were invading Judah, and they were defeated."[48]

The battle was won in praise. Let that sink in.

Maybe, like me, you don't feel inclined to break out in song when you are in a battle. You can still surround yourself with praise music. Let other worshipers sing for you. Fill the atmosphere with praise. When you get your bearings, then you can begin praising too. As we praise God, it puts the enemy in his place, defeating him and his purposes against us. Not only that, to sing and praise is fitting for those who belong to Christ. As His, we praise because we know He is with us and for us.

Today I will remember:
• Singing with joy to the Lord is fitting for those who belong to Him.
• Praising God silences the enemy.
• Worshipping sets up an ambush against the attack of enemy armies.

Lord, though I don't naturally break into song when troubled,
I acknowledge that doing so is powerful in breaking the power of
the enemy. May I remember to fill the atmosphere with worship
when my heart is troubled or my day is spinning out of control.

---

48 2 Chronicles 20:22.

JOY RESTORED

Restore to me the joy of your salvation and
grant me a willing spirit, to sustain me.
PSALM 51:12

I became a Christian right before entering college. Seeing *The Jesus Revolution* reminded me of those early days of fresh faith and walking with Jesus. I don't often think of those days, but remembering them brought back the joy I had then—the joy of my salvation.

Moving an hour south to Orange County, California, right after graduation was more than a move—it was God orchestrating the pieces of our lives. I was a broken girl from a dysfunctional family, filled with self-doubt and on my way to teenage alcoholism. My mother was a hard worker and an occult dabbler. Daddy was a good man and a good drinker. Everyone was doing their best to survive.

But Jesus in His goodness made Himself real to us. The previous script was flipped, and all of our lives were radically changed. Over the years I had forgotten those early days of belief and change. I've had problems and pain—real life is full of both, even for those who trust Jesus. But the difference is that if we are His, He sustains us.

Maybe it's time to come back to your earliest memories of knowing Jesus and trusting Him. Or maybe it's time to come to Him for the first time. He is a life changer.

Today I will remember:
• God desires to restore the joy of our salvation.
• He can give us willing hearts and the spirit to follow His way.
• He sustains us in all things at all times as we look to Him.

Lord, thank You for my salvation and for Your grace that
made a new life possible for broken people like me.

DEVELOPING TRUST

Bring joy to your servant, Lord, for I put my trust in you.
PSALM 86:4

Trust is dependence. It is the belief in the reliability, character, or strength of someone or something. As Christians, we can talk about trust while living like we don't believe that God is who He says He is. When we are hit with a situation, a problem, a trial, or a waiting space, we don't like it. It's not fun or comfortable. But we all have a choice. We can forget whose we are and anxiously try to fix things on our own, or we can focus on the truth that we belong to God and He is on the throne and Lord over our life. We can learn to lean into the truth that He is good and He holds us together.

As we stretch ourselves to trust the character of God, it's important to pay attention to His still, small voice. He might not give us an immediate answer to our situation, but if we focus on His faithfulness and love we will receive just enough light in the dark to illuminate the step we are on. It's limited, but for today it's enough. Practice not obsessing over the plan, but instead, pray and put your trust completely in Him. Putting our trust in the Lord means living one day at a time, one step at a time, while listening for His leading. God will bring joy to our hearts as we put our trust in Him.

Today I will remember:
- Joy and trust go hand in hand.
- Everyone has waiting spaces while God is working but we can't see.
- Trust in God is often like walking in the dark while He lights one step at a time.

Lord, trusting You is often hard, but I know that when I trust You,
joy is the outcome. Remind me to keep focused on You, one step at a time.

UNDER THE CIRCUMSTANCES

As pressure and stress bear down on me, I find joy in your commands.
PSALM 119:143, NLT

Real life can be stressful, and joy is often elusive. Though we would like to push those hard seasons away, they seem to take their own sweet time in passing. We may seek relief in a number of things—food, alcohol, drugs, shopping, or new relationships. But when those things lose their shine, we are back to where we started—stressed out and living under the circumstances.

What if we could get out from under the problems and learn to live upon God's promises? This may seem simplistic, but it's not. There is protection in God's ways for us. But because His ways are different than ours, it's easy to brush them off or forget them entirely.

I was hurt recently, and the emotional toll was heavy. As long as I focused on trying to understand or fix it, the weight bore down on my soul. I was tired of living buried under my emotions. So I found a verse—one single verse—that promised me God saw, knew, and would work on my behalf. And I held on to that promise. Though I was crushed by the situation, I was encouraged when I was reminded of truth. It was God's Word that brought me joy long before things turned around. That is what it means to learn to live upon the promises instead of under the circumstances.

Today I will remember:
- Pressure and stress are part of life.
- With each problem, I have a choice—live under the weight or upon God's Word.
- God's Word brings great joy to my heart.

Lord, thank You for Your Word, Your commands, and Your promises.
Remind me to find Scripture to cling to when life is hard. May I find joy
when living upon Your Word rather than buried underneath my problems.

WAITING IN JOY

Be joyful in hope, patient in affliction, faithful in prayer.
ROMANS 12:12

I was naive about the Christian life. I was young and assumed that having God in my corner meant that life would be really good all the time. A little life resolved that naivete for me—after my first of a series of miscarriages and a diagnosis of an uncurable liver disease in my twenties. Life was disappointing instead of blessed—or so I thought.

The reality is, life in this world will have a variety of challenges and hardships. God doesn't promise differently. Scripture gives us instruction on how to live in the middle of the hard so that we might end up with a holy outcome. In other words, we go through things and grow through them when we pay attention to Scripture's instruction. Here we see three clear things we are to do in hardship—put our hope in God, remain patient, and pray. It actually says to be joy-filled in hope. In other words, when we put our hope in Christ and patiently wait for His work, we can wait in joy because hope says, *Jesus is over you*—and it's going to be OK.

How will you wait in joy today for your current place of hard to be made into a holy place where God works in you?

Today I will remember:
• I am to be joy-filled as I hope in God.
• I am to be patient in my afflictions.
• I am to pray faithfully and regularly.

Lord, I commit to remembering these three things and applying them to my life circumstances—in both the good seasons and the harder ones.

GROW IN PEACE

Those who promote peace have joy.

PROVERBS 12:20

Women can fill their lives with relational chaos. Perhaps it's because we are challenged with hormonal swings, or maybe it's because we haven't been challenged to live above all that female drama. As Christian women, God has called us to a place of peace. The opposite of promoting peace is gossiping, arguing, or being petty, selfish, or hurtful to one another. But what if you are in a situation where there is not an easy path to peace? Scripture says we are to be the ones who promote it—who actively encourage peaceful relationships and solutions.

Promoting peace might look like stepping away from our pride, our negative opinions, or our need to have the last word or take control. If we stay stuck in our heads and reasoning about things, we will be sour instead of having joy. Our reasoning might be affected by our own hurts and insecurities. We might not realize that holding on tightly to offense is robbing us. There is a joy that comes with promoting the things Jesus promotes. Friends, He is the Prince of Peace, so let's make it a life goal to do the things He does and learn what it means to live differently. When we do, we will find that promoting peace is the pathway to joy.

Today I will remember:
- If I promote peace, I will have joy.
- When I insist on my own way, I will miss joy I could have.
- It's not important to be right; it's important to reflect Jesus.

Lord, I ask You to forgive me for holding on to things rather than coming quickly to peaceful solutions. May I reflect You and surrender my rights to my way of treating people completely to You.

THE NIGHT WILL PASS

Weeping may stay for the night,
but rejoicing comes in the morning.
PSALM 30:5

The pain you are in today will not last forever. I have cried through the night when my parents died, when my marriage died, and when a friendship died. I thought I would never get over those losses. In the moment, I thought I would never feel joy again. The natural weeping and grieving that occurred subsided as I cried out to God over and over in those night hours.

It's important to know that we will make it through to the other side—we will be OK. Equally important is to realize that there will be times in life when lament and grieving are appropriate. Those dark nights of our soul can leave us deeply discouraged when we don't remember the sun will come up again.

Can you step back and look at the pain you've gone through and see how God has come through on your behalf? Remind yourself today that pain isn't forever. This life is not the last stop. But while we are here, we will have hope when we believe that we will be OK. We will get though our current problems, and we can still have joy.

Today I will remember:
- I might be in great grief today, but it will not last forever.
- Life may be hard, but I am going to be OK.
- The Lord will restore my joy, and this too shall pass.

Lord, I remember well the tears and the anguish of my soul during
painful seasons. I didn't like those times much, but now I realize
that I will get through to the other side because You are by my side.

ETERNAL PERSPECTIVE

*So with you: Now is your time of grief, but I will see you again
and you will rejoice, and no one will take away your joy.*
JOHN 16:22

Becky sets her heart toward heaven and is unflinching when life is hard. She is a spiritual influence—not perfect, as she is a very normal woman, but she certainly lives spiritually focused. In my immaturity, at first I thought maybe she was a little too spiritual. Have you ever heard the saying, "too spiritual for earthly good?" I suppose this means we are to keep our feet on the real soil of everyday life. It's crazy to think that we can be too spiritual. I know firsthand that I am not spiritual enough, meaning my perspective is easily tainted with the cares of this life rather than being settled on eternal perspective.

Jesus taught from an eternal perspective. He taught His disciples to look past the cares of this life into the eyes of the one who cared for them most and was preparing a place for them. Imagine how discouraged they were to see Him persecuted, and for everything around them to feel so dark. Jesus acknowledged their sorrow but brought a perspective of joy and hope to it. Today, He sees your sorrow too, and is gently reminding you that it will not be forever—your heart will find joy again.

Today I will remember:
• No one can take my joy when I am focused upward.
• Jesus sees my current sorrow and cares for me.
• Though life can be hard, I will rejoice again.

*Lord, without an upward focus, I tend to spiral down. Remind
me to tilt my head and heart up toward You, focus on the reality
of eternity, and find joy even when my life has sorrows.*

KINGDOM LIVING

For the kingdom of God is not a matter of eating and drinking,
but of righteousness, peace, and joy in the Holy Spirit.
ROMANS 14:17

It's easy to dismiss God's Kingdom when I assume it is a far-off, distant place. But the Kingdom of God is something to experience here and now. This truth is important enough that Jesus included it when He taught His disciples how to pray. He said, "This, then, is how you should pray: Our Father in heaven, hallowed be your name, your kingdom come, your will be done, on earth as it is in heaven."[49]

Kingdom here refers to God's sovereignty and rule both in this place and the place to come. Keeping that in mind, today's verse could read, *the rule and sovereignty of God is not a matter of finding fullness in this world but of being full as we live in faithfulness to God.*

It's not about filling our houses and bellies, but rather living with God's rule and reign in our hearts. When God's rule is present in our thoughts, we have a peace and joy that is given to us by the Holy Spirit. Living with a "your kingdom come" mindset is walking in the Spirit, and it will win over the flesh every single time. When we remember that God is the ultimate ruler of all things, it fills our cup and calms our anxious hearts.

Today I will remember:
- The Kingdom of God is to be a present-day reality in the life of believers.
- Kingdom living is not about what we can get for ourselves, but how we surrender to God.
- A Kingdom mindset is Spirit-filled living.

Lord, You are holy and above all things. I ask You to adjust my mindset.
I want to walk in Kingdom living—filled with the Holy Spirit
and a joy that is not changed when my circumstances change.

HEALING JOY

Satisfy us in the morning with your unfailing love,
that we may sing for joy and be glad all our days.
PSALM 90:14

The morning routine of sitting in Scripture became consistent after my life fell apart in my thirties. Before then it was hit and miss, but in days of depression after an unwanted divorce, God met me when I made space for Him each new day. That morning time, even if it was brief, was my lifeline in a season where not living seemed much easier than walking forward. Coming out of the pit of discouragement, hopelessness, and depression still seems like a personal miracle, but I know that it's something God invites us all into every single day. And though sitting with God can be done anytime of the day, there is something good about stopping at the front of each day and acknowledging God and praying for His Kingdom rule in our lives. Thanking Him for His constant love and presence makes all the difference in how we go about the rest of our day.

Spending time with God opens you up to receiving from Him in your most vulnerable places.

Ann Voskamp says, "Letting yourself be loved is an act of terrifying vulnerability and surrender. Letting yourself be loved is its own kind of givenness. Letting yourself be loved gives you over to someone's mercy and leaves you trusting that they will keep loving you, that they will love you the way you want to be loved, that they won't break your given heart."[50]

Today I will remember:
- God will satisfy me in the morning with His love.
- As I receive His love, I will have joy.
- Gladness rests in coming to receive both love and joy from the Father.

Lord, may I desire You in the morning and be filled
with You so completely that my heart swells with joy.

---

50 Ann Voskamp, *The Broken Way: A daring path into the abundant life* (Nashville: Thomas Nelson, 2016), 100.

RENEWED DAY BY DAY

When anxiety was great within me, your consolation brought me joy.
PSALM 94:19

All through Scripture we see accounts of God's people being under pressure that was too much for them to bear. The psalmist here speaks of anxiety that was great within him. Have you ever been anxious? Have you felt heart-pounding, soul-crushing anxiety? Many have and speak of God comforting or consoling them in the middle of the situation. Paul spoke of this when he said, "We are hard pressed on every side, but not crushed; perplexed, but not in despair; persecuted, but not abandoned; struck down, but not destroyed…Therefore we do not lose heart. Though outwardly we are wasting away, yet inwardly we are being renewed day by day."[51]

The image of someone outwardly wasting away is quite a visual. And yet, God comforts and soothes the inner person that is being renewed while everything else is falling apart. In these times God's Word can be a source of comfort and joy. Thanking Him for the truth and filling our minds with it redirects our thoughts. Even though we don't like our current circumstances, we can practice and learn to lean into truth over time. And, just like Paul, we can say with joy—circumstances are bad, but I am not losing heart, I am not abandoned, and I won't be destroyed. Repeating God's intent for us and reminding ourselves of His faithfulness comforts us when times are hard. And that comfort brings us joy.

Today I will remember:
- God reassures me when anxiety is great within me.
- Though I am being stripped, I am really being renewed.
- Knowing I won't be abandoned brings me joy.

Lord, may I look to You when I am in despair and things are harder than I can handle. Help me to live in joy as I note the ways You comfort and console me.

---

51 2 Corinthians 4:8-9, 16.

THE LIFESTYLE OF JOY

Rejoice in the Lord always. I will say it again: Rejoice!
PHILIPPIANS 4:4

There are some things that need to be repeated. Paul knew that finding joy in the Lord was not natural, and that everything in our flesh, emotions, and natural reasoning goes against the grain of finding our joy in the Lord. To *rejoice* here means to be glad. Be glad in the Lord. Glad that He has you and that He loves you. Glad that you can give Him your cares and He will work on your behalf. Glad that His covering is over you in all things, in all days, and in all ways. Earlier in the letter to the Philippians, Paul told them to rejoice and said he didn't mind repeating things because it would keep them safe. Now as the letter continues, he tells them again to rejoice. This repetition is something to pay attention to. Joy is a way of life that bears repeating.

Let's not overlook the word *always*, which is an important component to what he is saying. Rejoicing, being glad, and finding joy in the Lord should be a continual way of life. Paul knew that life itself does not warrant this attitude of heart and mind, but that rejoicing changes a believer's outlook, which changes the way we live. Imagine framing your problems with the thought, *this is happening, but I will be glad in the Lord because He is with me and always working His purposes.*

Today I will remember:
- Being glad in the Lord is a lifestyle to be practiced and learned.
- I learn to rejoice by focusing upward and remembering God is over me.
- Joy is a byproduct of a heart focused on God's presence in all things.

Lord, thank You for repeating themes in Your Word. These themes teach me what is important. May I learn how to be glad in You regardless of my circumstances.

May

PERSEVERING IN PROBLEMS

Problems are inevitable—Living overwhelmed is optional.
Debbie Alsdorf

IN THE MIDDLE OF PAIN

*The Lord has heard my weeping. The Lord has
heard my cry for mercy; the Lord accepts my prayer.*

PSALM 6:8-9

Tucked in a corner of my closet, I cried longer and harder than I ever had before. My heart was broken from rejection. And though I had friends who would listen, it just wasn't appropriate to burden them with friendship drama because they knew all involved. So I cried in my closet. Have you ever cried tears in private, wishing that things were different than they are?

What a comfort to realize that the Lord not only sees our tears, but He hears us when we call out to Him. Whether our pain is physical, relational, circumstantial, or financial, our tears are a form of prayer and a calling out for help. Tears are not a sign of weakness but a sign of pain. Safe in God's care, we can let the tears flow, call out in our distress, and find peace in knowing that He accepts our prayers, no matter how insignificant they might seem to someone else. Each cry for help is important to the God who loves us.

We all experience the sting of hard things in our lifetime. Some face more difficulties than others, but none of us is exempt from experiencing hurt. The first and best thing we can do is cry out for help, knowing the Lord hears and acts on our behalf.

Today I will remember:
- God hears me when I cry.
- He sees every tear and cares for what caused each one.
- He accepts my prayers as I come to Him for help.

*Lord, the days are long when my heart is hurting. Thank You for inviting
me into a relationship with You and for caring about every single
hurt and all of my cares. May I never hold back my pain from
You, but learn to bring each pain into Your presence.*

THE PIT OF MY DOING

*Whoever digs a hole and scoops it out falls into the pit they
have made. The trouble they cause recoils on them.*

PSALM 7:15-16

Not every problem is caused by others. Some pits and problems are of our own doing. Moved by triggered emotions, selfish desires, or attempts to control a situation, we sometimes do crazy things that we never thought we would do. Overthinking and dragging others into every little detail can be a form of digging our own hole. Yet we are surprised when we fall in.

In the realm of problems and pits, it's good to recognize when we are part of what caused things to go south. When we are the problem, nothing will change until we turn to God. If we have the humility to quit pointing a finger at others, we will intersect with God's grace and find solutions. The words, "I'm sorry" and "I was wrong" are powerful tools in climbing out of self-made pits and into a healthier place. Yielding to God after we have caused havoc is yielding to His Spirit and resisting the nature of our flesh that wants its own way at all costs.

Today I will remember:
- I can dig a hole that ultimately swallows me up.
- I can create my own pit, fall into it, and drag others with me.
- When I cause trouble, it will come back on me in the end.

*Father, I come to You with my stubborn heart and pride. I ask
You to forgive me for unkind actions, words of gossip, and any way
I have contributed to my own pit and problems. I want to live in Your
love and repair any areas of drama in my life and relationships.*

IMMOVABLE IN PROBLEMS

Take up your positions; stand firm and
see the deliverance the Lord will give you.
2 CHRONICLES 20:17

How do we stand firm when things are hard? What does this mean in the middle of grief, problems, and relational wars? This verse follows a word from God that King Jehoshaphat would not have to fight the battle before him. He was told two things he would need to do—take up his position and stand firm.

I have wondered over the years how this relates to me, an ordinary woman going through the real and regular battles of life. I have come to realize that taking up my position and standing firm in battle is standing in who I am in Christ and whose I am as His. Reminding myself and finding courage in these truths changes my stance when I am in any kind of trouble.

When I am focused on God's love for me, I am immovable. The army, in this same story, went before the battle singing, "Give thanks to the LORD, for his love endures forever."[52] Love was their battle cry, not just fluffy sentiment. As they declared the truth of who God is and how He loves, the enemy was ambushed and the battle won.

Today I will remember:
- My position is in Christ—I am loved and cared for.
- Standing firm is what is required of me—God fights the battles.
- I must remind myself daily who He is and how He loves.

Lord, may I stand firm in Your love, feet locked secure in the power of a
loving God who is my victory in every battle. Teach me how to take my
position daily so that my problems are positioned squarely on You.

LEAPING THROUGH OBSTACLES

*The Sovereign Lord is my strength; he makes my feet like
the feet of a deer, he enables me to tread on the heights.*

HABAKKUK 3:19

The feet of deer are graceful, swift, and sure. They enable the deer to climb rocky cliffs without stumbling and scamper without a care, unafraid and undeterred by the obstacles before it. This is an illustration of the surefooted, unafraid, reliance we can have in God.

The psalmist repeats this same idea: "He makes my feet like the feet of a deer; he causes me to stand on the heights."[53] Repeated themes are worth paying attention to. I wish I could say that I was skilled at standing on the heights and undeterred by obstacles. The truth is, I am good at freaking out and becoming afraid. I have always needed to learn how to stand strong in the midst of obstacles. Maybe you can relate.

Friends, when relying on God, we can face any height of circumstance. We can do hard things, leaping over the obstacles of our lives. In practical terms, this is living above our circumstances. God gives us the strength, patience, stamina, and grace we need. We can move past our enemies and gain freedom, stepping boldly into whatever God is calling us to do.

Today I will remember:
- The Lord makes me someone different than I could be on my own.
- He gives me sure footing in rough or uncertain times.
- He enables me to stand in freedom, against all odds.

*Lord, when I look at the challenges before me, I stumble and fall.
Teach me to run upon the heights of Your strength, with Your face
always before me, giving me stability even when I don't feel capable.*

---

53 Psalm 18:33.

STRENGTH BORN IN WEAKNESS

*He said to me, "My grace is sufficient for you, for my power is made
perfect in weakness." Therefore I will boast all the more gladly
about my weaknesses, so that Christ's power may rest on me.*

2 CORINTHIANS 12:9

Unbearable pain has stopped me again. A car accident in my twenties wreaked havoc on my spine, and I still feel the effects. Through discouragement, I wonder if God is doing something deep within me when I walk through hard things. Can circumstances that rob me of my physical strength teach me more about God's power within me?

The ways of God seem upside down—always upside down. God's power perfected in times of weakness goes against the grain of everything the culture understands. We value strength, but God works in weakness.

Do you ever get disappointed in weakness, illness, or trials? Like the apostle Paul, I have prayed repeatedly to be relieved from some of the things I go through. Those prayers are often unanswered—or so it seems.

God's answers are often different than what I expect. I want a problem removed, and He might want to use the problem to change me—to grow something beautiful in me. I beg, and He blesses with, "my grace is sufficient for you" and "my power is made perfect in weakness."

Today I will remember:
• God's grace is sufficient—enough to meet the needs of the situation.
• God's power is made perfect in weakness—in pain, problems, and inability.
• I will boast in God's grace in my weakness—and He will rest upon me.

*Lord, You know my wrestling with the weakness associated with physical
illness and pain. Teach me to boast in Your strength, to look for Your grace,
and to find all I need, even in the middle of struggles, illness, or pain.*

THINGS HAPPEN TO ME
SO SOMETHING CAN HAPPEN IN ME

*Now I want you to know, brothers and sisters, that what has
happened to me has actually served to advance the gospel.*

PHILIPPIANS 1:12

I have countless memories of being in the middle of unfair or hard situations. I wish I learned my lesson the first time around, but it's taken a repeated theme for me to see God working in hard circumstances. We must learn to believe that things happen *to* us so God can work *in* us! I have held on to that for many years and through many hard times.

In our own reasoning, hard is only bad. And Paul's friends in Philippi viewed his unfair treatment and imprisonment as bad too. I can imagine the fury they must have felt and maybe even the demonstrations they considered staging. But Paul knew something that he wanted them to know too—God works in the hard, and God's Kingdom is either advanced within us or around us. He even said, "through your prayers and God's provision of the Spirit of Jesus Christ what has happened to me will turn out for my deliverance."[54] If we believed this, we would have more hope in the hard moments of life, knowing that a greater purpose will be served as a result.

Today I will remember:
- God is fully aware of the things that are happening in my life.
- God works within the context of things happening in me and around me.
- God brings me to a better place despite hardships.

*Lord, I thank You that You can be trusted with all unfair treatment,
hard situations, and things I don't understand. You are at work,
and I want to remember this as I walk out this life with You.*

---

54 Philippians 1:19.

COMFORT IN TROUBLE

Praise be to God...who comforts us in all our troubles... This happened that we might not rely on ourselves but on God, who raises the dead.

2 CORINTHIANS 1:3-4, 9

I rely on myself more than I care to admit. I like to proclaim that I only rely on God, but truth be told, I try to control my life and turn to God only when it falls apart. I am working toward making the space smaller between the start of a trouble and the moment I start relying on God rather than myself.

God comforts us in ALL our troubles. In the small things and the larger things, He covers us with Himself and assures us of His presence. God has met me in my tears, frustrations, fears, and angst. He has met me in my questioning. He has used troubles to mellow the part of me that fights for control when things aren't going my way. Relying on Him has quieted my soul in a way that made me stronger.

If you are facing troubles of any kind today, look up and be encouraged. God is inviting you to a personal relationship where His Spirit comforts you. It's OK to let go of control and trust God with the pain of the pieces, the fear of the diagnosis, or the disappointment of cancelled dreams or plans. It's OK to cry, plead, and process your angst before Him. Let the comfort in. Don't resist the hand of God on your heart.

Today I will remember:
- God comforts us in our troubles.
- He continually invites us to rely on Him rather than ourselves.
- He invites us to a place of love, peace, and support.

Lord, thank You for being a God of comfort. Remind me not to blame You when I am in the middle of troubles, but instead to run to You for comfort. Teach me what it means to rely on You more than I rely on myself.

NOW I KNOW YOU

I had only heard about you before,
but now I have seen you with my own eyes.

JOB 42:5, NLT

Why do God's people suffer? Only God knows why things are allowed in our lives or happen as they do. One thing we know is that our suffering is never wasted. God catches every tear and uses everything we go through this side of heaven.

Job was a righteous man who was tested. He had a life of prestige, possessions, and people when suddenly he was assaulted on every side. The book that bears his name is a gripping account of suffering and a biblical rags-to-riches story. After seasons of questioning the plan of God, doubting His love, despising His hand—Job reconsidered and realized that God was enough. It seems the hard things shaped Job. He came to know God by being in His presence when he was at the bottom, relying on nothing else in life besides the God who created it all. The story ends with Job being restored to happiness and wealth. But was the road to get there necessary? None of us would like to say the suffering was necessary—even Job's wife told him to curse God and die!

Hard things are part of real life. In every hard place, we will find God and see Him when we look for Him. When we search our heart for sin or doubt, we will begin entering into a space where God speaks to us and shapes us in the middle of the situation.

Today I will remember:
- God allows hard things and never leaves us.
- We, like Job, will have our faith tested.
- In the end, we will be restored and know God more as we trust Him in the hard.

Lord, I have spent much of my life being a fair-weather believer.
I want to trust You when the storms come as much as
I do when the sun shines. I want to know You more.

INEVITABLE TROUBLES

I have told you these things, so that in me you may have peace. In this world you will have trouble. But take heart! I have overcome the world.

JOHN 16:33

Think of your favorite podcast or motivational speaker. Now imagine them telling you to count on having troubles. Not just any troubles, but tribulations and crushing distress. Would you be encouraged, or would you want to run away from them and their message? I think I'd want to run away!

Jesus was preparing His disciples because He knew troubles are part of life. These words of Jesus were meant to bring comfort and peace—peace in being forewarned that life would have times of unrest and difficulty, and comfort in knowing that Jesus has overcome this world with all its drama.

Jesus wasn't proclaiming negativity over the disciples; He wanted the best for them. The best life isn't necessarily problem-free, but having peace in the midst of the things we go through is possible. Knowing there would be troubles, Jesus assures us that He has overcome this world and its challenges. The important thing to remember when things are hard is that God is with you, hardships are part of life, and these things are temporary. This is how we keep moving forward and how we practice taking heart and finding comfort in the here and now of everyday problems.

Today I will remember:
- Jesus Himself said life would be hard.
- Jesus told them this so they could have peace.
- When we accept that He has overcome all things, we can take heart in anything.

Lord, You came to give us abundant life, but often my life looks like an abundance of problems. May my heart find peace in knowing You are with me in every trouble.

CHANGE THE MENTAL CHANNEL

I remember my affliction and my wandering... I well remember them,
and my soul is downcast within me. Yet this I call to mind and
therefore I have hope: Because of the Lord's great love we
are not consumed, for his compassions never fail.

LAMENTATIONS 3:19-22

The best of us can have the worst of days or seasons. Sadness can drive us to a place of discouragement. The longer we focus on the negatives, the more downcast we will be. I know from experience how to spiral down. What I need most is to learn how to direct myself back up.

Jeremiah speaks about his affliction and hardships, and how his downward focus led him to an emotional pit. But then something happened. He changed his focus—he turned the channel of his thoughts upward. When he did, his hope was restored. Could it be that easy? Can a change of focus lift us to a better place?

When we consider that God is loving, compassionate, and faithful, we begin to shift our attention from the negative to the positive. Jeremiah ends with speaking truth to himself:

"I say to myself, 'The LORD is my portion; therefore I will wait for him.'"[55] Let's speak words of hope to our hearts today. Let's tell ourselves the truth as we wait for the hard to pass or the season to change.

Today I will remember:
- When I rehearse the negatives, I will be discouraged.
- When I remember the positives, I will begin to have hope again.
- Speaking the truth to myself can change my perspective.

Lord, forgive me for spiraling down into a negative place.
Give me the grace to look up so I can focus upward. May I tell
myself the truth of who You are and how You are with me.

WHEN PROBLEMS COME

Power and might are in your hand.
2 CHRONICLES 20:6

I don't know about you, but if I am going to fall apart, it's usually because troubles have come my way. There's great comfort in knowing that many of God's people struggled when faced with problems too. King Jehoshaphat was alarmed when he heard that a vast army was coming against him and his people. It was an army too big for them to defeat. Maybe you'd get alarmed too. Fear and alarm might be our initial response, but they don't have to be our last. We can move from fear to faith when we remember to look up at the beginning of every problem.

What is causing you concern today? God can handle your initial fear. Though He understands that natural response, He invites you to something different. After that first alarmed response, Jehoshaphat "resolved to inquire of the LORD" and "to seek help from the LORD."[56] When he was afraid, he resolved to look up. Everyone has an initial response when facing something hard. Sometimes fear is a deeply engrained habit. The path ahead can be different. You might not see or feel His power today, but as you believe in the mighty power of God, you will move through the day differently.

Today I will remember:
- Power and might are in God's hand.
- God has authority over my life.
- Living in fear is a choice that can be changed by looking up.

Lord, thank You for understanding that sometimes I am afraid. Help me to learn to respond to fear by turning to You. Let me live out the truth of Your mighty power by the way I face my problems and by the faith in which I handle daily life.

HOLDING FIRM IN SUFFERING

We glory in our sufferings, because we know that
suffering produces perseverance; perseverance, character;
and character, hope. And hope does not put us to shame.

ROMANS 5:3-5

Most of us don't grow up lacing suffering and hope together. None of wants to suffer, because we know it isn't going to feel good. But what if we turned that narrative around to a biblical view of suffering as something necessary to shape us in ways nothing else can?

Not only is suffering a normal part of life, we are told to *rejoice* in it, which is to feel or show great joy or delight. It seems crazy to think of showing delight when emotions are all over the map. Our feelings are important indicators—when we feel afraid, it signals us to go to God in prayer. But sometimes we have to "faith it" until we make it, no matter what we are feeling. Don't fake it—but faith it!

Rejoicing in hardship is not fake, it is demonstrating our faith God. God's plan is to develop in us a forward movement during difficulties. This forward movement develops a depth of character in us. We become women who have learned to rely on God's faithfulness, and in the end we have more hope in God than when we first began. Maybe today is the day to stop hiding from the hard and begin rejoicing in it.

Today I will remember:
- God is at work in my life when things are hard.
- Suffering has a purpose, and therefore it's nothing to be afraid of.
- When I suffer, character is developed within me and I learn to withstand hard things well.

Father, in the middle of my problems remind me to rejoice in who You are and how You faithfully love me. Let me not cave to my problems, but instead bear up under them because I know they are developing something beautiful in me.

SEEK AND FIND

*"You will call on me and come and pray to me, and I will listen
to you. You will seek me and find me when you seek me with
all your heart. I will be found by you," declares the Lord.*
JEREMIAH 29:12-14

I will never forget the angst and despair I felt going through an unwanted divorce.
The end of the dream felt like the end of my life. My heart felt like it was bleeding,
crushed under the weight of rejection. In that place I called out to the Lord—
over and over again I called upon Him. There was something beautiful about the
simplicity of my calling out to Him. No eloquent prayers, but rather a simple and
often teary, "Help!"

I found Him close to me in that season. I look back on my prayers, and though
there weren't immediate answers, He gave me peace each time I called upon His
name. I cried for months as His presence dried my tears. The verse before says, "'I
know the plans I have for you,' declares the LORD."[57]

God knew His plans for my life, and that is what I had to stand on, hope in, and
believe. It required a daily practice of rehearsing the truth of God's love for me to
my own head and heart. In the end, I learned how to draw near to God. He's always
there, but when we seek Him, our heart finds Him.

Today I will remember:
• I am invited to call out to God in my distress.
• I am encouraged to pray with my whole heart leaning on Him.
• I will find Him as I call out to Him.

*Lord, thank You for all the times You have met me in my need.
It's not about following rules, but about Your invitation to an
intimate relationship with the God who knows me and sees me.*

---

57 Jeremiah 29:11.

SAFELY TO THE OTHER SIDE

The Lord will rescue me from every evil attack
and will bring me safely to his heavenly kingdom.
2 TIMOTHY 4:18

When I am going through something hard, I choose an anchor verse to repeat several times each day. This has been an anchor verse. There were days I found myself repeating, "the Lord will rescue me from every attack" over and over again. Before long, it was shortened to, "the Lord will rescue me."

I wasn't raised in a Christian home, and when I became a Christian in college, I had rose-colored glasses on. I assumed that my life would be blessed, carefree, and successful. After all, now God was on my side. The truth is, even though God is good, life is hard. Some of us are surprised by how hard it can be. The words *every evil attack* strike a little angst in my heart. I don't want evil attacks or hardships. Who would? But the attacks will come, and there are a few key things we need to hold on to.

God will rescue us. He will free us from danger or evil and save and deliver us. This is who He is—our deliverer, our safe place, our shelter from every storm. He will bring us safely home when this life is done, but in the meantime we might have to go through some things and count on His rescue here on the streets of real life.

Today I will remember:
- There will be attacks in this life.
- God will rescue me from every attack against me.
- God will bring me safely through to the other side.

Lord, thank You for being my deliverer. In a world filled with danger and unknowns, I put my trust in You and how You rescue and save Your people. Teach me to remember the truth of Your rescue when I am in need of it.

FALSE ACCUSATIONS

Because the Sovereign LORD helps me, I will not be disgraced.
Therefore I have set my face like flint, and I know
I will not be put to shame. He who vindicates me is near.

ISAIAH 50:7-8

Have you ever been falsely accused of something? What about having someone lie about you or misrepresent you? I'm raising my hand on all accounts. I still vividly recall sitting in family court defending false claims about me. I felt hurt, angry, and helpless. In that moment, God whispered to my heart that He would vindicate me. I didn't understand what that meant, but I knew that word was in the Bible. I later looked it up and discovered it means that He protects us from attack, harm, allegation, and blame. God would take care of all the accusations because He had my back. He was my vindicator.

Court went on for weeks, and it was one of the lowest times in my life. Daily I would remind myself that God would be my vindicator. In the end, that is exactly what happened. It didn't happen on day one, but it happened before the case was over. Every single accusation against me was thrown out by the judge and the court evaluator. Sometimes we forget that God is near and that He works in us, through us, and for us. He works in every aspect of our lives.

Today I will remember:
• The Lord helps me in my life situations.
• I will stand firm and strong in believing He has my back.
• God is near—to help, defend, and protect from attack.

Father, thank You for seeing me, knowing me, and protecting me from harm
that comes from others. I entrust myself and my life circumstances to You.

ATTITUDE IS EVERYTHING

*Set your hearts on things above,
where Christ is, seated at the right hand of God.*
COLOSSIANS 3:1

It's time to get serious about life—redefining it and reclaiming it for God's purposes. One thing is certain: He has a purpose for each one of us, and His plans are good. But those plans can't take place when we are living our lives on our own terms.

Life often surprises us with circumstances we didn't see coming and troubles that aren't a welcome gift. We might find ourselves wanting to run away, but in real life running from problems isn't the best idea. Looking to God in the middle of every problem is better than running, and that is the very thing that will help us get through to the other side.

Though we can't control all our circumstances, we do have control over a few things—the attitude we carry in them, the direction we take each day, and where we put our hope and trust. When we pay attention to what we can do rather than stressing over how awful the problem seems, we will not only be setting our hearts straight, but we will be planting ourselves on a solid foundation of focusing on God, who is greater than every problem we will face.

Today I will remember:
- To set my heart on things above.
- To guard my mind and where I allow it to be planted.
- To live in the reality of a picture bigger than my temporary problems.

Lord, I need Your help when I am in the spiral of my problems. I stress, overthink, and stir in anxiety. Teach me what it means to lift my gaze to You and trust my heart to the One who loves me in the middle of every single problem I face.

NO THING WILL SEPARATE ME

Who shall separate us from the love of Christ?
Shall trouble or hardship?
ROMANS 8:35

Troubles often settle in and are seldom over as quickly as we'd like them to be. It would be ridiculous to think we could wave a magic wand or sprinkle some fairy dust over our real-life problems to make them go away. But God does promise to be with us in every trouble we face and to hold us close in the meantime.

Are you in the "meantime"? The meantime is the middle—that place between a prayer and the answer. I have the hardest time in the middle of my problems. It's hard when I don't know how long it's going to take to get through and it doesn't seem like God is hearing or answering my prayers. The dictionary defines *meantime* as the interval between things. I like to think of my problems as providing some interval training in my spiritual life. More than a cliché, biblical truth is our gift from God to guide us along in every "meantime" place. And, friends, let's be real—we need all the help we can get because sometimes the meantime feels long, frustrating, and downright mean!

Regardless of the length or severity of our troubles, God's love never leaves, and He holds us in the meantime places in life.

Today I will remember:
- When I feel like God has left me, I will remind myself that He never leaves me.
- Nothing—and No Thing—can separate me from God's love.
- Trouble, problems, and hardships are temporary; God's love is eternal.

Lord, when I am in the middle of my messy life, help me to remember
that You are in the mess with me. No problem is a surprise to You,
and nothing can separate me from Your strong arm of love.

DISCERNING WHAT'S BEST

*And this is my prayer: that your love may abound more and more...
so that you may be able to discern what is best...filled with the
fruit of righteousness that comes through Jesus Christ.*

PHILIPPIANS 1:9-11

The apostle Paul knew about problems. He knew they could take our breath away, bully our faith, and leave us worn out. Knowing this, he prayed for his friends who had messy lives filled with everyday problems. His prayer wasn't for the problems to go away, but for God's love to go deeper and be experienced in a richer way than ever before. He prayed God's love would rise stronger than the circumstances squeezing the joy out of the day.

When we walk through hard things, discernment is important. We need to ask God for wisdom and for a fresh assurance of His love. Praying about our problems and asking God to sort them out will make all the difference, whereas overthinking will only defeat us. Oswald Chambers said, "Subtle irritability caused by too much thought over our circumstances robs joy."[58] We can *go* through our situations, or we can *grow* through them. God's love being worked out in a life of faith enables us to grow through every single thing we go through.

Today I will remember:
- To pray for myself and others as problems threaten to steal our joy.
- God's love is not a fluffy rainbow of hope, but a solid foundation to stand on.
- Growing through my problems produces the fruit of righteousness.

*Lord, help me to discern Your voice and Your will for me in the
middle of my problems. Remind me to pray for myself and others
and to allow myself the space to grow in the hard places in life.*

---

58 Oswald Chambers, *My Utmost for His Highest*, August 31.

FOR A LITTLE WHILE...

For a little while you may have had to suffer grief in all kinds of trials.
These have come so that the proven genuineness of your faith—of greater
worth than gold, which perishes even though refined by fire—
may result in praise, glory and honor when Jesus Christ is revealed.

1 PETER 1:6-7

Why do we have trials? Why is life filled with problems? We are told it's because we live in an imperfect world since the Fall. That's true, but if you are anything like me, you need a little something more to hold on to in the midst of problems. This verse gives it! There are two little words in today's verse that are important—*so that*. Pay attention, because there is purpose hidden in every problem.

We all will have grief and problems—for a little while—meaning they aren't forever. While they are present, it's *so that* our faith can be refined. Being refined is not fun. Yet it's the faithfulness of God burning away the things in us that keep us locked in self instead of freed in faith.

Friend, our problems are hard in the moment, but they are not forever. Lean into Jesus so that He can do His amazing work in your heart and mind through the hard. Look up! He is with you even now.

Today I will remember:
- My problems aren't forever, but for a while.
- Everyone faces problems; I am not a victim but subject to real-life difficulties.
- Each trial has a purpose—so that my life can be refined to bring Jesus glory.

Lord, in the midst of pain, suffering, and trials, it's easy to be discouraged.
But today I hold on to the truth that every problem has a purpose.
Refine me, Lord, and may all that You do through this current hard
change me more into Your image, bringing You glory when it's over.

RESHAPED BY GOD

I went down to the potter's house, and I saw him working at the wheel.
But the pot he was shaping from the clay was marred in his hands;
so the potter formed it into another pot, shaping it as seemed best to him.
JEREMIAH 18:3-4

When was the last time you tossed and turned or were hounded by an endless cycle of trying to make life behave again? There is nothing fun about a problem—not one thing. It's important to remember there is always a plan. We can't see God working, but He never ceases. He uses the things we go through to take what was marred and reshape it into beauty.

I have always liked this story of the potter's house because it illustrates how when something is not turning out as I planned, God reshapes it into something new and beautiful. Take note that it says the clay was not only marred in His hands but reformed into beauty in His hands. We are always held by God, and in His hands our story is safe. Life might be turning on the wheel and not making sense, but you—the clay—are forever in His hands, and He is forever faithfully working according to His plan for our individual lives.

Today I will remember:
• I am the clay, God is the potter, and I am on His wheel.
• I am always in His hands, and He will reshape me when necessary.
• The potter knows the plan and only wants to create beauty.

Lord, for years I have heard of the potter and the clay but have not related it to my real life. Today may I take this story and hold tightly to the truth that I am clay in Your hands and You are shaping me as You see fit. What a glorious realization and a reason to exhale in the spin of my problems.

LOOK UP!

Why, my soul, are you downcast? Why so disturbed within me?
Put your hope in God, for I will yet praise him, my Savior and my God.
PSALM 42:11

Sometimes it's easier to be down than to look up. When faced with hard circumstances, the emotional pull to discouragement is real. In sadness, even as Christians, we can wallow in our feelings. Though being downcast is an easy route, it's not the only one. We must train ourselves to look up and praise God even when our problems warrant spiraling down.

When discouragement hits, acknowledge it and sit with it a bit to understand what is making you feel the way you feel. Though feelings aren't what should lead our lives, they can be indicators of what is going on inside of us. After sitting with that indicator light for a while, get as far from it as you can by looking to God for His help and strength.

We can put our hope in God—it's just that we don't. If, like me, you forget to stop and look up, begin trying something different. Practice walking the opposite of the emotions that are causing you to be down and move toward the hope in Jesus that will help you trust His promise and live with peace and endurance.

Today I will remember:
- I will be downcast from time to time. That's not a sin, it's human.
- What I do when discouraged is important—praise can be a breakthrough.
- I will practice looking up to find hope in God, one negative emotion at a time.

Lord, I wish I were never discouraged or down. But the reality is,
it happens more than I care to admit. When I find myself in that place,
remind me to look up and anchor my hope in You. May my mouth
praise You even when I do not understand why things are as they are.

MY SAFE PLACE

You are my hiding place; you will protect me from
trouble and surround me with songs of deliverance.

PSALM 32:7

I once had a little dog named Bubba. He routinely tried to hide under the living room couch. Silly dog, he didn't fit under the furniture and his fluffy white Bichon bottom poked out and gave him away every time. We found him hiding when he was unsure, it was too noisy, or he did something wrong. It became his safe place.

God wants us to be our safe place, the place we run to when life feels unsure. We can learn to routinely hide ourselves in Him. It's not a tangible hiding, like Bubba and the furniture, but it is hiding our soul, our emotions, our problems, and our fears within the shelter of His care. The truth is, though we are protected, we often don't feel like we are—and so we hide behind the wrong things. It's time to realize that God protects us from things we aren't even aware of. It is a fact that He protects us from trouble while the angel army sings all around us. The sounds of such warfare are mute to us, but real nonetheless. Let's live like the few but powerful statements in this verse today are real. It just might change our perspective in problems.

Today I will remember:
• Jesus wants to be my hiding place.
• God is a protector and deliverer.
• I will learn to find that place of soul care where I hide all of me in all of Him.

Lord, forgive me for the many times I forget that I am protected. I want to remember
daily that You surround me and protect me in my troubles. And, though I can't
hear the songs of deliverance around me, by faith I thank You today for them.

COURAGE IN OUR PROBLEMS

I will take you as my own people, and I will be your God.
Then you will know that I am the Lord your God.

EXODUS 6:7

I was mad at God, discouraged about life, and didn't feel like praying. One day, alone in my misery, I told God that I no longer believed. I knew the Bible promised that all things were working for good, but nothing seemed good. I yelled out a desperate prayer. The way I saw it, God could have prevented all I was going through, but He didn't. How could I possibly trust Him?

The Children of Israel were frustrated too. God had seen their troubles and sent Moses to lead them, "but they did not listen to him because of their discouragement."[59] It's normal to be discouraged when we are engulfed by problems. As the circumstances get harder, our courage shrinks smaller. That's what discouragement is—a loss of courage.

Maybe you don't feel like praying. God wants to speak to you. He speaks through His Word, in His still, small voice, or through the people you trust. The day I called out to Him, He spoke tenderly to my heart, "especially in this, trust Me." I cried myself to sleep. When I woke, nothing had changed—my problems were still there. But I had changed. I had courage to face whatever I had to go through because I heard that still, small voice assuring me that I could trust Him.

Today I will remember:
• God sees me in my distress.
• God hears me when I pray; my words and wails are safe with Him.
• God delivers me in and through every problem I face.

Lord, thank You for knowing my emotions and not shutting me out
when I am discouraged. Help me to trust You, listen for Your voice,
and expect deliverance in and through the hard things in this life. Amen.

---

59 Exodus 6:9.

DON'T ALLOW FAITH TO FADE

Watch yourselves closely so that you do not forget the things your eyes
have seen or let them fade from your heart as long as you live.
Teach them to your children and to their children after them.

DEUTERONOMY 4:9

I recently passed a sign that said, "What doesn't kill you makes you stronger, so I should be able to bench press a minivan." I laughed, because I've felt like the weight of problems was going to kill me more than once. Much of how we walk through hard things is based on our emotional response. Because emotions are a product of our thought life, it's important that our faith doesn't fade based on how we are thinking about things.

What we think about a problem determines how we handle the problem itself. If what we think does not reflect truth, then what we feel does not reflect reality. Here's an example: While waiting to hear the results of an important job interview, you hear a false rumor that someone else got the job. How would you feel? Probably disappointed. But in reality, you got the job but just haven't been told yet. The enemy likes to plant F-E-A-R—False Evidence Appearing Real—in our minds to produce an emotional response that draws us away from hope and faith in God.

Today I will remember:
- To watch closely how I'm thinking about things.
- To prevent faith from fading by remembering God's faithfulness as long as I live.
- It's important to pass faith on to those following after me.

Lord, my thoughts are often all over the place and not centered on Your
goodness. In that place it's common to react emotionally to life. I desire to
change that and to watch my thoughts, patterns, and what I am believing.
May I pass on stories of faith to my children and their children.

FROM STRENGTH TO STRENGTH

*Blessed are those whose strength is in you, whose hearts are set
on pilgrimage...they go from strength to strength, till each appears before God.*
PSALM 84:5, 7

Our life is a pilgrimage—a journey with God. We pass through barren times. "As they pass through the Valley of Baca, they make it a place of springs."[60] This valley is symbolic of weeping, tears, or the struggles people must pass through to meet God. This is a beautiful account of not just passing through but turning hardship into something holy along the way.

I live in the desert, where the air is dry, and the summers are hot. Water in any form is welcomed here—misters, pools, and the ordinary garden hose. When I think of the Valley of Baca, I think of those hot, barren months that people in the desert endure. Problems are like that. We endure—waiting it out, sometimes complaining all the way. What would it look like to make our deserts a place of springs?

If you are in the heat of a problem, you can cool down the emotion and make it a place of refreshment as you trust God. Set your heart on Him, and no matter what life throws at you, you will go from strength to strength. When your heart is set on God, your strength is secured.

Today I will remember:
- I am blessed when my strength is in God.
- I am to set my heart on God and my life on the journey with Him.
- When my heart is set, my strength is secured.

*Lord, in the heat of my problems, remind me that setting my
heart on You is the most important thing. May I find strength
in any circumstance by changing my view and looking up.*

FACING THE PROBLEM

Endure hardship as discipline.
HEBREWS 12:7

It all started with a few freak accidents. I blew my calf muscle, then a tendon, and ended up in a wheelchair. I wasn't happy with the sudden halt in my schedule. But I needed surgery and a physical therapy called gait training—basically, learning to walk again. I cried, alternated ice and heat, took pain meds, and learned a lot about enduring hardship.

To *endure* is to suffer through difficulty patiently. The opposite of enduring is to quit. I felt like quitting. But I began to believe that hardship was disciplining me for my good. We often aren't aware of what God is working in us, but we can trust that He's working out of love.

Living with faith in God is not natural, but something we learn. If someone you know glides through hardship with stellar faith, they have been disciplined and trained along the way. Probably the most important thing is being aware that God hasn't left us, but is working in us through our circumstances. "God is treating you as his children. For what children are not disciplined by their father? If you are not disciplined—and everyone undergoes discipline—then you are not legitimate, not true sons and daughters at all."[61]

A change of attitude will help us face hardship and give us the faith to show up in the middle of each problem and be open to God's work in us.

Today I will remember:
• I have a choice in each problem—endure or quit.
• Enduring requires me to trust God.
• Quitting is the easier choice, but I will miss out on being shaped by God.

> *Lord, problems require me to trust You. In the middle of the hard stuff, You shape me as I wait on You. Thank You for loving me enough to treat me as Your daughter. May I honor You.*

---

61 Hebrews 12:7-8.

CHOOSING TO BE UNMOVED

I cry to you for help when my heart is overwhelmed.
Lead me to the towering rock of safety.
PSALM 61:2

Have you ever been utterly stressed and frantic? Too much on your plate, too many problems, no solutions in sight? You spin the facts 101 times, fret over the outcome, and worry more than trust. That is what it looks like to be overwhelmed. Even though it feels as if we must be overwhelmed to be human—as if there were no other option—the truth is, there is always a choice. Oswald Chambers said, "we must battle through our moods feelings and emotions."[62]

The opposite of being overwhelmed is to be unmoved. It's not denying the problem, but rather choosing to be unmoved by it because you are trusting God with the outcome. Surrendering the current situation to God is an important step in trusting. Surrender is intentionally giving up control to another. We must stop and purposely give it to God in prayer. This isn't wishing He would take it, but knowing we have given it over to Him.

No matter what the situation is, surrender it to the Lord. Ask Him to work out the details, lead you through the particulars, and give you the grace and strength not just to go through the annoyances, but to actually grow through them.

Today I will remember:
• When I am overwhelmed, I can stop and turn to God.
• Being overwhelmed is a choice—a sign that I'm not trusting.
• Being unmoved means to battle through fears and feelings, standing in faith.

Lord, I desire to live differently than my normal default of fear, worry,
and being overwhelmed. I thank You that I can come to You in all situations.
May I run quickly to the rock that is higher than any problem I will ever face.

---

62 Oswald Chambers, *My Utmost for His Highest*, November 13.

PRUNING AND PROBLEMS

*He cuts off every branch in me that bears no fruit, while every branch
that does bear fruit he prunes so that it will be even more fruitful.*

JOHN 15:2

Pruning is painful but necessary. Jesus is the true vine—our source—and we are the branches. Pruning is not to harm us, but to make us more fruitful. Though it hurts because pruning cuts deep, the end result is always more fruit. Since most of us want fruitful lives, pruning is something we should welcome even though it's uncomfortable in the moment.

Problems and pruning go hand in hand. Problems cut away at us and often leave us feeling bare. I've heard it said that not all problems come to disrupt our life—some come to clear the path. Just like we clean out cupboards, purge our closets, and toss food that has seen better days, problems clear away the parts of us that are cluttering up our growth. While in the hard circumstance we most likely don't realize this, God uses problems to cut away what is prohibiting more fruit in our lives to bring us to a place of new growth.

We view problems as bad, but what if we began viewing them as necessary, asking God while we are in them what He is doing in us. Problems clear the path for more fruit when we are seeking God in and through each new hard circumstance.

Today I will remember:
- Problems can be God's pruning tool.
- Problems and pruning aren't fun in the moment.
- Pruning is necessary for my future growth.

*Lord, I want to grow and live a fruitful life until my very last breath.
Though I don't like problems or pruning, I thank You that everything
You use to shape me can be trusted because You are good and You
always work to form more of Yourself and Your ways in me.*

PROBLEMS HAVE A PURPOSE

We do not lose heart. Though outwardly we are
wasting away, yet inwardly we are being renewed day by day.
2 CORINTHIANS 4:16

Things happen to us. None of us likes pain, but pain brings us to a place of dependence on God. Remember, things happen *to* us (tests, trials, hardships) so something can happen *in* us (maturity, completeness). .

C. S. Lewis said, "pain is a megaphone."[63] Those words couldn't be more descriptive or more accurate. Pain calls out to us until we are reached at the deepest level. We don't want to go there, but pain does have a purpose. And this purpose makes pain our friend—not usually an invited guest, but a friend nonetheless.

When pressed by pain, remember this: "We are hard pressed on every side, but not crushed; perplexed, but not in despair; persecuted, but not abandoned; struck down, but not destroyed... So we fix our eyes not on what is seen, but on what is unseen, since what is seen is temporary, but what is unseen is eternal."[64] These words are from Paul, who learned to trust the process of purpose in each trial he faced. He fixed his eyes on Jesus and His love—the unseen power holding life together.

Today I will remember:
- Today might be hard, but I will not lose heart.
- I see myself crumbling, but God sees what He is building.
- I will fix my eyes on Jesus instead of my problems.

> *Lord, thank You for using all things in my life for good. You take*
> *problems and repurpose them to growth. May I live with eyes on*
> *You and faith in Your process during any test or trouble in my life.*

---

63 C. S. Lewis, *The Problem of Pain* (New York: Harper Collins, 2001), 88.
64 2 Corinthians 4:8-9, 18.

NOT DESTROYED

We are hard pressed on every side...but not destroyed.
2 CORINTHIANS 4:8-9

To press my clothes takes the heat of an iron. To press a pretty flower takes the steady, prolonged pressure of being placed between two heavy books. We are pressed in life when stress or hardship flattens us.

Have you ever been pressed by pain? I have, and at times it seems like only yesterday. I can remember the weather, the flowers that were blooming, and the deadness taking over my heart. Life happened, turned my world upside down, and left me feeling like I was suspended in midair. That in the story of my real life, but the pain brought about something new and real in my faith walk. To my surprise, my heart has grown stronger, warmer, and more pliable in the hands of God. I have confidence this can happen for you, too.

If you are hurting, remember that Jesus is working in you. I know it's brutally hard some days, but Romans 8:28 says all things are making us more like Jesus. That's it. The eternal crystallized. The pieces of the puzzle put together. The pain given purpose. We are being changed daily and being made into people we could never be without the brokenness of our problems. The game is on. We are in the middle of the field, and we can't give up now. Let pain call you and inspire you to take heart as you focus on the bigger picture.

Today I will remember:
• My problems are pressing, but I won't be destroyed.
• God is using everything I go through to make me more like Jesus.
• Some pieces of my life make no sense to me, but God knows where they fit.

Lord, sometimes the heaviness in the moment is more than I can bear. But You promise that You are working. Thank You that though I feel like my problems are destroying me, I will not be destroyed because You hold me fast.

PROBLEMS CAN POISON US

Resentment kills a fool, and envy slays the simple.
JOB 5:2

We've looked at problems from different angles. But there is one important thing we must remember: If we make our problems precious, they will poison us. Sit with that a minute.

How do you make a problem precious? By giving everything to God except your pet problem. By holding it close, feeding it with overthinking, and talking to everyone about it. I have made plenty of problems precious, and they have nearly killed me emotionally and spiritually. The enemy uses the problems against us when we hold them tightly. He is a liar, thief, and destroyer.[65]

While I was going through my divorce, I kept my "precious problem" of unforgiveness and resentment close. I held it, made excuses for it, and talked about it with others. Friends took sides and fanned the flame of my resentment. But by not yielding to God, I was becoming bitter and ugly. No girl wants to be ugly!

I realized that the enemy didn't have to look far to trigger me—he looked at my storyline and hit me where it hurt. Since I was excusing it as normal divorce war stuff, I was being poisoned spiritually. We are not instructed to forgive because it feels good, but because it is God's will.

I have no idea what hard thing you are making precious today, but believe me, it's going to poison you. Given to God, our problems prosper us into new life and growth. Held close and managed by us, they are a slow ugly poison.

Today I will remember:
• Resentment destroys me.
• Jealousy will kill peace in my life.
• I must give all things over to God.

> *Lord, I know You have forgiven me for every time I have handled myself or my problems in a way that made them worse. Teach me Your ways and shape my heart toward beauty, not ugliness.*

---

65 John 10:10.

June

LIVING WITH PURPOSE

Without God, life has no purpose, and without purpose,
life has no meaning. Without meaning, life has no significance or hope.
Rick Warren[66]

66 Rick Warren, *The Purpose-Driven Life* (Grand Rapids: Zondervan, 2002), 30.

GOD PROTECTS OUR STORY

I am the gate; whoever enters through me will be saved.
They will come in and go out, and find pasture.
JOHN 10:9

I never could have anticipated the path my life would take, but God knew. And though purpose is often connected to things we do, real purpose is about our journey with God. Jesus lays a foundation for this concept in John 10 when He speaks of being our Good Shepherd. He came to give us life in its fullest. But, as in every story, there is drama—in this case, it is the thief. Jesus told us clearly that there is a thief waiting at the gate to steal, kill, and destroy. God's purpose is life—not just mediocre life, but a full, abundant life. We are invited to daily find the pasture of intimacy with the Father. God wins.

Back to that sneaky thief—if God has a purpose, the thief wants to steal that purpose. His main ploy is to go after our minds. Louie Giglio writes, "In the garden of Eden, the serpent didn't shout his temptations to Eve over a loudspeaker. He planted seeds in her mind and waited. He prompted her to question God's goodness. He coaxed her to wonder if God was withholding something good from her. Eventually Eve relented and let those seeds take root. Eve acted out what she had been thinking about. That's how the enemy works."[67]

The thief wants you to question God's goodness and love.

Today I will remember:
• Jesus is the gate to salvation and purpose.
• His purpose is to give me a full life.
• His purpose doesn't mean I won't have problems, but that He is with me in them.

Lord, what a beautiful contrast, as well as a real and present challenge.
May I walk confidently in purpose today, finding what I need in You.

---

67 Louie Giglio, *Don't Give the Enemy a Seat at Your Table: It's Time to Win the Battle of Your Mind* (Nashville: Thomas Nelson, 2021), 117.

TO KNOW HIM

I am the good shepherd; I know my sheep and my sheep know me.
JOHN 10:14

My granddaughter comes into my room, going through makeup and jewelry at will. I love that she is comfortable with me. Familiarity is a beautiful thing. Jesus invites us to know Him. The word *know* here is *ginosko*, which can mean to understand and be sure of. That is the kind of familiarity that Jesus has with us. He fully understands us. The abundant life is one of fellowship and intimacy with the Father—knowing Him and believing He knows us. Purpose may be lived out in the things we do, but it starts with the foundation of knowing God.

Charles Stanley reminds us, "Activity, though essential to practical faith, is not a substitute for personal fellowship. It can never outweigh intimacy with God. Our relationship with Christ erodes and cools when our primary focus is taken off the Messiah and placed on other things. That is the beginning of idolatry, and it is a dangerous path for the saint to tread. The gods of this age—sports, work, money— are cleverly disguised and ensnare many Christians with their compelling allegiance. Too much of a good thing can be wrong if it distracts you from devotion to Christ."[68]

Our greatest purpose in life is to know Jesus and to be known by Him.

Today I will remember:
• Jesus is the Good Shepherd, and He has good plans for me.
• Jesus knows me intimately and is familiar with all my ways.
• I know Jesus better and grow in intimacy with Him as I set my focus on Him.

Lord, I want to know You more—being intimately acquainted with You and walking with You daily. Help me to push back distractions or anything else that would rob my commitment to following Your purpose for me.

---

68 Charles Stanley, *A Touch of His Love: Meditations on Knowing and Receiving the Love of God* (Grand Rapids, MI: Zondervan, 1994), 67.

LIVING IN HIS PRESENCE

Come, let us return to the Lord...He will heal us...He will bind up our wounds...
He will revive us...He will restore us, that we may live in his presence.

HOSEA 6:1-2

The purpose of being a Christian isn't being good, doing the right things, or hanging with the right people. Oswald Chambers says, "This salvation which comes from God means being completely delivered from myself, and being placed into perfect union with him...It means the Spirit of God has brought me into intimate contact with the true Person of God Himself. And as I am caught up into total surrender to God, I become thrilled with something infinitely greater than myself."[69]

God's purpose is that we be caught up in Him more than being concerned about ourselves. When we seek first His Kingdom, all things are added to us.[70] These additions are practical, but more importantly, they are things we can't do for ourselves—healing, revival, restoration, and intimate relationship with God. The word *revive* here means to bring back to life and strength, while *restore* means to bring back to the original state.

Sometimes we get off course and need to be brought back around to what the original plan was. Other times we need to be revived and brought back to life spiritually. In either case, be assured of walking in purpose today by turning to God, and when you do, He will clear all paths so you may live in His presence—unreservedly committed to your life journey with the Father.

Today I will remember:
- God's purpose is not to straighten me up.
- God's purpose is to fill me up with Himself.
- God will complete His purpose as I live in His presence.

Lord, lead me daily to Your best for me. When I need healing, heal me.
When I am exhausted, revive me. And when I am broken and off track, restore me.

---

69 Oswald Chambers, *My Utmost for His Highest*, March 13.
70 Matthew 6:33.

THE PRACTICE OF RETURNING

Let us examine our ways and test them, and let us return to the Lord.
LAMENTATIONS 3:40

Our walk with Jesus is a series of returns. We return to Him for help in hardship, peace in anxious times, light in darkness, and rest for our minds and emotions. This practice of returning is needed because we get distracted with all the highs and lows in life. In either space it's easy to lose the focus of following Him—and lose our sense of purpose.

Pain is a teacher. Whether the pain is physical, emotional, or relational, it gets our attention. When things are going great, it's easy to lose focus on the real purpose of life—being a disciple or follower of Jesus. But when life is pinched with inconvenience or pain, we run back to Him. Both the hard and the good hold value, but the most important thing is that we return to God many times over while we are learning and growing as disciples of Jesus Christ.

The Lord's ways may be foreign to us or grate against the way we do things. His way may bump up against our flesh and how we want to live. Letting go and returning are spiritual practices to be embraced and practiced. Stop to pray, examine your ways, and return once again to the Lord. You will be glad you did.

Today I will remember:
- It is important to examine my ways.
- I should test my ways to see if they align with the truth in God's Word.
- I need to return to the Lord so He can redirect me.

Lord, may I return to You over and over again throughout my life.
May returning be a theme that leads me to a place of wisdom, grace, and maturity.

NEW ATTITUDES

In your relationships with one another, have the same mindset as Christ Jesus...
He made himself nothing by taking the very nature of a servant...
He humbled himself by becoming obedient to death—even death on a cross!
PHILIPPIANS 2:5, 7-8

When my neck is stiff or my back is out, I make an appointment with my chiro-practor, who skillfully adjusts me and makes me straight again. Perhaps when my attitude is out and I am filled with pride, anger, unforgiveness, or the need to control everything I need to make an appointment with Jesus for an adjustment. I know He can make the crooked parts of me straight and the narrow parts wide.

As I read this passage, part of me cringes because I know that my pride changes my attitude from a humble servant to a woman who wants her own way. But I see a key phrase here—*He humbled himself by becoming obedient to death.* Let that sink in. To humble ourselves is to freely lay our will down in favor of another. He laid down His will before God out of obedience. Living purposefully surrendered and yielded to Jesus and His way over mine can become a lifestyle. I want to live a life with the attitude Christ had rather than living a life to prove myself, protect myself, or perfect myself.

Today I will remember:
• Jesus made Himself nothing—He gave all glory to God the Father.
• Jesus humbled Himself in obedience to God—praying *not my will, but yours.*
• Jesus' obedience led Him death—a death which gave life to all mankind.

Lord, I need an attitude adjustment. So I come to You and ask You to
transform me and my attitude, making me more like You. May I be like
You in surrendered obedience, even death to myself and my pride.

KNOWING HIS VOICE

He goes on ahead of them, and his sheep
follow him because they know his voice.
JOHN 10:4

There should be an intimate exchange between Jesus and His people. We were not meant to follow Him out of strict obligation, but rather out of choice to respond to His love and care for us. Following out of obligation produces people who are rigid and miserable. Following because we believe He loves us still might be hard, but it produces an obedience born in expectancy that He knows the best way for us.

When people talk about hearing God, it can sound a bit strange. But it isn't. God's voice isn't a loud audible boom from heaven, but rather a knowing that He is pressing something deeply into our heart and mind. Sometimes it's something we would have never thought of ourselves. His voice is not something scary to be afraid of, but a voice that we can learn to listen to through His word speaking to us and His still, small stirring in our hearts and circumstances that point us in His direction. It might be an idea that keeps passing through our mind, or a phrase that won't leave our thoughts. When we are filled with the Holy Spirit, what we tend to think are brainstorms might actually be Spirit storms. One thing is certain: We can know His voice and learn to follow it, finding daily direction and purpose. Mark Batterson says, "I'd rather have one God idea than one thousand good ideas."[71]

Today I will remember:
- I am His.
- He goes before me.
- I can hear His voice and follow Him.

Lord, help me to know when You are speaking to me. May I always be
open to Your Spirit and ready to follow You and Your leading in my life.
Thank You that You go before me because You know the path I am to take.

---

71 Mark Batterson, *Whisper: How to Hear God's Voice* (Colorado Springs: Multnomah, 2017), 14.

THE CENTERPIECE

He must become greater; I must become less.
JOHN 3:30

Every ticket for the conference had been sold, and over a thousand women were going to be coming through the doors in less than an hour. As I surveyed the set, the decor, the teams gathered for prayer, and the worship team finishing their rehearsal, I stood in awe. God did it. A conference was born.

I was reminded that Jesus was the one we were there for—not the artists, speakers, or attendees. The team worked hard for months, but it wasn't about us. We were simply those who came before Him, praying that He would be lifted up once the curtains were drawn. John the Baptist left this example for us. He wasn't the Messiah; he came to prepare the way for Him.

We must remember that our role is to prepare the way too, making paths for others to come to know Jesus. We draw the curtain and let Jesus shine. We learn to step back so that in His time we can boldly step forward. He loves us, but we aren't the big deal—Jesus is. Jesus must increase in our lives, our relationships, and our ministries. It might do us good to remember this: I must decrease so that the life of Christ can increase. We need to humble our hearts before Him and make Him the centerpiece of all we do.

Today I will remember:
- Jesus is the only One to be lifted up.
- I obey by humbling myself to make room for His will through me.
- Living the decrease is an act of obedience in all my relationships.

Lord, let me not forget to always point any applause to You. In my relationships, may I learn to take a step back so that others can be heard and take a step forward. May I trust You to increase in me as I acknowledge my need to decrease.

GOD ASSIGNS OUR DAYS

Lord, you alone are my portion and my cup; you make my lot secure.

PSALM 16:5

She met me at the door, beautifully dressed and ready for visitors. It seemed as if I were visiting a friend recovering from surgery rather than someone dying of cancer. She took out a small gift, and folding my fingers over it said, "remember me." I could barely hold back the tears, while she had joy in being able to give me something to remember her by.

She was not afraid of dying, nor was she bitter that her doctor missed her cancer until it was stage four and too advanced for treatment. She had a grace about her. She knew something we all need to know—God assigns, appoints, and even secures our lot in life and our days. She leaned in, and looking me straight in the eyes said, "we are all going to die, and how wonderful that I get to say good-bye in a meaningful way."

I left that morning with tears streaming down my face. I was shaken by the confidence and peace she had. I often don't live that way, much less go through trials that way. And she was dying that way. She knew God and believed He was big enough to be Her portion and cup in this life and the one to come. She went to heaven a week later—and I will never forget her.

Today I will remember:
- God assigns—appoints, directs, and designates—my place in life.
- God gives different portions to each of us, and I will be content with mine.
- God's love is the boundary line around my life, and this makes me secure.

Lord, how I thank You that You alone are my portion and my cup. You assign things for me that are secured by Your will and purpose. Help me to rest secure in You.

HIS WAYS ARE PERFECT

As for God, his way is perfect; The Lord's word is flawless;
he shields all who take refuge in him.

PSALM 18:30

Do you understand all the intricacies of your computer hard drive? I'm pretty sure there's a lot going on in those wires that is beyond us. God working in us is like that. We don't fully understand, but God's Spirit is always working in the background of our lives. He is doing things that we can't see to get us where He wants us to go and make us who He's called us to be. To top it off, His way is perfect.

Think back to a time when you were concerned about the purpose for your life. How did that season turn out? Was God faithful to you? As you waited for His answers to your problems, were you anxious or worried? If so, did His faithfulness in the end build your trust? Here's the truth: We don't understand His will or ways, but we have undoubtedly seen his faithfulness time and time again. You might have heard of the movie *Yes Day*, where parents say Yes to their kids for one whole day. Let's make today a Yes Day between us and God, where we yield to His purpose for us and declare Him faithful over our lives—our problems, challenges, and all that concerns us. His way and purpose are perfect, even when we don't understand them. Perhaps saying yes will act as a faith shield as we keep growing, learning, and building strong spiritual foundations.

Today I will remember:
• I will say YES to God, all day.
• He shields me as I place myself under His care.
• His ways are perfect, and His purpose is firm.

Lord, today I want to yield to You with all of me. I place my yes before You
and look for You to multiply my yielding by leading me in Your ways.

—§—◇◈◇—3—

THE RIGHT PATH

So I say, walk by the Spirit, and you
will not gratify the desires of the flesh.
GALATIANS 5:16

On a speaking trip, I picked up a suitcase at the airport that looked like mine. But when I got to my hotel and opened it, I found a nice business suit, a flashy tie, and some men's boxers. It definitely was not my bag.

I had a choice—wear the suit to speak or get to the airport and make the exchange. I don't look good in men's suits and couldn't stand the flashy tie, so my choice was easy. If only it were so easy to decide to swap our personal baggage for God's power and purpose. But if we don't make the exchange, we will forever be wearing the wrong thing, living as carnal people rather than by God's power as the spiritual people that Scripture says we are.

We came wired for living according to the flesh, which Scripture refers to as our carnal nature. But being born again released us to live in the power of the Spirit. We can choose to keep in step with the Spirit by yielding our will, emotions, and choices to God. The most important thing to remember is that it is a choice—a daily choice. We will naturally drift to our own ways, but if we pay attention, we will notice the pull of God drawing us to His way.

Today I will remember:
- The carnal nature—the flesh—will always be a pull.
- The Spirit is where I live in peace, purpose, and power.
- Every day I have a choice: flesh or spirit.

Lord, it seems so clear—walking in the Spirit will bring me all my heart
truly longs for. But the pull of the flesh is so strong some days. Teach me
to lean into the Spirit and hear You leading me into Your purpose.

THE DIFFERENCE MAKER

*"Come, follow me," Jesus said, "and I will send you out to fish
for people." At once they left their nets and followed him."*

MATTHEW 4:19

This story might be familiar to you. Perhaps you have a ho-hum attitude right now. But stretch with me here and look at the deeper meaning in what Jesus is doing, what He was saying, and how it relates to us today. He asked them to follow. We've heard that before, and we may have also heard that they immediately put down their nets. All good things to know. But do you see the promise Jesus was offering them?

Jesus told them that if they followed, He would make them something different. Rather than fishing for fish, they would fish for people. They would be changed, and the outcome of their lives would be changed too. This is amazing! I want a different outcome than life lived for myself. I want a life that is an expression of Christ. I want to live in the context of a faith that is beyond myself.

God is the difference maker in our life. Jesus changes us and makes our life something different when we turn and follow Him. He has always invited His followers into a life of purpose. What might God do when you lay down your figurative net and follow Jesus? I dare you to find out.

Today I will remember:
- Jesus invites us to follow Him.
- To follow, we must lay down things that we are holding.
- When we follow, our life is changed. He is the difference maker.

Lord, thank You for inviting me to be part of Your plan when I follow You and do the things You have purposed for me to do. I lay down my net—anything that I'm holding on to—and ask You to change me the way You changed those fishermen.

FOLLOWING GOD INTO PURPOSE

Come with me.
MATTHEW 4:19, MSG

Following is key in living a purposeful life, so let's sit with it again today. For some the idea of following Jesus means going to church. That might be a good start, but you can follow Jesus without a church building. To follow Jesus is personal, intimate, and sometimes private. To follow Jesus is to journey with Him through life—pursuing a relationship with Him, paying attention to His directions, and obeying His lead. Maybe this is the key to change for some of us. Three simple yet profound words invite us into a different life: "Come with me."

Most of my Christian walk has been spent following God ideas, not following God. Because of this, I've spent significant time spinning my wheels and not seeing much life change. But in those times when I dare to follow, He changes me. Jesus didn't approach the fishermen with a five-step plan to create new and better fishing nets. He simply said lay down the nets you have and you will be more fruitful and more effective. Ken Gire speaks of following God as joining Him in the dance: "he doesn't ask us to write the notes to the music or choreograph the steps to the dance. He asks us merely to take his hand and follow him. To move when he moves. To speed up when he speeds up. To slow down when he slows down. And to stop when he stops."[72]

Jesus invites us to follow, and the result will be a life of daily, God-led purpose.

Today I will remember:
- Jesus invites me to get up close and personal with Him.
- I am to follow God, not God ideas.
- If I dare to follow Him, my life will change.

Lord, I want to follow You, dance with You, and move
with You, daily living in Your purposes for me. Show me how.

---

72 Ken Gire, *The Divine Embrace* (Wheaton: Tyndale, 2003), 89.

BE WITH JESUS

When they saw the courage of Peter and John and realized
that they were unschooled, ordinary men, they were astonished
and they took note that these men had been with Jesus.

ACTS 4:13

Before Jesus called the disciples to go out and represent Him, He called them to be with Him. Before He sent them out, He drew them close. This same Jesus wants to draw us close today too. But we get it backwards, don't we? That's natural for us doers. We want to do things for God, in His name—things earmarked with Kingdom purpose. It's easier for us to say yes to a position than it is to say yes to seeking the heart of God.

The very thing that will lead us into purpose is being with Him in thought, through frequent prayer, by looking up for heaven's perspective and living in heaven's actions. The point is, it starts with being with Jesus, then becomes doing for Him—not the other way around. Luke tells us that the credentials by which the disciples were recognized were not based on their position or influence. Instead, the disciples were known as those who "had been with Jesus." Being with Jesus each day changes us. It makes us passionately enthusiastic. It energizes us spiritually to lay down our nets, listen to His voice, and look for the power and supply of God.

Today I will remember:
- I don't have to have special credentials to have purpose.
- I find a life of purpose by following Jesus daily.
- I am gifted with all I need as I lay down my net—my life—before Him.

Lord, it's easy to think that I have to be specially trained to have purpose
in Your Kingdom. Thank You that You receive ordinary me and fill
me with extraordinary gifts of service as I follow You. My first purpose
each day is being with You. Draw me closer to Yourself, Jesus.

CHRIST ALIVE IN US

I have been crucified with Christ and I no longer live, but Christ lives in me. The life I now live in the body, I live by faith in the son of God.
GALATIANS 2:20

We are to live by faith in Jesus. This is the Biblical norm, but it is far from how most of us live. Since Christ is now living in us, Paul instructs us to no longer be conformed to the culture that we live in.[73] Take a moment and think about what is normal in our culture. Think of the laws that are passed—what has become normal in our lives? Think of the social media we look at—what is normal in our expectations? Think of what entertains us—what has become normal in our thinking? When I process what is normal in the culture, I think that learning to live beyond normal is a good idea.

I admit it's safe and predictable to live within the confines of what is culturally acceptable. But that's not what the Bible teaches. Instead, I see people like the apostle Paul, who turned his life around after God stopped him—blinded him—in his tracks on the road to Damascus. Paul's normal became a thing of the past and a wild devotion to Christ became his new life.

Friend, Christ lives in us! I often forget this powerful truth, but I am finding the need to keep returning to it. When I remember this truth, I live differently—with humility, appreciation, conviction, and a different compass for each moment, each day, each season. Beautiful purpose begins with Christ in me.

Today I will remember:
- I have been crucified with Christ.
- Christ now lives in me.
- I am to live by faith, not conformed to this world.

Lord, I don't want to waste my days living in unbelief and insecurity.
My purpose is to walk out a life of faith in You. Lead me.

---

73 Romans 12:2.

PUT AWAY CHILDISH THINGS

When I was a child, I talked like a child, I thought like a child, I reasoned like a child. When I became a man, I put the ways of childhood behind me.

1 CORINTHIANS 13:11

Remember the nursery rhyme about little girls? It tells us that little girls are made of sugar and spice and everything nice. I envision pretty little princesses sitting in fluffy pink tutus, smiling while waiting for the next performance. With the exception of a polite giggle here and there, they are silent. Little girls are watching their steps—or, as the nursery rhyme says, being sugar and spice and everything nice.

How many of us are still talking, thinking, and reasoning from the immature place of that little girl of the past? Is that God's best for you? Do you think you will find the purpose and radical shift you seek by living in the patterns you always lived in? You probably won't. Neither will I.

To live differently, I will have to put that little girl to rest and begin to live as the woman of God that His Word says I am. I want to laugh—and laugh out loud. I want to live—expecting that sometimes real life gets messy. I want to smile— at strangers, enemies, and those I love. I want to say what I mean and live what I say. I want to trust God to sort through my processing and bring me to inner healing. I want to run toward the goal of God's purpose for me, faster and harder than I ever have before. How about you?

Today I will remember:
- I learned things in childhood that need to be challenged.
- Some of my patterns are not good for me anymore.
- I am a grown woman, and God has a purpose for me.

Lord, show me the things from my past that need to be put aside. Heal me from old hurts and hang-ups, and give me courage to live in Your purpose now.

PURPOSE NOT PERFECTION

Remain in me, as I also remain in you. No branch can bear fruit by itself;
It must remain in the vine. Neither can you bear fruit unless you remain in me.

JOHN 15:4

Life doesn't always flow perfectly. Our story isn't tied up with a bow at the end of each season. But one thing is certain: God has purposed for us to get all that we need from being connected to Him. If we want to be part of things that have eternal value, we must remain in Him. Remaining connected is staying submitted to God's plan—even when things don't make sense or when life is interrupted.

Oswald Chambers said, "A saint's life is in the hands of God is like a bow and arrow in the hands of an archer. God is aiming at something the saint cannot see, and he stretches and strains, and every now and again the saint says—'I cannot stand any more.' God does not heed, he goes on stretching till his purpose is in sight, then he lets fly. Trust yourself in God's hands."[74]

Jesus is inviting us into a life of purpose. This bears repeating! Think about it: Jesus is inviting us to a life of following His lead into the places He has purposed for us to be. We try to perfectly figure out the plan, and He keeps inviting us to come closer to listen, learn, and be led. Perfection is overrated, temporal satisfaction. God's purpose is eternal.

Today I will remember:
• Jesus invites me to be securely attached to Him.
• I can't bear eternal fruit on my own.
• Remaining in Jesus leads me to His purpose.

Lord, may I daily remember Your
invitation to find purpose by remaining in You.

---

74 Oswald Chambers, *My Utmost for His Highest*, May 8.

PURPOSE AND PROMISES

Lord, you are my God; I will exalt you and praise your name, for in perfect faithfulness you have done wonderful things, things planned long ago.
ISAIAH 25:1

Next to me is a magazine, the cover of which promises 122 quick changes for health, body, home, and happiness. I must admit I am a sucker for this stuff. It also promises that I can lose 30 pounds without even trying and redo any room in the house in just 48 hours. But the most alluring promise for me is that I can look five years younger fast—and with no surgery!

I like promises. Promises offer hope and possibility. Unfortunately, all the promises for quick fixes end up leaving me more hopeless and less hopeful. They draw me in and suck me dry when I don't perform well enough to get the prize. Sometimes life seems like a lot of promises that never get fulfilled or a bunch of dreams that we never really get to live. This longing to "arrive" plagues us, drives us, and keeps us from enjoying the moments that make up a day— and the days that make up a life. We miss out on the beauty of life in the moment when we are chronically trying to fix ourselves.

I made a wild decision some time ago to step off the wheel of perfection and find the peace that awaits when I trust God. Psalm 138:8 (NLT) says, "God will work out his plans for my life." Sometimes the work seems slow. Slow is not popular, but speed is not usually how God works His way in us. God works the purpose of His heart for us—in faithfulness—over time.

Today I will remember:
- God has plans and purpose for my life.
- He faithfully works out His plan.
- He promises to perfect all that concerns me.

Lord, thank You for Your promise to work in me according to Your purpose for me.

GOD KNOWS THE PLAN

*"I know the plans I have for you," declares the Lord, "plans to prosper
you and not to harm you, plans to give you hope and a future."*
JEREMIAH 29:11

While looking for something, I happened upon several loose rolls of used film in the
bottom of a junk drawer. Film? I hadn't seen a roll of film in ages. I dropped off the
film at the local photo center, and what happened next is where the beauty began.
Film was made to capture images, but in order to do what it was made for, it has to
be developed. As simplistic as it sounds, in order for us to experience the life God
has purposed for us to live, we must be developed. For us, development is a lifelong
process. We don't drop our little hearts in a bin and pick them up the next day, glossy
and ready for framing. With film, yes, but not with real lives. Before I got those
glossy prints in hand, the film had to go through a process. The same is true with us.
It's God's purpose to bring about His plan in our lives. And we are in the processing
solution of His Spirit.

Many things shape us in life. God knows exactly what He is bringing to life
through every circumstance. Like the film, God has the image of His plan for us,
and today He is working in our lives because He knows the intended picture. The
plan will unfold. The picture God has for you—and of you—will happen because
He is faithful.

Today I will remember:
- God has plans and purpose for my life.
- His plan is to prosper me and give me hope.
- He is developing me now to be ready for His plans.

*Lord, may I remember daily that you are working in my life—snapshots of Your
plan that I cannot yet see. In Your faithfulness, You are developing me. Thank You.*

DIVINE GUIDANCE

*His divine power has given us everything we need for a godly life through
our knowledge of him who called us by his own glory and goodness.*
2 PETER 1:3

What did we do before we had GPS or map apps? One of my first experiences with
GPS was on a speaking trip. I had been to the retreat center before and knew where
I was going, but I wanted to play with the my GPS in a new car, so I entered in the
destination. As I was driving down the freeway, the little lady in the box began to
speak up. "In a quarter of a mile, exit to the right." I didn't agree with her, so I kept
driving like a rebellious teen. After all, I knew where I was going. After two recal-
culations, she finally got in sync with me, telling me get off right where I thought I
should. I arrived at the retreat center smug in the knowledge that I beat the little lady
in the GPS, only to find out later that the first two exits were both quicker. Insisting
on following my own way took longer.

This is a lot like our lives. We think we know how to get where we're going, devise
a route—and then God intervenes, giving different instructions. We say, "no thanks,
Lord, I know what I'm doing." In His love, He keeps recalculating our course because
He wants to get us back on track. Sometimes we turn off the guidance system, telling
the Lord we don't want to hear Him anymore. But just like the navigation system,
God is ready and waiting for us to choose to hear His voice again.

Today I will remember:
• God has all we need for life.
• He knows the way we should take.
• His way is always leading us to the best.

Lord, may I listen to You more than myself and more than the opinions of others.

GOD'S RE-APPOINTMENT

I press on toward the goal.
PHILIPPIANS 3:14

When things don't happen as we had planned, we face disappointment. This is normal. There is nothing wrong with being disappointed, but we must know how to deal with that feeling or it will take us down. We will always have disappointment, but we can make the choice to believe and behave as if our disappointment is actually God's reappointment. It is God's recalculation and provision for us, because He is always leading us into His purpose.

The apostle Paul had to learn how to live differently. To be a follower of Christ, he confronted the way he had lived before and everything he believed in. He spent the rest of his life and ministry teaching others how to live. I think one of the greatest things he said to us was, "but one thing I do: forgetting what lies behind and reaching forward to what lies ahead, I press on toward the goal."[75]

He showed us how to turn disappointment into reappointment by pressing forward. It takes faith to believe that God has a purpose. When we let go, we get a new vision, plan, or idea. We get a fresh outlook, a new mindset, and a change of focus. Throughout the Bible God instructs us to be filled with joy and to rejoice because of who God is and how He loves. We believe God plans good things for us and will always lead us into purpose.

Today I will remember:
• With each situation, I have a choice.
• I will choose to believe God has a purpose for my life.
• I will stay focused and press on toward the goal

Lord, I am easily distracted with disappointment and looking backwards. I ask for Your help to focus forward, look ahead, and press toward the new things You are doing.

75 Philippians 3:13-14, AMP.

THE HOLY SPIRIT AT WORK

And the Lord—who is the Spirit—makes us more and
more like him as we are changed into his glorious image.
2 CORINTHIANS 3:18, NLT

The Bible is very clear that "God is working in you."[76] To become more Christlike is one of God's purposes for your life. It is the Holy Spirit's job to produce Christlike character in you. You can't produce Christlikeness in your own strength or through resolutions, best intentions, or willpower. At the mention of the Holy Spirit, many have thoughts of extremism or intense emotions. But most of the time the Holy Spirit works in unassuming and quiet ways. The Spirit often nudges us with quiet whispers that are part of the personal work He is doing in the private as we seek God.

We allow Christ to live through us in the choices we make. We make a choice to do what is right and then trust the Spirit's power to give us the love, faith, or willingness to change what we need. And because God's Spirit lives inside of us, everything we need to live in God's purpose is available to us. The key is cooperating with the Holy Spirit's work. We act first, by faith, not waiting to feel confident or capable. We move ahead in our weakness, doing the right thing even when we don't feel like doing it. This is how we yield to the Spirit and cooperate with His work. The result is that we will become more like Christ, which is God's ultimate purpose for us.

Today I will remember:
- The Holy Spirit is working in me.
- The Spirit works to make me more like Jesus.
- I reflect Jesus as I cooperate with the Holy Spirit though obedience.

Lord, thank You for Your work in me. When my feelings pull me in
the wrong direction, pull me back to You. Be glorified in my life.

---

76 Philippians 2:13.

A LONG PROCESS

...that we will be mature in the Lord,
measuring up to the full and complete standard of Christ.

EPHESIANS 4:13, NLT

God left us with a big responsibility—to make disciples. If we had to fulfill this command alone, we would probably give up before we even started. But as the body of Christ, we can do this together when each person does their part—each one committed to their own spiritual growth. In the end, when one grows, we all benefit.

One of the many purposes of God is our spiritual growth. God is more interested in who we are than what we do. Becoming more Christlike is a slow process; it's not instant or automatic. Trying to change overnight leaves us discouraged. I like to think of it as baby steps in His direction. Every "Yes, Lord," is another step—not a leap, just a step. Small steps add up over time. Paul goes on to say, "Then we will no longer be infants, tossed back and forth by the waves, and blown here and there by every wind..."[77] To be honest, it only takes a good hearty emotional trigger to get me veering in the wrong direction. How do I rein it in? By reminding myself that the trigger is a small thing that can help me grow. Acknowledging what trips us up and turning it to God for lessons and growth yields another step in growth and maturity.

Today I will remember:
- God cares about my personal growth.
- Maturing in Christ is part of God's purpose.
- I will look for ways to say Yes to God.

Lord, I want to be mature and measure up to what You have called
me to. Draw me near and help me to say yes to You, even when
I don't want to. Stretch me to the place of growth in godliness.

---

77 Ephesians 4:14.

GOD FULFILLS HIS PURPOSE

The Lord will work out his plans for my life—for your faithful love,
O Lord, endures forever. Don't abandon me, for you made me.
PSALM 138:8, NLT

I made my way to a friend's house in tears. My mama heart was hurting for my teenage child, who was going through something hard. Seeing that I was falling apart, she quickly ushered me in, sat me down, and told me to claim this psalm over my child's life. I began to repeat it out loud, declaring that the Lord would indeed fulfill His purpose for my child. I thanked God for His love and that He never abandons us. Peace flooded me as I sat with this one single verse in the Psalms. I have since claimed it countless times over my own life in the darkest of situations.

There is so much here to hold on to. God will fulfill His purpose for us. He will accomplish it. We might go through hard things, but God will see us through, never abandoning us in the process. This brings hope and security when it seems like we have messed up our lives, our situation, or when it appears that someone else wants to mess with us. Despite what happens and regardless of what others do to us or say about us, God will make sure His purpose for us is ultimately fulfilled.

Today I will remember:
• God has a plan, and He plans to accomplish His will in my life.
• God is committed to me with enduring love.
• God will never abandon me.

Lord, in the times when my life looks like it's a mess, You are still there,
working things out. I might not see You accomplishing Your will, but by
faith I thank You that You are. Today I declare that You will do what
You said You would do—fulfilling Your purpose in and through me.

GOD HAS FUTURE PURPOSE IN MIND

*"For I know the plans I have for you," says the Lord, "They are plans
for good and not for disaster, to give you a future and a hope."*
JEREMIAH 29:11

Dangling between one life season and the next, there is uncertainty about God's plans for me. I want to have the next step figured out, make a vision board to anchor it, and maybe outline a map of God's instructions in a well-worn journal. In other words, I want to have some control.

It's interesting that Jeremiah wasn't assuring the people that God would outline the plan, just that God Himself knew the plan. They were to trust that God had their best in mind—that's the hope and future promise. The same is true for us today. But is knowing that God knows the plan enough? Can we trust the character of God even if we don't know the details of the path?

This is what I do know: God wants what is best for us. He always goes before us in each season. Even in the hard seasons, He is there. I struggle with not knowing the plan but am becoming increasingly comfortable with trusting that He knows, and it's becoming enough. He knows—so let's exhale the doubt and breathe in the security of His involvement in our life.

Today I will remember:
• God wants what is best for me.
• He alone knows the plan for my future.
• He desires to prosper me, not harm me.

*Lord, I want to trust You so much that the details are of little
importance, but Your promise of knowing the plan is the biggest thing
I hold on to. Help me to walk in the confidence of one who is being
led through life by a God who knows the plans He has for me.*

THE FOUNDATION OF PURPOSE

All things were created through him and for him...
and in him all things hold together.
COLOSSIANS 1:16-17

When we get clear on our God-given purpose, things will change in our lives. It is then that we begin to live a life of intention—to walk in what God has for us. Why is this important? Most of us don't grow up being told that we were created by God, and that it's in Him we find our path and purpose. *By Him and for Him* is a powerful truth that can become a mission statement that steers us away from people-pleasing and approval-seeking. This one single truth can create courage to live in our deepest significance in this life.

God knows the places He will take us in this life. He is writing our story one day at a time. And, though life gets complicated, He holds us together. We might not have the details of this season carved out, but we can be assured that He holds us together and directs our way.

Maybe today, in a new time and season, we are in need of a friendly reminder that our life is on purpose—for His purpose. I like how it reads in The Message: "Everything got started in him and finds its purpose in him."

Today I will remember:
- I was created by God.
- I was created for His purposes.
- He holds me together, and I find myself in Him.

Lord, thank You that in each season You hold me together and are
underneath me as my foundation. Thank You for creating me for
Your use. May I daily remember that and live to honor You.

COMING TO JESUS FOR LIFE AND PURPOSE

You study the Scriptures diligently because you think that in them
you have eternal life. These are the very Scriptures that testify
about me, yet you refuse to come to me to have life.

JOHN 5:39-40

As a young senior pastor's wife leading the women's ministry, I studied diligently to teach the weekly Bible study. When I started, I had no idea what I was doing. I just loved the women and loved Jesus. And we needed a women's study, so tag, the inexperienced pastor's wife was it. I learned so much in those years about what Scripture teaches. Sadly, I also gained a lot of head information without much life transformation. I taught the Scriptures but didn't spend much personal time with Jesus. I was too busy for that—I had kids to feed, places to be, events to plan, and Bible study table leaders to train. I preached the Word and lived in a frenzy far more than I learned to live in His presence.

Jesus spoke boldly to the Jews who were scoffers about the folly of head knowledge over real relationship with Him. And, though we may know that the only way to have eternal life is through Jesus, we too might forget the invitation to come to Him, be in relationship with Him, hear His voice, and follow Him. No Scripture can save us; only coming to Jesus can bring us new life.

Today I will remember:
- The Scriptures testify about Jesus.
- I study to learn what the Scriptures say and to know who Jesus is more fully.
- I find new life by coming directly to Jesus, and Him alone.

Father, I want to know You. I want to know Your Word, too,
but I don't want to be guilty of making Scripture my god while ignoring
Your invitation to be in a personal, intimate relationship with You.

EVERYDAY DISCIPLES

Go and make disciples of all nations, baptizing them in the
name of the Father and of the Son and of the Holy Spirit,
and teaching them to obey everything I have commanded you.
MATTHEW 28:19-20

Being diagnosed with liver disease in my twenties prohibited me from going on mission trips. Over the years I felt like a less-than Christian because I didn't have my hands in the soil of other countries. I mistakenly thought that the mission field was only in faraway, impoverished places, not realizing that God called me to make disciples right where I was planted.

It is God's purpose to save and restore lives. Each of us has been called to share in that purpose. You don't have to be an evangelist—you just need to be you. A disciple is simply a follower. We are first called to follow, and then to lead others to follow too. When we ourselves become true followers—not perfect disciples, but women growing closer to Jesus—our life changes. Jesus came to change how we experience life. Life will always be hard, but there is purpose in following Jesus through real life, experiencing His faithfulness in all we walk through. We share Jesus by first being interested in others, and then sharing the gospel and how it's changed our life. This call of God is not out of our reach, but when we are open, God will prompt us at just the right time, and how we respond might save someone's life.

Today I will remember:
- I am called to share Jesus with others.
- God has people for me to reach.
- I am to be open to the people and places around me—God is at work.

Lord, forgive me for not paying attention to my real purpose, which is
helping others know You and follow You. Use me to influence others with
the truth of the gospel and how knowing You changed me forever.

GOD POSITIONS US FOR PURPOSE

If you remain silent at this time, relief and deliverance for the Jews will arise from another place, but you and your father's family will perish. And who knows but that you have come to royal position for such a time as this?

ESTHER 4:14

God's plans are bigger than we can comprehend. We see this in the story of Esther. God positioned her in the right place at the right time. God raised Esther up to become a King's wife so that she would have an influence in sparing the Jewish people. Esther had to persuade her husband to stop the plot to have the Jewish people wiped out. Speaking up was dangerous for her because her husband could likely have killed her along with the others. Her uncle Mordecai sent her the message in this verse to remind Esther that if she did nothing because of feeling helpless or afraid, she and others would perish. God had ordained her for this specific time and purpose. Esther and Mordecai believed in God's care, and because they acted at the right time, God used them to save God's people.

Do you ever hold back, remain silent, or wait for other people to step up? When you begin to realize that God has ordained you for a specific time and purpose, you will be empowered to say yes, take risks, and see God work—for such a time as this.

Today I will remember:
- God desires to use me for such a time as this.
- God has prepared me and placed me where I am for His purpose.
- If I remain silent and don't answer the call, God will use someone else.

Lord, I desire to fulfill Your purpose for me.
I want to honor You with faith, obedience, and a sacred yes!

THE SACRED PATH OF PURPOSE

Consecrate yourselves, for tomorrow
the Lord will do amazing things among you.
JOSHUA 3:5

Sun-kissed and college bound, I practically ran down the aisle to commit my life to Jesus. I wasn't sure of all it entailed, but I knew that I wanted to know God and make a difference. It was the 1970s, a time filled with protests and change. I went from the sandy beach to being baptized and never looked back.

But what I thought was purpose then is different than how I view it now. Looking back over fifty years, I realize that purpose is something we journey into one day and one season at a time. It's a solid and steady dedicating of our lives to Jesus for the present use before us. Making a difference starts with the consecration of our lives to God. Then purpose carries on and will be present with each of us until our last breath.

Consecrate is a big-sounding word that means to dedicate something to a divine purpose. There is much in this one single word. It's a set-apart life viewed as sacred unto God. Amazing things will happen through our lives, but we must get in position by dedicating ourselves to Him completely. Declare to yourself today that you have been called to a purpose bigger than you can see and frame your life by devoting yourself to making space for God to work in and through you.

Today I will remember:
• God calls me to declare today that I am His.
• The Lord has a plan to work through my life.
• God's plan starts with the dedicating of myself completely to Him.

Lord, I come laying my life down before You once again today. You are the difference maker, and I'm asking you to make a difference through me in my relationships, my family, and my daily endeavors. Use me, Jesus, for Your divine purpose.

LIVING BEYOND MY SELF

Pardon your servant, Lord. I have never been eloquent...
EXODUS 4:10

Insecurity threatens to rob purpose out from under us. When usefulness gets wrapped up in performance, we will be tempted to shrink back and be afraid to stand out. Moses reminded the Lord of his inadequacy: "I am slow of speech and tongue." The Lord responded, "Who gave human beings their mouths? Who makes them deaf or mute? Who gives them sight or makes them blind? Is it not I, the LORD? Now go; I will help you speak and will teach you what to say."[78]

But Moses still said, "Please send someone else."[79] I'm sure we can relate to Moses. God assures us of His help—and we still say, "no thank you."

Listen, God knows we are not capable on our own. The human heart is complex, and so is life. He invites us into this amazing purpose of walking with Him and being empowered to do His good work in this world. But it's all Him. We can accept the invitation and live an extraordinary life—even though we are ordinary women—because of His Spirit. Or we can argue with God and waste our lives away. We get to choose. What will you choose today? Will you settle for allowing your inadequacies to hold you back or lean into His power lifting you up to His call on your life?

Today I will remember:
- God is not expecting me to be qualified.
- God made me who I am to work His purposes through my life and story.
- God will be the help and power I need to be used by Him.

Lord, thank You for inviting me into Your purpose in this world.
Continue shaping me and preparing me for Your plan. May I be
a "yes" woman—saying yes to Your power and purpose in me.

---

78 Exodus 4:10-12.
79 Exodus 4:13.

July

LIVING IN FREEDOM

"Christian freedom does not mean being free to do as we like;
it means being free to do as we ought."
William Barclay [80]

---

80 William Barclay, *The Letters of James and Peter* (Louisville, Westminster, John Knox Press, 2003).

FREEDOM FROM THE SLAVERY OF FEAR

You have not received a spirit that makes you fearful slaves.
Instead, you received God's Spirit when he adopted you as his own.
ROMANS 8:15, NLT

Fears come in all shapes, reasons, and sizes. When we add "do not fear" to our vocabulary, we get wrapped in shame for not having enough faith. In a perfect world there would be no reason to fear. But in the real world, where people go through hard things, life can seem scary. Some days we walk into the world afraid—fearing what can happen to us or doubting that we are enough.

Friend, Jesus comes with an invitation to trust His heart. He met a woman at the well[81] who was rejected by five husbands. She must have wondered what was wrong with her—and likely feared she wasn't enough. Jesus invited her to take living water from Him. He didn't bother with who she should be; He invited her into who she could be when she began worshipping God in Spirit and truth.

Let the truth sink in—you have not received a spirit of fear. If fear is ruling your life in any area, it's not from God. It may be a natural by-product of life and hard circumstances, but it's not from God.

Today I will remember:
- God has not given me a spirit of fear.
- I am not a slave to expectations or insecurity.
- I am not on my own, but invited into a relationship with the living God.

> *Father, I admit that I struggle with fears—fear from without and*
> *fear from within. I know You are inviting me into a place of*
> *greater freedom, as fear is never from You. I come expectantly.*

---

81 John 4.

THE FREEDOM OF TRUSTING HIS PRESENCE

You hem me in behind and before, and you lay your hand upon me.

PSALM 139:5

I was four months pregnant and finally feeling well enough to do routine errands with my three-year-old son. I circled around the car to get him out of his seat—and heard a rush of steps coming toward me. I was grabbed, thrown to the ground, and covered by a heavy body, wrestling for my purse. I let go, and the stranger sprinted to a getaway car. In the ensuing days I questioned God, asking, "Where were You?" The fear that something could have happened to my son or the baby haunted me. I didn't leave my house for days.

A detective brought pictures, and I quickly identified the attacker. "Looks to me like God protected you. He and his buddies were armed and on drugs. It could have been much worse." As that was sinking in, he told me my attacker held up three women at gunpoint after leaving me on the ground. The detective helped me realize that God had been with me. Since I was attacked, it never occurred to me that I was also protected. This began changing my thinking, helping me understand that no matter what I go through, God is covering me.

The word *hem* here means to enclose or to shut in. In the KJV it is translated *beset*, which means to confine with borders. I began to see God's border around me as my protection, a type of God-box, behind—before—upon me. Slowly I began to realize that I can be safe even through the ugly things that happen.

Today I will remember:
• He protects me.
• God puts a border around me—even in unsafe situations.
• He goes before me, covers behind me, and lays His hand upon me.

Lord, life is scary and filled with things that make me feel vulnerable and unsafe.
Help me to believe Your Word that says You are a border around my life.

THE FREEDOM OF A BALANCED MIND

For God has not given us a spirit of fear and timidity,
but of power, love, and of self-discipline.

2 TIMOTHY 1:7, NLT

Going back to a place where I was hurt was hard, but attending my friend's memorial service was important. My stomach twisted and churned until I was worked up and stressed out. I had let the spirit of fear take over.

In the car, I began to pray out loud. "Lord, help me to get through this." Suddenly I remembered this verse out of 2 Timothy. Some versions use the words "sound-minded" and "balanced" instead of self-discipline.[82] That stuck with me. God gives me a sound and balanced mind. I needed that. On repeat I claimed it and prayed it, "God you have not given me a spirit of fear, but a sound mind." Parking at the church where I worked for nearly fifteen years, I again thanked God that He had not given me a spirit of fear. I rebuked the enemy and stood tall. The rest is history, as the day was absent of the fear I was worried about.

It is normal for fear to be a first thought, but it doesn't have to be the last. When we linger in fear, dwelling in dark discouragement, it is contrary to the power that God has given us. He hasn't given us a spirit of fear—period. When was the last time you felt afraid, timid, or insecure? The truth is, whenever we sink into fear, it is not of God and it's something we have the power to stand up against. God wants to assure us that in everything, He is with us.

Today I will remember:
- God does not bring me to a place of fear.
- God gives me power to rise above.
- God enables me to have the courage to live in love and self-discipline.

Lord, thank You for the spirit of love and a sound mind.
Remind me when fear sneaks up on me that it is never
from You. May I have a sound and balanced mind.

THE FREEING COURAGE OF HIS PRESENCE

Be strong and courageous. Do not be afraid; do not be discouraged,
for the Lord your God will be with you wherever you go.
JOSHUA 1:9

Sometimes it seems like we are trusting God until every prop is pulled out from under us. Try as we might to work up courage, it can easily collapse in the heat of a situation. That is, unless our courage is based on the character of God. Recently I was sick and on five different medications. The doctor called to tell me that I actually tested positive for three viruses and the medications would not help. I began to panic. *If I don't take anything, how will I get better?* It was then that I realized I was trusting the familiar more than having faith that God was with me and could heal me. Fear began to do its creepy-crawly thing in my thoughts.

If we dare to believe that God is with us, we will have courage. There are four directives that the Lord gave Joshua to enable him to lead the people, but the exquisite promise that underlines it all is the most important thing—the Lord your God will be with you. Join me today in declaring with courage, "The Lord is with me, whatever I go through and wherever this day takes me."

Today I will remember:
• The Lord is with me.
• I can have courage in the midst of all situations.
• I do not have to be terrified of problems because the Lord has me.

Lord, forgive me for the many times I trust familiar
things rather than putting true faith in You.
May I walk in courageous faith as I remember
the truth that you are with me in all things.

A LIBERATED REALITY

If the Son sets you free, you will be free indeed.
JOHN 8:36

In a world of facades, we are invited into the freedom of a liberated reality. Jesus talked about real-life things like sin and weaknesses. He was open about being enslaved by fears and longings. But the people he was addressing weren't relating to being enslaved, they simply didn't understand: "We are Abraham's descendants and have never been slaves of anyone. How can you say that we shall be set free?"[83]

Often we are like those people. *Why freedom? I am fine the way I am.* Jesus knew we needed freedom—and He is on a freedom mission in our lives. Regardless of personal circumstances, Jesus wants to free us from all that holds us back and keeps us stuck. In particular, He wants to free us from our self so that we can be truly liberated to trust His work of grace in our lives. Nothing is too big or too small for His reach. Though we may still struggle with the bondages of our past, it's our own limitations that keep holding us back. Ask Jesus to free up those parts of you that keep getting you tripped up and distanced from all God has called you into.

Today I will remember:
• Jesus has the power to set me free from myself, from my sin, from my past.
• When Jesus frees me, it's a supernatural work.
• I may still get triggered and tempted, but I can stand on my freedom in Christ.

Lord, thank You for setting me free. Though old
memories pop up, I stand in the reality of freedom today.

83 John 8:33.

FREEDOM FROM THE "NOT ENOUGH" LIE

Such confidence we have through Christ before God.
Not that we are competent in ourselves to claim anything
for ourselves, but our competence comes from God.

2 CORINTHIANS 3:4-5

Confidence is tricky. We think it all depends on us—enter performance. So we have confidence when things are going well and lose it when things aren't so great. For those who struggle with feelings of not being enough, the push to prove ourselves through perfection and performance is actually the catalyst that trains us to place our confidence in the wrong source—self.

When placing our confidence in self alone, we are not on a solid foundation. The word *competent* here in the original is *hikanos*, and it can mean the following—good, great, worthy, or enough. With that in mind, it could read, "...not that we are good in ourselves, great in ourselves, worthy in ourselves, or enough in ourselves."

We need freedom from the "not enough" voices that follow us. We were not created to be enough in ourselves. Scripture goes on to say, "He has made us competent [good, great, worthy, enough] as ministers of a new covenant—not of the letter but of the Spirit; for the letter kills, but the Spirit gives life."[84]

Friend, it gives me life today to know that I am not called to be enough. He is enough, and I am in Him. The same is true for you.

Today I will remember:
• I can live in confidence as I live in Christ.
• I was not meant for self-competency but Christ sufficiency.
• I am enough because of Christ in me and through me.

Lord, forgive me for the codependent way I rely on others' opinions of me to
feel confident or competent. I wasted too much time feeling "less than"
when You never called me to measure up, but only to be measured in You.

---

84 2 Corinthians 3:6.

SET FREE FROM ME

*Now, the Lord is the Spirit, and where the
Spirit of the Lord is, there is freedom.*

2 CORINTHIANS 3:17

If the Lord sets us free, then why do so many of us circle back to the bondage and old triggers of the past?

The Bible says we can quench the Spirit—meaning we can live or behave in such a way that does not encourage the movement of God's Spirit in our midst. First Thessalonians 5:19 says, "Do not quench the Spirit." How do we quench the Spirit? We put out the Spirit's fire by living like people who do not believe—lying, anger, stealing, unforgiveness, selfishness, jealousy, etc.

There are many times the Bible speaks of living in the Spirit as opposite of living in the flesh. When we are not experiencing the freedom of the Lord, we are most likely walking in the flesh or perhaps bound up in habits, hurts, and hang-ups that trigger the flesh to respond louder than the Spirit.

Often disappointment or frustration can leave us feeling defeated. In that place, it's easy to take things out on others. When our focus is on ourselves, we easily get tripped up in responding and living according to our old habits, giving way to our flesh nature.

Simply put, I am not free when I am bound up in me.

Today I will remember:
• The Lord is the Spirit—with a will and personality.
• There is freedom when living in connection with the Spirit.
• I can quench or stop the flow of the Spirit in my life by my attitudes and actions.

Lord, thank You that You have given Your Spirit to lead, guide, direct, and empower me. The Spirit sets me free, and I desire freedom from self. Teach me what quenches Your Spirit's fire and how to live free by walking in the Spirit daily.

FREED FROM COVER-UPS

*Live as free people, but do not use your freedom
as a cover-up for evil; live as God's slaves.*
1 PETER 2:16

We landed in Hawaii ready for a much-needed week of rest. But soon after unpacking, I discovered that I had forgotten my cover-up. Ugh! I couldn't possibly go out and about the resort without the very thing that would make me feel comfortable, hidden beneath fabric. Most women know about a good cover-up. Whether it's makeup or clothes, we have learned how to hide our imperfections.

Sometimes as Christians we cover up other things, like bad attitudes and behaviors. We become adept at living safely beneath the confines of acting right when our heart is filled with wrong. Where Jesus wants to free us, we keep at arm's length from God and others by expertly covering up the imperfections. Knowing we have been set free from sin and death by the blood of Jesus, we can easily slip into not taking responsibility to live in that freedom. Living free means to go about our lives as God's servants, being His hands and feet in this broken world. It is living by the rhythms of His grace with difficult people and letting go of lingering offenses. To be free in Christ is to live covered by Him, not covering our sin with the right words or actions.

Today I will remember:
- I am called to live in freedom.
- I am not to cover up my sin as a means of looking free.
- I am to be surrendered and submitted to God—and live as His.

*Lord, it's easy to masterfully cover up the ugly things in me. I want to walk in
the light and live as a freed woman, who though imperfect, is perfectly loved.*

ALIENS AND STRANGERS

Dear friends, I urge you, as aliens and strangers in the world,
to abstain from sinful desires, which war against your soul.
1 PETER 2:11, NIV 1984

The word *alien* brings up images of creepy-looking characters in sci-fi movies. It's not a word in my everyday vocabulary, but maybe it should be. An alien owes allegiance to another country, being different in nature and character. And as foreign as that sounds, it's exactly how Scripture describes us as Christians living in this world— aliens and strangers.

I wonder if I have become so familiar with this life that I've lost interest in the one to come. Some days I know that is true. The early church was urged to live with this alien and stranger mentality and to allow that to change their choices and their lives. We are strangers in this place and are to live by a different playbook than the one we grew up accustomed to.

How do we do this? One way is to pay attention to the desires that go against all we know to be true about God's Kingdom. It says these desires are at war in us—the flesh warring against the things of our souls. These desires pull us down to a level of bondage that is never God's best for us.

Today I will remember:
• I am not of this world—and am being prepared for a heavenly Kingdom.
• The ways of this world are at war within me, fighting against God's ways.
• I am to abstain from the sinful desires that keep me from my freedom in Christ.

Lord, forgive me for my distraction and preoccupation with this life,
and for not giving much thought to the life to come. Heaven is my
real home, and I am asking You to make that a reality to me so that
I willingly turn from those things that are at war within me.

FREEDOM TO LIVE CORRECTED

*If anyone, then, knows the good they ought
to do and doesn't do it, it is sin for them.*

JAMES 4:17

I grew up with an aversion to the words *should* and *ought*. Both led to a feeling that I was never doing enough. Over time I developed a belief that at my very core, I was not enough.

That old baggage left me resistant to the parts of Scripture that tell me what I ought to do. It took work to turn those words around from a negative to a positive. Jesus wants us to have abundance of life and knows that there are many things that lead us to bad choices, keeping us from true abundance. *Should* and *ought* are actually safeguards, not shame creators.

The good we are directed to do in Scripture has nothing to do with our value—it's always for our good and growth. If you resist being told what to do, like I did, submit that to Jesus and be freed to begin living in His best instead of your habitual ways that might not be leading you to your best. It's clear that to know the right and live the wrong is sin. Sin is missing the mark, being off target and not living in the best that God has for us. Thankfully, there is a remedy for sin and missing the mark—forgiveness in Jesus. We are freed by being forgiven.

Today I will remember:
- I need to pay attention to the good I know I am to do.
- I can pray and ask God to give the grace and strength to choose His best.
- When I stopped resisting instruction, I can be set free.

Lord, help me not to resist any instruction for my good in Your Word.

FREEDOM THROUGH APPLICATION

Do not merely listen to the word,
and so deceive yourselves. Do what it says.

JAMES 1:22

Are you living in the truth of God's word or letting it go in one ear and out the other? To live the word is all about walking it out truth by truth, situation by situation. Listening without applying what we have heard will not lead us to the freedom that we hope to find in our Christian walk. We can know a lot of verses and preach poetic on their meaning, but if we don't try stepping into those truths in our daily lives, we may drift the other direction. I have found that I can help lead others to freedom but stay in bondage myself. It's not what you know, but how you live.

James go on to say, "Anyone who listens to the word but does not do what it says is like someone who looks at his face in a mirror and, after looking at himself, goes away and immediately forgets what he looks like. But whoever looks intently into the perfect law that gives freedom, and continues in it—not forgetting what they have heard, but doing it—they will be blessed in what they do."[85]

I like the results of paying attention far more than the effects of drifting from truth.

Today I will remember:
- I am deceived when I look at God's Word and don't apply it to my life.
- God's Word is a perfect law that gives freedom.
- I am blessed when I hear and pay attention to God's way.

Lord, I need You in all that I do. I want to hear Your Word, live Your
Word, and know the blessing of living by the truth of Your Word.

---

85 James 1:23-25.

FREEDOM IN BEING HIS

It is for freedom that Christ has set us free. Stand firm, then,
and do not let yourselves be burdened again by a yoke of slavery.

GALATIANS 5:1

My friend Lori found a lump in her breast and was diagnosed with breast cancer at thirty-nine. She could have walked away from faith in God, but she learned to stand firm. After ten years, I stood before her family and friends eulogizing her. Though cancer devastated her life, she remained undevastated. She stood firm.

I wear a silver bracelet engraved with *His*. It reminded me that I did not belong to myself, but to a loving God. I began experiencing freedom in areas that had long held me back. Funny thing is, I wasn't wearing a bracelet engraved with *freedom*, but rather with the reason for my freedom—being His. I could stand firm when I remembered that I was His.

God never promised to change our circumstances, but He did promise to change us. We aren't set free so we can do whatever we want, whenever we want—that kind of life would lead us right back to being a slave to our desires, sin, and selfishness. Because of Christ we are free to do what was impossible before—live unselfishly. Freedom isn't about rules and regulations but rather a journey into a relationship with God that changes our desires and how we approach life—regardless of our circumstances.

Today I will remember:
• Christ cares about my freedom.
• If I am not careful, I can go back into my personal bondages and slavery.
• I am to stand firm in who I am in Christ and how He set me free.

Lord, thank You for setting me free and caring about my life being
different because of the way You break the chains of fear and doubt.
Teach me in each season to stand firm in my circumstances.

—◦⧉◦—

THE FINAL FREEDOM

My Father's house has many rooms; if that were not so, would I have told you that I am going there to prepare a place for you?... I will come back and take you to be with me that you also may be where I am.

JOHN 14:2-3

Three times she repeated her last words to us—"Live like it's real, because it is." As we stood by her hospital bed, surrounded by crumpled tissue and broken hearts, nothing could have prepared us for that final good-bye.

My mother was afraid to die. But as she journeyed closer to her eternal home, heaven became clearer and her attitude changed to desiring to go to that "fancy" place that was becoming more real to her. She went from dying in fear to fully alive in faith. God revealed himself to a woman losing her grip with this life. We say it, we sing it, but I wonder how many of us spend time believing it. I witnessed the final freedom, and it was beautiful.

Heaven is not a pink cloud filled with harp music. Heaven is operated by God's principles—eternal and unshakable. Scripture tells us we are citizens of a different Kingdom, and our forward hope is to settle one day with God in our eternal home. If it weren't so, Jesus would not have told His disciples. But He did. It is settled. One day we will face the final freedom, and until then we are to live like it's real—because it is.

Today I will remember:
- God is preparing a place for me.
- This world is not my home; I am a citizen somewhere else.
- He will be faithful to take me home with Him when it's my time.

Lord, it's hard for us to live as citizens of heaven with so much invested here on earth. I pray that I will live like heaven is real, and that the focus of eternity will change the way I live.

FREEDOM FROM THE THINGS WE LEARNED

We were like children; we were slaves to
the basic spiritual principles of this world.
GALATIANS 4:3, NLT

Our story begins at home, and our belief system starts forming in our earliest days. The apostle Paul uses strong words here—saying we are *enslaved* by the principles of the world we grew up in. We need our minds renewed daily so that we don't keep turning back to the old thought patterns, self-rejection, or the principles of the world we live in. The greatest thing that can happen to us is learning to lean into the truth of God's Word and learning to live in the freedom of being His children. But for some reason, we stay stuck. We turn back to our old ways of thought and reasoning.

Paul goes on to say, "Formerly, when you did not know God, you were slaves to those who by nature are not gods. But now that you know God—or rather are known by God—how is it that you are turning back to those weak and miserable forces? Do you wish to be enslaved by them all over again?"[86]

The years we spent being programmed by the world have affected all of us. Old thought patterns don't just disappear. We must establish a new way of thinking biblically as Christian women who are known by God. Being known by God is the key, and knowing Him is the path to freedom.

Today I will remember:
- When we did not know God, we learned to live as the world lives.
- The Bible calls these earlier principles *weak* and *miserable*.
- Once we know God, we are to live as new people known by God.

> *Lord, I don't want to turn back to my old thinking*
> *and patterns. When I am moving in that direction,*
> *nudge me and lead me toward You and Your ways.*

---

86 Galatians 4:8-9.

FREEDOM TO STAND

*Put on the full armor of God, so that when the day
of evil comes, you may be able to stand your ground.*

EPHESIANS 6:13

We are in a spiritual battle. It's not *if* the attack of the enemy will come, it's *when*. As long as we are alive, there will be an adversary who will come against us. How do we wage war in our daily life against an enemy who is invisible, powerful, and a dedicated threat to humankind? By standing our ground.

The devil is the ringleader of all the fallen spirits cast out of heaven and is determined to do all he can to wean us away from Jesus. His focus is not on those who do not believe, but on believers like you and me. The Bible pictures him as a roaring lion looking for victims. Even as he tempted Christ, he tempts us. His temptations are subtle, sinister, sneaky, and often sugarcoated. We are told, "Resist the devil, and he will flee from you."[87]

Only with Christ and through what He did for us on the cross can we resist the devil and defeat him. Jesus has overcome Satan for us. With Him at our side, the victory is always won. Put on the full armor of God, standing your ground, so that you can be more than a conqueror through Him who loves you.

Today I will remember:
- Daily spiritual clothing is to include the armor of God.
- I step into this armor by faith, placing myself under God's authority daily.
- The day of evil will come, and I must be aware and prepared.

*Lord, thank You that I am a conqueror through You, and that You
conquer the power of hell that seeks to come against me. Show me
what it means to live adorned in the armor of God each day.*

---

87 James 4:7.

FREEDOM IN WEAKNESS

That is why, for Christ's sake, I delight in weaknesses, in insults, in hardships, in persecutions, in difficulties. For when I am weak, then I am strong.

2 CORINTHIANS 12:10

Like most people, I don't like weakness. But, like the apostle Paul, I have come to accept and embrace weakness when it's part of my life. Paul might have been flat on his back in the weakness of the thorn in the flesh, bent over in the hardships of traveling from one city to another, receiving insults and persecutions at every turn. Yet he said that this is when he was the strongest, for then he received the full power of God.

When weak, have you experienced God's power? Once when I was scheduled to keynote a retreat, I had no voice. The women's leaders were equipped to take over, but I felt that God wanted me to step up to the podium. It began with the women leaning in as my voice was a whisper and ended with a full-strength voice as God moved. It wasn't me. I was weak—and God showed His strength. I just had to step up to the plate.

When we imagine ourselves to be strong, that is when we have the greatest weakness—for it is only our strength. But when we are weak, the fullest strength of God comes to carry us on. Paul seems to say, "bring on the problems, the sickness, the difficulties." He knew that in weakness, the all-encompassing power of God would come. Freedom comes in trusting God more than ourselves.

Today I will remember:
- I can delight in times of weakness.
- When I am weak, God will be strong through me.
- It is never me, but Christ who is in me.

> *Lord, this is my hope—Christ in me. Living in and through me when I am weak and when I am strong. When I am weak, Your power is made perfect.*

⸺⟡⸺ 3 ⸺⟡⸺

FREEDOM FROM FENDING FOR MYSELF

There is no wisdom, no insight,
no plan that can succeed against the Lord.
PROVERBS 21:30

Sometimes it seems like everything is against us. Fear rises as we watch things fall apart. Will we ever find ourselves where we hoped to be? Or will people, circumstances, and even the enemy bully our dreams away? Fear has been said to be False Evidence Appearing Real. While the circumstances may be very real, what is false is the idea that God has left us to fend on our own. Fear says He has left the building, while faith knows that He is near.

In the history of God's people, there are many instances when they sought to fend for themselves without God's help, and sometimes were even defiant to His commands. Here, we are told that God is in control and that any human ambition apart from God's design will come to nothing. God does not leave us to our own wisdom, insight, or plan. God is about the business of rescue. Our wisdom, insight, and plans often fail. God's ways always succeed.

There is a freedom in trusting that we are not on our own and that God has a plan. While the enemy will be quick to try to steal from us, God is present to provide for us. The next time fear rises and doubts are persistent, stop and tell yourself the truth—nothing will succeed against the plan of the Lord, and there is nothing that can collapse the plan of God in my life.

Today I will remember:
- God is at work in all things.
- God has a plan for my life and reigns in wisdom over me.
- Nothing can take His place or His plan in my life.

Lord, forgive me for the times I overthink and doubt Your plan in
my life. Keep me focused on You and Your presence with me.

FREEDOM FROM STRIFE

Starting a quarrel is like breaching a dam;
so drop the matter before a dispute breaks out.
PROVERBS 17:14

It's easy to start a fight. All we have to do is take the bait of offense Satan dangles before us. We internalize something more negatively than intended, slinging words and emotions that can't easily be taken back. We've all been there. It's ugly. And, if we are going to be honest, most of us don't want to be ugly girls, but beautiful women.

We have beauty treatments for skin and hair, but there is none for the part of the body we use most—the tongue. The Bible says, "the tongue is a small part of the body, but it makes great boasts."[88] The tongue can start a quarrel and break open a dam of poison or remain silent and drop a matter before a dispute breaks out. Our words can make marriage a paradise or a prison. It can kill a church, break down relationships, and destroy a family. But dropping a matter can be the beginning of building bridges.

Next time you want to quarrel, think about a dam busting lose. Do you want to build up or tear down? There is freedom when we put strife to rest.

Today I will remember:
• Quarreling is a choice. Not everything has to be a fight.
• When I start a quarrel, I open up floodgates that affect others.
• When I drop the matter, I make room for peace.

Lord, thank You for freedom in Christ, freedom to choose to do the right thing
when I want to do the opposite. Remind me of this verse the next time I am quick
to argue or worked up in my emotions. Help me to drop a matter in favor of peace.

---

88 James 3:5.

FREEDOM FROM LONELINESS

The Lord your God goes with you;
he will never leave you nor forsake you.
DEUTERONOMY 31:6

Have you ever felt lonely in a crowd? When you don't feel connected to people or feel like you are misunderstood, you might feel completely alone. Most of us have experienced feelings of loneliness. For me, the feeling of loneliness increased when transitioning from one life season to the next—the empty nest being one of the greatest times of lonely angst. Loneliness is a normal part of life, but as Christians, when we draw closer to God, we can claim some freedom in this area.

Though loss and changes in relationships with others might bring a season of loneliness, we are never truly alone. God says, "I will never leave you." Reminding ourselves that God is always with us, repenting of the negative spiral we get ourselves into, and refocusing on the truth are all ways that we can stand in freedom when we are down and lonely. Perhaps it's time to accept loneliness, as it can draw you closer to God. Give thanks for the promise of God's presence. Refuse self-pity. Offer up your loneliness, asking God to transform it.

When you are lonely, remember that God knows how hard it is. One way to begin turning loneliness around is finding others to serve—giving of your time and talents to others is a sure way to begin the climb out of the pit of lonely days.

Today I will remember:
• The Lord goes with me everywhere I go.
• God will never leave me alone.
• God will never abandon or forsake me.

Lord, forgive me for the times I allow a negative spiral in my life
when I feel sorry for myself or alone. Though change is hard,
You are always near. Thank You for Your promise of being with me.

FREEDOM FROM PEOPLE PLEASING

*Am I now trying to win the approval of human beings,
or of God? Or am I trying to please people? If I were still
trying to please people, I would not be a servant of Christ.*

GALATIANS 1:10

Do you ever say "yes" when you want to say "no"? The overwhelming need for acceptance and approval can cause us to be nice and agreeable because we are afraid of facing rejection or disapproval. Living like this can be a bondage that keeps us from the freedom of balance in relationships. People-pleasing can become an approval addiction that leaves us focused on others more than on what pleases God. When we are focused on what others think of us, we lose focus on what God is requiring of us.

From the time I was young, I learned that making people happy made my life easier. To disappoint someone was completely unacceptable. So I learned to say I was OK, even when I wasn't. I studied what pleased the people in my life and did those things—even when they weren't what I wanted to do. I am now a recovering people-pleaser. But I found that freedom starts with putting God first and having courage to give honest answers without comment or apology. Start simple, trusting God as He guides you along your life path.

Today I will remember:
- I can't serve two masters—God and people.
- When I live for people, I'm not living to please God.
- When pleasing God, I will be free to honestly love people.

*Lord, help me to keep my focus on pleasing You and loving others—
not the other way around. Remind me that I can love others
even though I might not be doing all that pleases them.
May I live for You, pleasing You with my choices and my life.*

FREE TO LIVE UNSHAKEN LIVES

I keep my eyes always on the LORD. With him at my right hand,
I will not be shaken. Therefore my heart is glad and
my tongue rejoices; My body also will rest secure.

PSALM 16:8-9

I pictured imaginary skid marks all the way from Southern California to Northern California when a necessary move disrupted everything I knew, landing me and my kids in an unfamiliar city. I stressed and worried over the future. I like familiar, and life was anything but that.

Worry and fear about what tomorrow might bring doesn't help us—it holds us back from peace today. Jesus talked about the future, encouraging His disciples to resist worrying about their future because "each day has enough trouble of its own."[89] He predicted hard times, but told His disciples to be of good cheer because He had overcome the world. With that overcoming truth in mind, instead of wasting our cares on tomorrow, Jesus wants to give us the freedom to live today—full, rich lives.

Here is the hope: God goes before us, and He knows us and His plan for us. We can choose to worry and fret or resist fear by living an unshaken life. We can count on Him. I don't know what tomorrow brings, but I'm going to rest in the knowledge that He is steps ahead.

Today I will remember:
- I have committed my life to Christ—it is set before Him.
- He is always with me, so I will not be shaken.
- I will praise Him and rest in security.

Father, I have wasted so much of life worrying over the future.
Now I want to rest secure in knowing that You go before me, and because
of that my life no longer has to be shaken by the threat of circumstances.

---

89 Matthew 6:34.

FROM HERE TO ETERNITY

*No eye has seen, no ear has heard, and no mind has
imagined what God has prepared for those who love him.*
1 CORINTHIANS 2:9, NLT

Most of us are focused on the here and now. To be heaven focused would change everything for us. Some become more eternally focused when they have loved ones waiting for them there. Suddenly heaven seems more real than they ever imagined before. Yet there is freedom in training our thoughts upwards. Rather than forgetting our eternal home, we begin thanking God for our heavenly home today.

While we can't imagine what heaven will be like, we know that it is more beautiful than anything our eyes have ever seen. Look around at the most beautiful things here on earth, and think of how much more beautiful heaven will be. Sunsets hint at God's glory, rainbows remind us of His promise, and dancing porpoises delight us out in the ocean. Add to the list the glory of a newborn baby, the first blush of love, the fun in growing older—all things that we experience here and now, and yet heaven is so much more. For now, the goal is to live in the freedom of eternity's promise. He has indeed prepared a place for those who love Him. We have no need to fear—God is with us from here to eternity.

Today I will remember:
- I have never experienced the wonders of what awaits me in heaven.
- My ears have not heard a sound as beautiful as the chorus there.
- God has prepared a place for me, so I can live in the freedom of eternity.

*Lord, heaven is such a mystery. Yet Your Word promises mysterious wonder
and exciting glory waiting in that place You have prepared for those who are
Yours. Thank You for always being near, even to our last breath here.*

FREEDOM OF EXPRESSION

*The only thing that counts is faith
expressing itself through love.*

GALATIANS 5:6

I ranted and vented until even I was sick of hearing myself. With each complaint, my feelings of frustration took root. The last thing on my mind was faith or love. I was upset and was free to express it, right? Well—sort of. What might seem like free expression in the moment could be bondage to myself, my flesh, and all that is opposite of what really counts—faith and love.

The apostle Paul was clearing up a response over the battle of circumcision versus uncircumcision. The argument was about who was right. The bottom line is that obeying the law and doing the right thing is not the main thing; we are made right with God through faith and the love of Jesus. Trying to earn our standing through deeds only further separates us from God.

Paul says, "You were running a good race. Who cut in on you…?"[90] He goes on to say that being persuaded off the main thing does not come from the One who called us. That applies to us, too. We can get so fixated on our rights and opinions that we no longer express the most important thing—faith expressed through love. Next time we express only the negative, let's ask what or who cut in on us.

Today I will remember:
- There are two things that count—faith and love.
- I can express myself in many ways, but only faith and love count.
- Self-expression can become selfish, cutting in on the good that God can pour through me.

Lord, I desire to be an expression of faith and love and am asking You to make that a living reality in my life. If anything is cutting in on my race toward You, expose it that I might turn completely in Your direction.

THREE FREEING TRUTHS

To those who have been called, who are loved
by God the Father and kept for Jesus Christ.

JUDE 1:1

To those who have been hurt, rejected, and disregarded, life can become a quagmire of self-doubt, fear, and apprehension. Doubts creep in, leaving us to wonder if we are talented enough, good enough, or significant enough. The spinning "not enough" thoughts can spiral us negatively unless we take hold of the truth and turn upwards to find freedom in the truth of God's involvement in our lives. When it comes to who we are and how we are loved, there are three words to place on repeat—called, loved, and kept.

You are called by God, you are loved by God, and you are kept by Jesus Christ. All three truths establish our security and keep us emotionally stable. Freedom is always found through the truth. Jesus said, "you will know the truth, and the truth will set you free."[91] The truest thing about your life and mine is that we are kept by God. One of the definitions of *kept* is to retain possession of. Think of this—Jesus has a retainer on your life. You are His, and His covering over you is love. Believing the truth will set the path for free thoughts that replace the fearful ones. Tell yourself the truth today and begin walking out your freedom in Christ.

Today I will remember:
- I am called by God—He has a plan for my one and only life.
- I am loved by God—He gave His life for my freedom.
- I am kept in Christ—His grace covers over my many imperfections.

Lord, may these three truths be on repeat in my mind, becoming
the truth that my heart holds on to. Thank You for Your love,
for calling me to Your story, and for keeping me every step of the way.

---

91 John 8:32.

FREEING FAITH

*Build each other up in your most holy faith, pray in
the power of the Holy Spirit, and await the mercy of
our Lord Jesus Christ, who will bring you eternal life.*

JUDE 1:20-21, NLT

When my sons were little, they loved making things out of nothing. Now my grandkids pull out the building blocks or MAGNA-TILES, putting together their own special creations—they, too, make something out of nothing. That's what faith is like. We believe that God has the ability and power to make something out of nothing. We might not be building with actual blocks, but we are always building too. What are we building with our lives? Are we building things that don't matter, or are we building on a holy faith in God, one day at a time?

The writer of Hebrews tells us that "faith is confidence in what we hope for and assurance about what we do not see."[92] It is this set-apart faith that we are to build our lives upon, believing in something bigger than what we can see. We are to build upon faith, pray in the Holy Spirit, and keep ourselves in God's love. This is how we live in freedom. Let's build our lives upon an assurance and guarantee of God's pledge to us.

Today I will remember:
* I am to build my life on the foundation of faith.
* I am to pray daily, as led by the Spirit, in the Spirit, always.
* I am to keep myself in God's love by remembering who He is and how He loves.

*Lord, it's so easy to build on wrong foundations. I want to build
a life of faith, a habit of prayer, and a language of Your love.
Today I commit myself to this kind of freedom living.*

---

92 Hebrews 11:1.

FREEDOM TO STAND IN HIS STRENGTH

*To him who is able to keep you from stumbling and to present you
before his glorious presence without fault and with great joy.*

JUDE 1:24

To him who is able—what does that mean to you today? What is God able to do in
your life? Through your life? Because of His Spirit alive in you? There is a freedom
that comes when we quit striving and begin standing on the truth that God is able.

Able means capable, strong, powerful, makes things possible, gives favorable
circumstances.

God keeps us from falling and presents us without fault. Both are nothing short
of a miracle. Left to myself, I stumble around a lot. I say the wrong things, do the
wrong things, and often mess things up. But God is able to keep me from falling into
sin or falling all over myself due to insecurity or fear. And it's not just catching us, it's
presenting us before God. Think about that. It's incredible to realize that though we
are imperfect and make all sorts of mistakes, God presents us without the faults—
and with great joy.

Friend, you bring God great joy. Not because you have it together, but because
you are His. The next time you doubt yourself, look up and thank God that He is
able to accomplish anything and everything in your life. Then pause and receive the
joy of a Father who adores you without limitation.

Today I will remember:
- God is able to keep me in all my ways.
- God is able to keep me from stumbling and falling.
- God brings me into His glorious presence with great joy.

*Lord, I declare today that You are able.
When I am not able, You remain the one who keeps
me steady and who will bring me into Your purposes.*

FREEDOM TO HONOR GOD WITH MY BODY

I have the right to do anything—but not everything is beneficial.
I have the right to do anything—but I will not be mastered by anything.
1 CORINTHIANS 6:12

We aren't all the same. Each of us has the freedom to live according to what would be best for us. Because we are different, what is right for me might be very wrong for you. What you can handle might lead me down a very slippery slope. It's important to be aware of what is and isn't beneficial for each of us.

The early church was misapplying the meaning of the phrase "I have the right to do anything." Some were excusing their sins, insisting that because Christ had taken away their sins, they were now free to do whatever they pleased. Even something being a Scriptural standard was not enough for them to move from their place of proclaimed freedom. Paul addressed this by telling them that Christ taking their sin did not give them free reign to do the things they knew to be wrong.

While it's true that some actions are not sinful in themselves, they might not be appropriate because they can control the life of the believer and lead them away from God. Other actions might hurt others—anything that hurts rather than helps is clearly not right and not a path to freedom. Our body is a temple of the Holy Spirit. We have freedom to care for ourselves and honor God in our choices.

Today I will remember:
• My body is God's temple, and my choices are important.
• Not everything benefits my body, His temple.
• All things are permitted—as long as those things don't master me.

Lord, help me to know clearly what is good for me and what isn't.
When I am aware of what isn't good for me, may I live to honor You by
making appropriate choices and not comparing my choices to those of others.

CALLED TO BE FREE

You, my brothers and sisters, were called to be free. But do not use your freedom to indulge the flesh; rather, serve one another humbly in love.

GALATIANS 5:13

There is a difference between freedom to sin and freedom to serve. The license to sin is not freedom, because it enslaves you to your own sinful nature. Paul taught that the works of the sinful nature are obvious: "sexual immorality, impurity and debauchery; idolatry and witchcraft; hatred, discord, jealousy, fits of rage, selfish ambition, dissensions, factions and envy; drunkenness, orgies, and the like."[93] While you might not relate to the entire list, pay close attention to the things that you do experience. Some of them are accepted things, like jealousy, selfish ambition, divisions, and discord with others. These are not just how we act out, they are works of our flesh. Jesus came to set us free from the power of the flesh and lead us to the freedom of walking in the Spirit. The walk of the Spirit includes "love, joy, peace, forbearance, kindness, goodness, faithfulness, gentleness and self-control."[94]

Do you want to know your calling? Friend, you are called to be free! What is freedom in Christ? Not being controlled by rules and religion, but being transformed by your relationship with Jesus. Freedom is being controlled by the Spirit of God rather than by our old habits and patterns. Freedom recognizes the emotional triggers and takes them to Jesus. Freedom experiences temptation and stops to pray and get re-centered. Freedom is your calling—and it's mine, too.

Today I will remember:
• Jesus came to set me free from the deadly self-life.
• Jesus came to empower me with the freedom of His Spirit.
• Jesus came to work into my life the very life of Christ.

Lord, thank You for calling me to freedom. May I remember the next time I am tempted or triggered to look to You and heed the call.

---

93 Galatians 5:19-21.
94 Galatians 5:22-23.

APPROACHING GOD FREELY

In him and through faith in him we may
approach God with freedom and confidence.
EPHESIANS 3:12

I was warned, "Mom, don't make it weird." I supposed that comment might have been warranted, since I was about to be around some "famous" people—up close and personal. I did behave myself, trying not to look too long or say too much. I didn't take a sneaky picture or ask for a selfie. It's amazing how different I felt just knowing I was sharing space in their presence. It's silly because they are people just like me. Have you ever been in the presence of someone important or famous and felt nervous, small, or like shrinking back?

What a privilege it is to be able to approach God with freedom and confidence. He is the one who made the earth and everything in it—the God of all people and things—and you and I are invited to step right up and approach Him freely. He isn't sizing us up, nor is He impressed with who we are or what we do. He also isn't disappointed if we haven't amounted to much according to this world's standards. All that matters is that we have been created in the image of God, and He is dedicated to love us for all time. This is why we can come to Him freely and confidently. Our confidence is this: "While we were still sinners, Christ died for us."[95]

Today I will remember:
• I am invited to approach God daily.
• I can come freely, by faith, to God with every need.
• I am made in the image of God, and He invites me to journey with Him.

Lord, thank You for inviting me into Your presence.
I stand in confidence today in Your commitment to my life—
I thank You for who You are and how You love me.

---

95 Romans 5:8.

SET FREE BY THE SPIRIT

*There is now no condemnation for those who are in Christ Jesus,
because through Christ Jesus the law of the Spirit who gives
life has set you free from the law of sin and death.*

ROMANS 8:1-2

What represents your life before Christ? You are no longer that woman, because now you have a new life in the Spirit. But how do we go from death to life in our thinking? So much of how we live is based on what we think, and unfortunately most of us have spent a very long time being governed by the mind of the flesh—or what Paul calls the mind of the sinful man—"The mind governed by the flesh is death, but the mind governed by the Spirit is life and peace."[96]

The beauty of the gospel is that Jesus came to set us free from the sinful flesh and the mind of the flesh, so that in the Spirit we can live in peace rather than chaos. If we were on death row and the decision was turned in the last hour to not guilty, everything would change. We would be given a new lease on life and a chance to choose differently because we've been given more than we deserved. Though we might not realize it, each of us has been on death row spiritually. And through faith, Jesus declared us "not guilty." Because of this, we are free to live a changed life. We are no longer bound by all that held us back. The proclamation over our lives took us from death to life.

Today I will remember:
- Any condemnation I feel is not from God.
- My life is now governed by the Spirit.
- I am free to live a changed life.

> *Lord, I sometimes do things on autopilot that are no longer part of who I am in Christ. When this happens, remind me of my new identity in You and the power of life in the Spirit.*

HE HEARD MY CRY FOR FREEDOM

In my distress I prayed to the Lord,
and the Lord answered me and set me free.
PSALM 118:5, NLT

My life seemed perfect—until it wasn't. Literally overnight everything changed. I went from loved to unloved, wanted to discarded. I remember the day, the way I felt and the pain bursting from my heart, spilling out in uncontrollable tears. Some things you never forget, and realizing you are unloved is one of those things. You can forgive, but the memory of what broke you remains part of your story forever.

The bigger part of the story is that God heard my cry for help. He knew my pain and cared. He held me as I cried in the night. The memories have faded a bit, but there is one thing that is worth remembering—God set free in me things that I could have never unlocked in myself.

I don't know your story, but I think it's safe to assume that you, too, need Jesus to set some things in your life free. Friend, He is here for that. He sees the pain and hears your cries. He doesn't pat us on the head and send us away—He touches us by His Spirit and begins the work of freedom within us. We never "arrive" this side of the story, but we can continually walk in growing freedom until we reach the other side. This is freedom—Christ and the power of His resurrection bringing new life to our ruins and rubble. The story isn't over. Cry out to God. Your freedom awaits.

Today I will remember:
- I should cry out to God when I'm in pain.
- When I call out to God, He hears and cares.
- His answer is always freedom in the Spirit of life.

Lord, thank You for the many times You have met me in my anguish. The many times You have led me to a new place of freedom. The many ways You love me.

August

LIVING UP

"For no matter how many promises God has made, they are 'Yes' in Christ. And so through him the 'Amen' is spoken by us to the glory of God."

2 CORINTHIANS 1:20

UNDER THE CIRCUMSTANCES

He has given us his very great and precious promises,
so that through them you may participate in the divine nature.
2 PETER 1:4

All of us have problems. We can live under the circumstances or upon God's promises. What will you choose—buried under the problems? Or standing firm in the hope of God's pledge to be faithful? A *promise* is a pledge that you can count on.

God has pledged things to us that would help steady our faith—especially when life challenges us. But we often forget His promises. Or we may have heard them so many times that they no longer impact us the way they were meant to. Peter encouraged the early church to pay attention because they had everything they needed: "His divine power has given us everything we need for a godly life through our knowledge of him who called us by his glory and goodness."[97] Friends, God's power has provided everything we need—including His Word that leads us to participate in the divine nature rather than living according to our sinful instincts.

I want to have spiritual instincts. When circumstances threaten to bury me, I want to stand up and be faithful to the call of what God has in that situation. Is this problem to teach me? To strengthen me? To draw me closer to Jesus? In each case, God has given us His Word and His promises of faithfulness to stand on as a bridge over the problems we face.

Today I will remember:
• God's Word is a pledge of His faithfulness.
• God's promises are a resounding YES and are meant to steady and direct us.
• I can live buried, or I can grab hold of a promise and stand strong.

Lord, thank You for providing all we need to be spiritually strong
in a world that tempts us to throw away our confidence and
abandon the faith. May Your promises steady me and lead me.

GOD GOES BEFORE ME

The Lord himself goes before you and will be with you;
he will never leave you nor forsake you.

DEUTERONOMY 31:8

Raising a family didn't leave much time to worry about the future—I was stressed just trying to keep clothes clean and figure out dinner every night. But as the nest emptied and grown kids began a life of their own, my life began changing too. With more time on my hands, I thought a lot about getting older and where life would take me. Those thoughts often were filled with fear and uncertainty. I had a crucial choice to make. I could worry and be anxious or I could find a promise from God's Word to stand on. I know this sounds obvious, but when you are in the tailspin of emotions, remembering to root yourself in a promise of Scripture might not be the first response.

What am I standing on? God goes before me and will always be with me. This is so important to remember, because everything changes but God never changes. He will continue going before me until my old age and gray hair.[98] That is something I can count on. Add to that, He will never forsake me. *Forsake* means to abandon, desert, quit, or strand. Though life changes, God won't leave me stranded. Guess what? The same is true for you. Your God goes before you. Your God will not forsake you or abandon you regardless of age or status. What does it look like to stand on the promise of His commitment to you today?

Today I will remember:
- The Lord goes before me.
- The Lord is with me.
- The Lord will never abandon me or leave me stranded.

Father, forgive me for the times I have lived in fear and constant
wondering about the future. Thank You that my future is in
Your hand. You go before me. May I stand on these truths.

GOD SHOWS ME THE WAY

I will instruct you and teach you in the way you should go;
I will counsel you with my loving eye on you.

PSALM 32:8

I was never going back into ministry. I was hurt while in the fishbowl of pastoral life and was certain that God was done with that part of my story. I was wrong. Many fruitful years of serving women came as a result of finally letting go of my own understanding and deciding to trust where God was leading me. While we process through hurt, God keeps leading according to His plan. There may be a cost to a hard decision, but when we base it on trust in God's lead we can have peace—even when it doesn't make sense.

Have you been confused about direction, decisions, and which choice to make? When you are confused, the first thing to remember is that God is not the author of confusion, but of peace.[99] Overthinking can send us down the path of confusing thoughts and internal dialogue that leaves us tied up in knots. Untangling confusion starts with acknowledging the frustration of not knowing what decision to make and then standing on these promises of God. He will teach you which way to go, and He will give you wise counsel as He lovingly looks after you.

These promises strengthen the believer when all options try to entangle us in a ball of nerves and fear. Friend, let's go another direction—straight toward where God is leading, one revealed step at a time.

Today I will remember:
- God knows the way I should go.
- God will instruct me and teach me, leading me on the right path.
- His loving eye is always on me.

Lord, there is power in standing on Your Word and trusting
in Your promises. May power to live according to Your divine
nature, wisdom, and strength be mine as I follow You.

---

99 1 Corinthians 14:33.

STRENGTH TO SOAR

*Those who hope in the L*ORD *will renew their strength.*
They will soar on wings like eagles; they will run and
not grow weary; they will walk and not be faint.

ISAIAH 40:31

Restless and contemplating the fear of motherhood, I held my large belly while gazing at the stars lighting the night. I began quietly singing the chorus that went with this Isaiah verse.

I remembered learning that most birds flap their wings to fly, while eagles stretch out their wings and hold them still to soar. Wing flapping can actually cause an eagle to die. I imagined stretching my arms out to God, my life in complete surrender as I waited on Him to provide all the strength I needed to be a first-time mother. As tears fell softly, I recited the promise of this verse over and over—"God, You will renew my strength. You will give me strength to be a mom. You will keep me from falling apart and growing faint."

Peace washed over me, but it was short-lived—within hours, I was in labor. I still remember the sights and sounds of that hospital, the angst of labor, and the joy of hearing my firstborn cry. But what I remember most is being internally focused on God giving me the strength I needed to bring our baby into the world. I'm grateful for that night, a mother's love for her son, and a God who is continually teaching me not to flap my wings so much!

The promise is there—we just need to receive the truth. What do you need to wait on God for? Take Him at His Word—wait and receive strength and peace.

Today I will remember:
- Strength comes with waiting on God.
- Eagles were made to soar, and so am I.
- As I hope in God, I will be energized.

Lord, thank You for the way You teach us through
the things You created. May I hold my arms out
and wait on You to lift me to higher ground.

TRANSFORMED THINKING

Do not conform to the pattern of this world,
but be transformed by the renewing of your mind.
ROMANS 12:2

The culture is pulling us in different directions. It's confusing, unsettling, and causing division between the best of people. How do we live amidst all the competing popular opinions? There is a promise regarding our minds, and it involves shutting out other chatter and aligning to the truth in God's Word.

To live a better story, we must pay attention to our thoughts. Norman Vincent Peale once wrote, "change your thoughts and you change your world." The apostle Paul taught that our lives would be changed by our minds being renewed. Transformed lives are the result of renewing our mind in God's Word. The Message says, "Don't become so well adjusted to your culture that you fit into it without even thinking. Instead, fix your attention on God. You'll be changed from the inside out."

Fitting into the culture without even thinking hits pretty close to home. How do we renew our minds? By addressing patterns of thought that are familiar to us but are contrary to God's Word. For instance, we often want to pay back when hurt, but Scripture teaches us to pray for those who mistreat us. It's a completely different attitude when we weigh our ways against the teachings in Scripture. God's Word changes us, rearranges our thinking, renews our joy, and gives us a firm foundation to stand on.

Today I will remember:
- My thoughts are important; they will lead me closer to God or tie me to the culture.
- I am not to pattern myself according to the world.
- God promises life change when my mind is renewed.

Lord, transform me by truth; Your Word is truth. Change me
from within, by aligning my thoughts with Your thoughts. Teach
me to recognize random negative thoughts so I can give them to You.

HOLY DEPENDENCE

They cried out and were saved;
in you they trusted and were not put to shame.
PSALM 22:5

I tend to run in circles when life gets crazy. When I fall flat, I cry for help. What if I practiced crying out to God before I collapsed from exhaustion or discouragement? Perhaps if I were depending on God and not myself, I would not be so disappointed. As I trust every outcome to Him, I can learn to rest in a way that is above and beyond myself.

Crying out to God is not a sign of weakness, but rather a holy habit, a spiritual practice, and the way we find help in times of need. When we cry out to God, we are returning again to our source of strength. For years we've learned how to move the needle forward in our strength when life calls for it—trusting in ourselves is our natural default. But although God will call us to do tangible things by faith, there is a foundational side of trusting before any movement on our part. This is the foundation that we can learn to live upon—total trust and reliance on God day by day. It starts with looking up, stating the present need, and thanking Him for His presence with us.

Today I will remember:
• Crying out to God is not a sign of weakness, but strength.
• Trusting God by coming before Him with my needs is a holy habit.
• Shame is present when I am blaming myself or others rather than trusting God.

Lord, may I cry out to You as a daily practice of dependence.
In this place, help me to count on not only Your answers, but also
Your covering. Teach me to walk in a way that trusts You in all things.

THE HABIT OF WORRY

Your heavenly Father already knows all your needs.
MATTHEW 6:32, NLT

Worry is as normal and predictable as the sun rising each morning. How do you feel when you are anxious and worried? Probably not great—no one does.

Jesus invites us into something better than worrying. In His own words, He said that the pagans worry and run after all the things they need. A pagan is an unbeliever, someone with little or no faith in God. Jesus compared the believer with the nonbeliever to emphasize a very powerful truth: "So do not worry, saying, 'What shall we eat?' or 'What shall we drink?' or 'What shall we wear?' For the pagans run after all these things, and your heavenly Father knows that you need them."[100]

You and I are invited into a relationship with a heavenly Father who not only knows our needs, but invites us to a place of calm in a world that is anxious. It's not a shame-filled, "Hey, sister, quit your worrying!" Rather, it's a loving God saying, "I understand that you worry, but I am telling you that you don't have to—I've got you covered." Memorizing this one verse and learning to stand on the promise of provision can change how we approach everything.

Today I will remember:
• I have a heavenly Father who loves me and will provide for me.
• He goes before me and knows what I need.
• I can exhale all worry and trust Him to take care of me.

Lord, help me to believe the truth that You know my needs.
Help me to trust that You are a loving Father.

THE HOLY WORK OF REST

*Then God blessed the seventh day and made it holy, because
on it he rested from all the work of creating that he had done.*
GENESIS 2:3

A season of injury laid me out, canceled scheduled ministry, and left me frustrated. I could have looked at it differently, perhaps viewing it as a planned time of much-needed rest. Instead, I wrestled with not being able to go and do. I was in pain while everyone else was moving on. God wanted me to take a soul rest. Falling asleep on a comfy couch is easy, but I am not good at soul rest. Soul rest is ceasing from all striving and surrendering once again to God.

God made the day of rest holy. It makes sense that He can have holy involvement in our lives when we slow our spinning wheels. I began to wait in anticipation, discovering what God was doing in the deepest parts of me. I wrestled with things like identity and lost ministry opportunity. For some of us, our work becomes our identity. For others our identity is wrapped up in what we do for our family. We feel lost if we stop for too long. God allowed me a season to solidify that who I am is not what I do. Who I am is a beloved woman of God—complete in Him regardless of my work.

What about you? Could you rest knowing you are complete in Him?

Today I will remember:
• God initiated rest into the rhythm of life.
• Rest is His plan.
• Rest can be a holy work when we surrender to God.

*Lord, thank You for speaking to me in my seasons of rest. I am convinced
that regular rest stops are what You have planned for us. May I always
live ready to rest from all my own striving, complete in You.*

HE GUARDS MY LIFE

I know whom I have believed, and am convinced that he is able to guard what I have entrusted to him until that day.

2 TIMOTHY 1:12

When things are hard or unfair, it is easier to fall apart than to believe. We all know how to fall apart, but most are not skilled in how to keep our conviction and faith in God strong when the heat is turned up. The apostle Paul, imprisoned, writes to encourage Timothy, whom he loved as a son in the faith. It's astounding that Paul learned, through repeated practice with hard things, to stand firmly on what he knew to be true about Christ. It would have been easy for him to lose his convictions after all he went through, but he remained convinced that God would be faithful to him.

It's one thing to know the promises and the Scriptures, but a different thing to be completely convinced of them. The bottom line is this—God is able. He is able to guard what you have committed to Him, able to keep you standing, able to come through at the right time. God is able. Whether it be family, finances, work, or relationships—God is able. Who do you believe in? God is able to keep you through life—in the good, the bad, and the in-between.

Today I will remember:
- God is able to take care of me and the details of my life.
- God guards me and all that I have entrusted to Him.
- Anyone can fall apart; it takes one convinced of God's faithfulness to "live up."

Lord, I want to be radically convinced that You guard what is mine and what I have turned over to You. I want to live in that conviction even when times are not easy. May I be a testament of one who stands strong in the One whom she has believed in.

WHATEVER HAPPENS

*Whatever happens, conduct yourselves in
a manner worthy of the gospel of Christ.*
PHILIPPIANS 1:27

How do you handle disappointment? You make plans, then the kids get sick. You look forward to something and it gets cancelled. You are on vacation and the weather is bad. It's one thing after another, isn't it? It's easy to apply this verse when things are going well, but much harder when we are discouraged or disappointed.

How do you act when disappointing things happen? Paul is telling us to conduct ourselves or to behave in a certain way—to behave as a citizen of heaven, worthy of the gospel of Christ. How does this play out in real life? It's a *whatever happens* attitude.

Whatever happens, I will trust God. Whatever happens, I will look up and pray for peace. Whatever happens, I will behave as if I am loved and I am held. *Whatever happens* is a stance of victory! It's a good way to live and a challenge to us all. Paul wraps up his thought on this with "For it has been granted to you on behalf of Christ not only to believe on him, but also to suffer for him."[101] So if your *whatever* today is a place of suffering, remember this—God uses both the believing and the suffering. Both are beautiful in His sight. We don't have to understand, we just have to lean in and trust.

Today I will remember:
- Whatever—anything and everything that happens—look up!
- Happens—whatever takes place and is out of your control, trust God!
- Conduct—live as if you are a citizen of a different country, a citizen of heaven.

*Lord, remind me of the word whatever when I am tired,
disappointed, hurting, or discouraged. May I live
to honor You as a citizen of a greater Kingdom.*

TO LIVE IS CHRIST

For to me, to live is Christ and to die is gain.

PHILIPPIANS 1:21

Many people love gospel songs about flying away to glory, and yet when a terminal diagnosis is confirmed, we probably won't be singing or clapping. We take life for granted, as if we will live forever, but life here on earth is limited. The truth is, all of us live limited lives. Yet in Scripture death is a positive, a gain and precious in God's sight.[102] This is hard for us to wrap our minds around. Paul struggled between life and death because he knew death would mean being with the Lord, while life gave him more time for fruitful service to God.

What does it mean that to live is Christ? Is it church attendance or serving the poor? It can be both, but is not limited to a descriptive of works. Living for Christ is a surrendering of our soul, our abilities, our resources—everything that makes up our life. In the end, it is all His anyway, so why be afraid to give it all now? To live for Christ reminds us of the reality that this world is not our final stop. My story here is important, and so is yours. But when our body dies, our soul lives on. We are human souls living in earthly tents—bodies of flesh. One day those will be gone, but we will live forever.

Today I will remember:
- I get one life, and I get to choose how to live.
- A life surrendered to Christ is useful.
- To die is a gain, not a loss, because His work is complete in me.

Lord, I am asking You to take the sting and fear of death from me.
I want to live free of fear so I can live fully for You while I am alive.

---

102 Psalm 116:15.

THE PROMISE OF ABUNDANT LIFE

The thief comes only to steal and kill and destroy;
I have come that they may have life, and have it to the full.
JOHN 10:10

There are two characters in our story: Jesus who offers abundant life and the thief who tries to destroy our life. Satan works by lying to us—he is the father of lies.[103] He is the accuser of the brethren.[104] And he waits to devour us.[105] Satan is not a fictional character with a red suit and a pitchfork. He is real, and if we are not alert, we will fall for his tactics every time and never experience abundant life.

Abundant life is not having everything we want, nor is it riches and comfort. Abundant life is a life with an edge or advantage. Faith gives us an edge over all the hard things we will experience. Things are still hard, but when we walk through with Jesus we have the edge on the situation.

In the KJV this verse reads, "I am come that they might have life, and that they might have it more abundantly. In NLT it reads, " My purpose is to give them a rich and satisfying life." God clearly has a plan, and it's for our good—freedom, abundance, and purpose. The thief also has a plan, and it's clearly not for our good—it is to steal, kill, and destroy.

Today I will remember:
- There is a Good Shepherd in my story.
- There is a thief in the storyline as well.
- I choose daily where I will stand—whose voice I will follow.

Lord, thank You for laying it out for us—the good and evil.
Thank You for triumphing over the enemy and for giving me the
victory when I trust in You. Because of You, I can live a better story.

---

103   John 8:44.
104   Revelation 12:10.
105   1 Peter 5:8.

A PROMISE FOR THE WEARY

Come to me, all you who are weary and burdened, and I will give you rest.
MATTHEW 11:28

I was frustrated with a silly hamster named Jif. All night long he ran the squeaky wheel, and in frustration, I cried out to God—*Lord, I hate Jif!* His response was different than I expected. He said, *you are just like Jif. You run, but your wheel is different—you run to be good, to be loved, to be noticed. You have been running so long that you are tired. Come to Me now.*

I knew the verse, but that night under my blankets I realized that I didn't take His invitation seriously. He was inviting me to come to Him—to move in a different direction and pivot my life toward Him. It was a kind invitation, but also one filled with promise and peace. There is peace in resting in Jesus. I just kept myself busy and running for so long that I never honestly knew the beauty of accepting the invitation.

Friends, we need to come to the Lord daily. He is calling us to draw near. Can you hear Him inviting you? Encouraging you to lay all your stuff down and pivot toward Him? Since that night many years ago, I can hear Him calling me on a regular basis—and in coming, I have found the unforced rhythm of a life of faith.

Today I will remember:
- Coming to Jesus is an action step—a change in direction.
- I can admit I am tired, weary, and burdened.
- When I admit my need and turn toward Him, I find the rest I long for.

Lord, forgive me for trying to carry the weight of life on my own. I come to You ready to get off my squeaky wheel of performance and perfection. I want all of You—all the time. Free me from the race I often put myself in.

A NEW WAY TO LIVE

And he died for all, that those who live should
no longer live for themselves but for him.

2 CORINTHIANS 5:15

My Christian experience has had many twists and turns. I learned how to say and do the right things. I had head information, but very little life transformation. My life crashed and burned, and I found myself searching for meaning as a Christian. I needed more than simply being part of a Christian club and began to hope for something more. I made a decision to start over and get more serious about my faith journey. I filtered everything through the simplicity of God's love for me, and my response to that love was to be surrendered to Jesus completely. This is where I found meaning in the middle of a broken life. The brokenness was no longer the focus, the love of my beautiful Savior was.

The verse that comes before the one quoted above is, "For Christ's love compels us, because we are convinced that one died for all and therefore all died. And he died for all, that those who live should no longer live for themselves."[106] *Compel* here means to influence. When Christ's love influences us, things change. We become set on turning our life over fully to the one who gave us life.

Friend, we were meant to live for more than ourselves.

Today I will remember:
- Christ's love for me was meant to be a strong influence that changes my direction.
- Christ died, opening up the possibility of me living a new and different life.
- I was created for more than just myself—I was created by God and for God.

Lord, thank You for new starts and second chances. Had I never known the reality
of Your love, I would still be living for me while saying it was all for You. But Your
love informed my heart of a new way to live, surrendered and present with You.

THE PROMISE OF BEING HIS OWN

*Do not bring sorrow to God's Holy Spirit by the way
you live. Remember, he has identified you as his own.*
EPHESIANS 4:30, NLT

As the kids became busy with their own lives, I bought a fluffy white dog that we named Bubba. Every day he would wait for me to get home from work, perched up on the couch looking out our front window. We were both excited to see each other. But instead of running into my arms once I opened the door, he would hide under the couch. Sometimes I'd find wrappers or other messes, but I didn't care—I just wanted him. Silly dog, all I wanted to do is love him, and he would run for cover in my presence.

Sometimes we are like Bubba. We don't hide under couches, but we hide behind facades and excuses. We are excited to be in God's presence, but if He gets too close, we run for cover. God calls us out and longs to have relationship with us as His own. You see, in God's eyes we are simply His, and that settles everything. The promise of being His is also our call to live up to something greater than ourselves. When we bring God sorrow through our actions and attitudes, He pulls us up and out from under our hiding place and says, "You are mine."

Are you ready to come into agreement with your God-given plan and identity? When we define ourselves as His, that identity will drive us and change everything.

Today I will remember:
- I can bring sorrow to God by the way live.
- I am His, and I am invited into a new life as His own.
- He promises a new identity when I come and commit my life to Him.

*Lord, I don't want to run and hide from Your love or Your presence.
May I remember that I am Yours and live accordingly.*

SUBMIT AND RESIST

Submit yourselves, then, to God.
Resist the devil, and he will flee from you.

JAMES 4:7

Scripture tells us that there is an enemy who must be resisted. I didn't grow up being taught to resist the devil, and maybe you didn't either. The apostle Paul taught the early church to put on the full armor of God so they would be able to stand against the devil's schemes.[107] Jesus included this same idea when He taught us how to pray: "Lead us not into temptation, but deliver us from the evil one."[108] As we submit to God and resist the devil, he has to leave! The promise is that there is victory over temptation and darkness.

Let's talk about *submit* and *resist*. *Submit* in the original language means under the obedience of or subject to. We are to put God above us and place ourselves under His authority. Once that's in place, we are to *resist* the devil, which means to stand against or oppose him. Let's think this through. The devil is a liar, accuser, and thief. He also is on the prowl looking for ways to devour us. He doesn't have to look farther than our storyline to find a way to bait us. We need to be aware. When standing on God's promises, we trust God and who He is. And when we resist the enemy, we are aware of who he is and spot his tactics. Then we resist him while standing on God's promise of victory over evil.

Today I will remember:
- Satan is a liar, accuser, and thief.[109]
- I am to submit my life to God each day.
- I am to stand against the lies and temptations of the enemy.

Lord, I didn't learn these things growing up. Spiritual realities were not my daily realities. Help me to stand strong against the enemy as I daily yield my life to You.

---

107 Ephesians 6:11.
108 Matthew 6:13.
109 John 8:44; Revelation 12:10; John 10:10.

THE PROMISE OF HIS NEARNESS

Come near to God and he will come near to you.
JAMES 4:8

Our family once lived near each other, but over time that changed. Now, when I see my grandkids, I open my arms, and they come running into my hug. They giggle, and my heart gets a size bigger. There is nothing that could stop this Grammy and GiGi from loving them. Hugging them, I can't help but think how the Father holds me when I come into His open arms. The love I feel for my grandkids doesn't compare to the love of the Father for us, but it gives me a taste of it.

To come near involves taking an active step toward something other than ourselves. Sometimes we hesitate to come near to God. Maybe we feel guilt over decisions or attitudes. Or perhaps we are mad at someone and not ready to yield to God. So we play keep away and stubbornly go off doing our own thing—living our own way. Note: this is not living upon but living under the circumstances! It's in those times that we need to be reminded of this promise—when we come near, He brings us in ever closer to Himself. It was Jesus who said, "Come to me, all you who are weary and burdened, and I will give you rest. Take my yoke upon you and learn from me, for I am gentle and humble in heart, and you will find rest for your souls."[110]

Today I will remember:
- God invites me to come close to Him.
- He promises to be near as I draw nearer to Him.
- Jesus promises soul rest when we come to Him.

Lord, forgive me for the many times I am purposefully distant, doing my own thing. I don't want to live under my emotions but upon Your promises. Thank You for promising to be near when I come near to You.

---

110 Matthew 11:28-29.

GOD KEEPS HIS PROMISES

Though I have fallen, I will rise.
Though I sit in darkness, the LORD will be my light.
MICAH 7:8

This promise is an affirmation of faith in the mercy of God despite all appearances to the contrary. No matter how ugly things are, God will not abandon His people. They are His, and in His own way, in His own time, He will be the light of rescue. Sometimes the assurance that God will not abandon us is the only thing we can hold on to and count on.

God always sought out people who had nothing of their own to offer. We are those people. We look down on ourselves, while God wants to lift us up. We reject ourselves, while God accepts us in our imperfections.

God began His search-and-rescue mission in Eden, and it climaxed on Good Friday and Easter, when God's Son demonstrated how far He was willing to go to forgive us and raise us up again. Jesus, the light of the world, has called us out of darkness into His light, where there is the promise of forgiveness, new life, and salvation. Let's *live up*—Upon the Promises—by remembering that God picks us up when we fall and brings us into His light.

Today I will remember:
- I will fall down sometimes, but I will rise again.
- There will be times of darkness, but God is my light.
- God promises forgiveness, new life, and salvation—and He's a promise keeper.

Lord, forgive me for the time I've wasted in self-rejection.
Thank You for the promise of being the One who always leads
me to a better place as I trust You and follow the light.

PEACE OF HEART AND MIND

The peace of God, which transcends all understanding,
will guard your hearts and your minds in Christ Jesus.
PHILIPPIANS 4:7

I have a plaque in my room that says, "Peace does not mean to be in a place where there is no noise, trouble, or hard work." Peace means to be calm in your heart in the midst of those things. Imagine being in the middle of chaos, but God promises to give you a peace that surpasses everything. It's more than you and I can understand. Peace here is the word *eirene*, which means quietness, rest, set at one again.

To keep this in context, we must look at what came before the peace promise. Paul said, "Do not be anxious about anything, but in every situation, by prayer and petition, with thanksgiving, present your requests to God."[111] There is a path to peace, and it is to refuse worry and instead pray, give God the details, and thank Him in advance for His answers. When we do that, Paul said, a peace that comes only from God will guard our hearts and minds. This is telling us that peace will guard the deepest inner core of us—mind, will, and emotions. I don't know about you, but I often need that kind of guardrail! I also need reminders to refuse doubt, fear, and worry—and instead pray. The promise of peace guarding our hearts and minds is for all of us.

Today I will remember:
• The peace of God transcends circumstances.
• Peace will be a by-product of praying over our concerns.
• When we give God our problems, peace is a guard to our heart and mind.

Lord, this verse, though familiar, is something I often forget to
put into practice. Remind me to make this my go-to spiritual
habit whenever I am troubled, worried, or stressed.

---

111 Philippians 4:6.

THE PROMISE OF GOOD

You are good, and what you do is good.
PSALM 119:68

I resisted believing that God was good. After all, in my twenty-five-year-old reasoning, sixty-eight was too young for my Dad to die. We prayed, cried, and begged God to heal my dad of cancer. Ten weeks later he met Jesus ahead of us. How could this be good? Some wiser, older friends began telling me that maybe my view of good was not God's view. Perhaps I had some things to learn about God and about what true goodness is.

"Precious in the sight of the LORD is the death of his saints."[112] I never knew that verse was in the Bible. Precious? Death? For my dad, healing was heaven. I realized that a new perspective was in order—not so much about death but about the reality and mystery of God's goodness. Scripture clearly says, "'My thoughts aren't your thoughts, neither are your ways my ways,' declares the LORD. 'As the heavens are higher than the earth, so are my ways higher than your ways and my thoughts than your thoughts.'"[113]

God is good—it's the nature of who He is. He can't act in any way contrary to who He is. The promise of God's goodness can bring a settled comfort as we rest in the truth that no matter how bad things look, God remains good.

Today I will remember:
- God's ways are higher than my ways.
- God is good.
- God always works out of His goodness toward me.

Lord, thank You for leading me on a path of knowing You are good,
even in the hard spots. May You always turn the hard
into a holy teaching for my soul as I put my trust in You.

---

112   Psalm 116:15.
113   Isaiah 55:8-9.

THE PROMISE OF GOD
WORKING IN ALL THINGS

In all things God works for the good of those who love him.
ROMANS 8:28

Going through an unwanted divorce, I'd pack the kids up and drive to my sister's house five hours north. One trip, I placed my youngest in a shopping cart and intense pain shot through me as the room started spinning. I passed out and was taken by ambulance to the hospital. The pain of divorce was bad enough, but now I also had herniated discs? I cried hot tears of frustration and anger. Little did I know, God was preparing me.

My mentor had been teaching me Romans 8:28. I didn't know how to believe that bad could work together for good. Those three numbers kept going through my mind—828.828.828. *But Lord, what about my back?* He spoke to my heart, "Especially about your back, trust me."

Months later, we sat next to a single dad and his daughters at a parade. When an ambulance went by, my son exclaimed, "the last time we were here my mommy broke her back and went in an ambulance!" There are so many details about what happened next, but had I not hurt my back months earlier, there would be no story. The dad happened to be a detective. He found me, and the rest is history. God put the pieces of my life together using a bad circumstance that ultimately worked for good and led to God providing the most wonderful husband whom I've been married to for 33 years. The darkest piece of the puzzle—the injury—was the necessary piece.

Maybe your life has some dark pieces right now. Trust the promise and hang on to hope. God is working in ALL things.

Today I will remember:
• God is at work in my life.
• God is working in the bad as well as the good.
• He is at work because I am called for His purposes.

Lord, thank You for 828 and all that
this promise can mean when we trust in You.

THE PROMISE OF BEING UPHELD

The Lord makes firm the steps of the one
who delights in him; though he may stumble,
he will not fall, for the Lord upholds him with his hand.

PSALM 37:23-24

My husband has been gone working security at a Christian music festival. We do almost everything together, so being alone feels strange. But in the quiet, I kept feeling that I wasn't alone. I don't know how to explain it, but I felt someone was right beside me. Looking down I realized that our dog, Teddy, had never left my side. If I moved, he moved. When I got up for water, he would tag behind me. Then it hit me—I can see Teddy by my side, following me around. But though I can't see God, the very real presence of God is with me too—at my side, getting up with me when I get up and keeping me company. Teddy was my reminder of something much bigger; the Lord is upholding me even in the regular moments of life. I can't see Him, but He is present.

There are a few promises wrapped in today's verse. God promises to be with us, to catch us, and to hold us. That's amazing. But let's go back to, "the LORD makes firm the steps... " *Firm* means secure, steady, not weak or uncertain. This is what the Lord does. Our steps are secure because of Jesus. We might feel weak and at times unstable, but He keeps us steady. Hold on to this promise, living in this truth the next time life feels uncertain, unsteady, or you feel alone.

Today I will remember:
• The Lord makes my steps firm.
• The Lord catches me when I stumble.
• The Lord holds me up with His hand.

Lord, truly You are with us. May I never forget that
these truths represent Your presence and faithfulness.

HE FIGHTS FOR ME

The Lord will fight for you; you need only to be still.
EXODUS 14:14

Most people I know don't find it easy to be still when they are in a battle. Whether it be relational, financial, physical, or spiritual, we just want to do whatever it takes to get it over with. Can I get an amen? But some battles have no quick fixes or easy answers. They are long and tedious and test every bit of our patience. And yet, the promise in Scripture says that the Lord will fight for us. We need to take our seat at the still table and let Him work.

To *fight for* us is a powerful word here. It means to contend in battle for us, to engage in fighting whatever is opposing us, to work to prevent the success of our opponent. Now apply that to your current battle. The promise is, the Lord will do the fighting for you. He will engage in the battle against the opposition—and the opposition is probably not what you think. "For we do not wrestle against flesh and blood, but against principalities, against powers, against the rulers of the darkness of this age, against spiritual hosts of wickedness in the heavenly places."[114]

The situation is not the enemy. The other person is not the enemy. You and I have an enemy, but it's not the physical things we see around us. It's time to learn to wait on God by being still—trusting the promise that He fights for us.

Today I will remember:
• My battles are not the things I see.
• I have an enemy, and he uses the practical things to take me down.
• The real battle is won by the Lord.

Lord, forgive me for focusing on the things I can see when the real battle is with things unseen. Teach me to be still and trust You to fight for me.

114 Ephesians 6:12, NKJV.

THE PROMISE OF HEALING

By his wounds you have been healed.

1 PETER 2:24

Years ago, I landed in the ER, then the ICU, on more than one occasion. After apparent "heart episodes" and many diagnostic tests that showed some blockages, I was off to the cath lab for an angiogram. I went in fully aware that the best-case scenario would be stents, worst case scenario would be heart bypass. What I didn't expect was to wake up being told I had no blockages and had the arteries of a much younger woman. Ecstatic, I was sent home with a clean bill of heart health.

I realized I had asked God to help me get through whatever I had to go through, but I had not asked God to heal me. Thankfully, others were boldly praying for a complete healing and God answered their prayers. Sometimes we don't ask Jesus to heal us because we've been let down before. But healing is more than the physical that we so often focus on. The most important healing is spiritual: "By his wounds you have been healed. For you were like sheep going astray, but now *you have returned to the Shepherd and Overseer of your souls.*" [115]

Yet throughout Scripture we do see Jesus restoring health. We read of the miraculous drying of blood, people rising from the dead, and leprous skin returning to normal. I personally have known people healed from cancer and those whose healing meant being ushered into God's presence. In the end, all were healed. God has all power and authority to heal, and He promises us that the greatest healing needed has been already done, while encouraging us to ask for His hand to touch us here and now.

Today I will remember:
- Jesus is my healer.
- Not all healing is physical.
- All healing miraculous.

Lord, thank You for providing both physical and
spiritual healing. Forgive me when I doubt that
You can do the very miracles that Your Word proclaims.

---

115   1 Peter 2:24-25, italics added.

GOD'S PROMISE TO BE WITH US

When you pass through the waters, I will be with you; and when you pass through the rivers, they will not sweep over you. When you walk through the fire, you will not be burned; the flames will not set you ablaze.

ISAIAH 43:2

Of all the promises in Scripture, this sums up how we can "Live-Up"—how we can live upon the promise that God will always be with us, no matter where we go or what we go through. This was written in a time when God's people were facing danger and God promised to be with them. The natural consequences of the water, rivers, and fire would not touch them because God would cover them. This is encouraging.

What are your waters, rivers, and fires? Perhaps you are sinking in the waters of financial hardship—God will be with you. Or maybe you are being overrun by the rivers of relational difficulties—they will not sweep over you and take you down. Maybe your fire is personal illness, and God is letting you know that He will be with you in the fire, and in the end it will not burn you. The promise to be with us is life changing. We forget. God reminds. When we live in the truth of it, we are different people in the middle of our real-life struggles. This Isaiah passage begins, "Do not fear, for I have redeemed you; I have summoned you by name; you are mine."[116] And that is the best promise of all—we are His, He calls us by name and has redeemed us. That is why the circumstances will not overtake us.

Today I will remember:
- God is with me in every season.
- God is with me in every situation.
- God promises to deliver me in and through all circumstances.

Lord, thank You for being with me. Let me always be aware of Your presence and find hope in Your power to deliver.

---

116 Isaiah 43:1.

THE PROMISE TO PROVIDE

*And my God will meet all your needs according
to the riches of his glory in Christ Jesus.*
PHILIPPIANS 4:19

A young couple I know were called to plant a church in a new area that necessitated a move across their state. Some friends felt called to move with them and found jobs, rental homes, and a moving truck. Meanwhile, the young pastor couldn't find a rental without a job. Rolling into town, by faith, with no place to live, the first stop was a real estate management company. Within an hour the pastor was offered a position to manage a brand-new property. This included a monthly stipend and free rent on a large three-bedroom unit. God provided more than they hoped for. It was a testimony of God going before them and providing for every need. Within days they secured a meeting spot and the Lord added to the church daily, until eventually it became well established in that city.

I think of this story when I am tempted to stress over material needs. I am reminded that God knows my needs and has promised to provide for them. What are your needs today? Jesus also said, "your heavenly Father already knows all your needs."[117] He told them that unbelievers worry and fret, but with a heavenly Father the worry can be put aside. God won't always call you to walk out in blind faith, but if and when He does, remember that He goes before you and promised to provide for you.

Today I will remember:
• My heavenly Father knows my every need.
• God promised to meet my needs.
• He meets my needs through the abundance of His riches.

*Lord, may I trust You, even when I don't see how the
situation can possibly work out. You have called
me Yours, and You have declared me provided for.*

FAVOR FOR THE HUMBLE

All of you, clothe yourselves with humility toward one another,
because, "God opposes the proud but shows favor to the humble."
1 PETER 5:5

God opposes the pride of putting ourselves before other people. When I live like that, I am placing myself in opposition to God and His best plan for me. Humility, on the other hand, involves shadowing the life and nature of Christ. The promise here is that living with a heart bent toward God also includes receiving favor from Him.

We need a humble heart if we are going to live in love toward others. We are told to clothe ourselves with humility, and that doesn't mean lying down on the ground while everyone walks over us. Biblical humility is a life submitted to God. Humility is saying to our Father, "You are God, and I am not!" Walking in humility toward others is simply putting them first. Not so simple, right? Part of the walk of "living up" is allowing God to shape us according to the new spiritual nature we have inherited in Christ—and that nature is humble and loving.

Christ gave us an example of humility by dying for people who didn't care, who were in their sins, and who were undeserving. This is the attitude that we are to carry through life. Rather than feeling entitled to receive, we are now free to give. Peter says, "Cast all your anxiety on him because he cares for you."[118] A woman who has properly placed her cares in God's hands has more space to humbly love other people.

Today I will remember:
- I am to clothe myself in humility each day.
- Humility is placing my life before God and thinking of others.
- Humility involves giving God every care so I am freed to love others.

Lord, I desire to walk in Your ways. Show me
how to walk humbly before You and others.

---

118   1 Peter 5:7.

SOWING AND REAPING

God cannot be mocked. A man reaps what he sows...let us not become weary in doing good, for at the proper time we will reap a harvest if we do not give up. Therefore, as we have opportunity, let us do good to all people.
GALATIANS 6:7, 9

Pauline lived on mission. Every day she thought of ways to bless people and lived out her faith by finding practical solutions that helped friends and neighbors in need. I was lucky enough to be her neighbor. During a tough time in my life, Pauline found ways to help me with my kids. She offered to take them for a few hours each day, pouring into them and making them feel loved.

Saturday mornings found her at garage sales buying boy toys—cars, trucks, and action figures. Before long, she had turned her garage into a play haven for two little boys. She bought an old dresser and filled each drawer with a different type of activity—art supplies, play-dough, and matchbox cars. That old dresser offered the boys things to do, giving them a space to belong. We will never forget her.

God calls us to this type of kindness, generosity, and unselfish love. It is the principle of sowing seeds and then reaping what we sow. God sees every seed sown. We will receive from God if we do not grow weary in doing good. As much as Pauline blessed our lives, God used this time to also bless hers. Part of "living up" upon the promises is living out the teaching of Scripture and then reaping the rewards.

Today I will remember:
- I will reap what I sow—that is God's principle.
- I might get weary in doing good, but God sees me.
- I am to look for ways to do good to others.

Lord, may I be on the lookout for how I can sow kindness and love into the lives of those around me.

CONTENTMENT AND STRENGTH

I have learned the secret of being content in any and every situation...whether living in plenty or in want. I can do all this through him who gives me strength.

PHILIPPIANS 4:12-13

There was a single woman who lived in a quiet house. Friends encouraged her to get a singing parakeet, and the pet store owner had just the bird for her. The next day she came home from work to a house filled with music. While feeding the bird, she noticed for the first time that the parakeet only had one leg. Feeling ripped off, she called the store to complain about being sold a one-legged bird. The owner said, "what do you want? A bird who can sing or a bird who can dance?" This is a good story for all of us who are disappointed with things in our life. It's all in how we view things.

Every woman lives in a tent—content or discontent!

As it turns out, we find the secret of contentment just a few verses earlier—finding the good and dwelling there.[119] This gives us strength to get through any circumstance. When we are content, we are free to live in Christ's strength. When we are discontent, we are constantly critical, tainting everything with negativity. Each of us can turn this around by making a daily choice to dwell in gratitude for our circumstances and relationships. This choice, as promised in Scripture, not only gives a peace that passes understanding, but it imparts a strength to do all things. This is solid gold!

Today I will remember:
• I can choose to look for good and dwell on that.
• I can do all things through Christ.
• I can live content and in peace.

Lord, forgive me for looking everywhere for answers
when the solutions to life are written in Your Word.
Thank You for giving me a guide to contentment and strength.

---

119 Philippians 4:7-8.

GOD PLACES HIS DESIRES IN US

Take delight in the Lord, and he will give you the desires of your heart.
PSALM 37:4

This was my first memory verse. I thought it promised that God would grant me all I wanted. That sounds so immature now, but it's the honest truth. Now I know that we don't always get what we want. But when we are delighting in the Lord, committing our lives to following Him, we open ourselves up to receiving His dreams, desires, and plans for us. Or as Paul said, "It is God who works in you to will and to act in order to fulfill his good purpose."[120]

The word *delight* in the original means to be soft or pliable. When we are pliable to be shaped by God, our desires change over time. I was sure my life path was to be a singer, taking private lessons and performing onstage when most girls were busy with dolls. It was my life. But after coming to Christ, leading worship, and later singing in a Christian band, my desires started to change. This was strange, because music had been my everything. God was shifting my desires. I could have never imagined being a writer, but I began to want to write spiritual growth resources for women. That grew into writing Bible studies for women in my community. God had changed my desire. The desires of our hearts are fulfilled because He puts His desires within us. Our part is to delight ourselves in Him—remaining pliable to His will.

Today I will remember:
- When I remain open to Jesus, the Holy Spirit works in me.
- The Holy Spirit changes my desires to align with God's plan.
- God fulfills the desires in my heart because He placed them in me.

> *Lord, I want to follow You and align my heart with Your desires for my life. May my heart remain open to receive Your desires for my life.*

GOD'S PROMISE IN OUR TEMPTATIONS

God is faithful...when you are tempted, he will also
provide a way out so that you can endure it.
1 CORINTHIANS 10:13

Flies were everywhere. Having flies buzzing around your face is disgusting, especially when you are trying to cook. I lost my appetite and gave up. I realized that I had felt like giving up all day. Tempting negative thoughts buzzed like flies around my mind, discouraging me. I had focused on a problem, and as the day wore on, the temptation to be defeated overtook me.

The way out of temptation has everything to do with stopping negative thoughts. Sometimes we are drawn to give in to a spiral of negative thinking while entertaining thoughts that are opposite of God's Word. This tempts us to blow up a simple problem. The best way to stop the temptation to doubt or make things bigger is to interrupt the negative thought and replace it with a positive truth. This helps us endure because temptation starts with our own desires. James says, "And remember, when you are being tempted, do not say, 'God is tempting me.' God is never tempted to do wrong, and he never tempts anyone else. Temptation comes from our own desires, which entice us and drag us away."[121]

Our desires bait us to turn away from God in favor doing what we want. But God provides a way out—and that way out starts with not taking the bait, and instead stopping the negative temptation before it causes us to sin.

Today I will remember:
- God is faithful.
- God will provide a way out when I am tempted.
- I am tempted when I am enticed by my own desires.

Lord, thank You for Your faithfulness to provide a way out
when I am being tempted. May I learn to refocus on Your
heart and desires when I am tempted to do the wrong thing.

September

LIVING THE RED LETTERS

When the red letters—the words and teaching of Jesus—
become our greatest direction, we change.

HANDLING SATAN'S TEMPTATIONS

Then Jesus was led by the Spirit into the wilderness to be tempted by the devil.
MATTHEW 4:1

Jesus was led by the Spirit to be tempted—does that blow your mind? If I were God, I would have wrapped Jesus in a blankie and given Him something to eat. Knowing He was hungry after a 40-day fast, Satan tempted Jesus with food. Note, the enemy doesn't have to look far to see where to poke us—obviously Jesus was hungry after a fast. "If you are the Son of God, tell these stones to become bread."[122]

My response might be, *bring on the bread!!* But Jesus answered, "It is written: Man shall not live on bread alone"."[123]

Satan went on to the next temptation—identity: "If you are the Son of God..."[124] And the last temptation was power: "All this I will give you...if you will bow down and worship me."[125]

Finally, Jesus stopped it. "Away from me, Satan! Then the devil left him, and angels came and attended him."[126] What can we learn? We, too, will be tempted by the enemy. Jesus talked back to Satan, resisting him with the Word of God. When we know our vulnerable areas, we can have Scripture ready to stand on when the attack comes. When the temptation is over, our loving God will attend to us just as He attended to Jesus.

Today I will remember:
- The Spirit of God leads us.
- Sometimes we are led into the desert.
- We must resist the enemy with the Word of God.

Lord, I am in awe of Your example and how You have prepared us for real life. Equip me to stand against the tempter and his lies.

---

122 Matthew 4:3.
123 Matthew 4:4.
124 Matthew 4:6.
125 Matthew 4:9.
126 Matthew 4:10-11.

AT THE END OF YOUR ROPE

Blessed are the poor in spirit, for theirs is the kingdom of heaven.
MATTHEW 5:3

Huge crowds were following Jesus. Unlike celebrities of our day, he walked the dusty roads as a human. He sometimes went without physical comforts, and His soul relied completely on God. Here we see that Jesus valued those in need or poor in spirit—which literally meant distressed and begging. Jesus called this dependence *blessed*. We would never equate blessed to begging for anything. And yet Jesus taught an upside-down gospel, different than anything other religious leaders taught. In large part, Jesus was challenging the religious leaders of that day and bringing people back to the basic message of heartfelt obedience over strict religious observances.

Jesus climbed a hillside and began to preach to the crowds. His words seemed to contradict each other—poor in spirit is the riches of heaven? To follow Jesus, we must be willing to give when others are taking, to love when others hate, and to help when others only care about themselves. By giving up our own rights and serving others, eventually we will receive everything God has for us. So here is where we start—"God blesses those who are poor and realize their need for him."[127] Another version puts it this way: "You're blessed when you're at the end of your rope. With less of you there is more of God and his rule."[128] The beatitudes are not multiple choice—they are a message of what it means to be Christ's followers.

Today I will remember:
• I am blessed when I am at the end of my resources.
• I am blessed when I am in need of God.
• I am blessed with God's Kingdom rule in my life.

Lord, I come to you once again, arms open to receive all You have for me.
Without You I am nothing. With You I am an heir to the Kingdom of heaven.

---

127 Matthew 5:3, NLT.
128 Matthew 5:3, MSG.

SEPTEMBER 3

THE GOD WHO HOLDS OUR PAIN

Blessed are those who mourn, for they will be comforted.
MATTHEW 5:4

There a few things you don't forget. My father's funeral is one of those things. After the service, I sat in the chapel motionless. My uncle was next to me, and we both stared at the casket until they came to close it. Like an out-of-body experience, I threw myself across the metal box weeping. I was ushered out to the graveside, where two godly church ladies came alongside of me. One whispered, "today you cry, but tomorrow you rejoice because people are watching you." Her well-meaning words almost made me throw up. I didn't know when I would ever stop crying. My daddy was one of my favorite people, and now he was gone. And I needed to be an example? No thanks. I was pretty sure Jesus cared more about my broken heart than my example.

Each beatitude illustrates how to be blessed—how to find more happiness. They are simple and humble, like Jesus. They speak to the human heart and human experience. While the Pharisees had superficial faith, Jesus taught that the deepest form of happiness came to those who experienced the pain of mourning but found comfort in Him. Paul taught about grieving, "You do not grieve like the rest of mankind, who have no hope."[129] Similarly, the psalmist wrote, "He heals the brokenhearted and binds up their wounds."[130] Jesus said those who mourned would be comforted because mourning is a necessary part of loss. It is a weeping that God cares about—because He is committed to loving you through every hard thing in this life.

Today I will remember:
• Mourning loss is part of life.
• I am blessed when I mourn if I feel my grief and give it to God.
• God comforts me when my loss is heavy and my heart is broken.

*Lord, thank You for being a God of comfort
and care. Let me never hide my heart from You.*

---

129 1 Thessalonians 4:13.
130 Psalm 147:3.

THE GIFT OF MERCY

Blessed are the merciful, for they will be shown mercy.
MATTHEW 5:7

"Good Morning, Mrs. Kenzie!" I said as I pulled the blinds on my mother's bedroom window. After days of being frustrated with her negativity, I prayed for patience. What God gave me was mercy. By definition, mercy is *compassion* and *forbearance*, two things that were growing thin once I became my mother's caregiver. After that quick but sincere prayer, I began getting a picture of what it must feel like to be her. She was growing older, had increasing illnesses, lost her independence, and was forced to live with her daughter—dependent, rather than the independent woman she had been for years.

It wasn't patience I needed, but a heart of compassion. So I entered her room like a kind nurse, and we began a little game of me starting her day by being her morning cheerleader, opening her room to light, checking her vitals, bringing breakfast, and giving her ideas for the day. She began to blossom, like a closed flower exposed to the light. About that time God began to pour His mercy over me, too. Hard situations became a bit easier. I poured into my mother, and God poured into me. You see, mercy is an important thing to Jesus. That's why he spoke these words. The message says it like this: "You're blessed when you care. At the moment of being "care-full," you find yourselves cared for." I recently saw a meme that said, "Mercy imitates God and disappoints Satan." That sums it up. Friend, let's imitate God with compassionate lives.

Today I will remember:
• Mercy is compassion for others.
• As I care for others, I will be filled myself.
• Being merciful is the lifestyle Jesus has called me to.

Lord, keep in tune with how You care for others. May I remain focused on treating others with the same mercy You have extended to me.

RISING UP AFTER HARD THINGS

For he will command his angels concerning you to guard
you in all your ways. They will lift you up in their hands.

PSALM 91:11-12

Sometimes I get blindsided when my emotions tank or when something happens that causes me to doubt. Knowing I am easily taken down when I feel afraid, rejected, or left out, I pay attention to Satan baiting me in those areas. Our attack usually comes with what we call triggers—those things that cause us to lash out in anger or emotionally spiral. For instance, some women are triggered by repeatedly scrolling curated social media posts—the enemy hisses, "They have more than you. You will never be enough. Your life is horrible."

We can deny the trigger, or we can ask God to give us wisdom—His wisdom—about why this is a vulnerable area for us. Perhaps each trigger is trying to give us information about where and how our enemy consistently goes after us. Knowledge is power, because it equips us. The psalmist goes on to say, "'Because he loves me,' says the LORD, 'I will rescue him; I will protect him, for he acknowledges my name.'"[131] Spiritual attack and temptation from the enemy is part of life. But when we are aware of them, we will be more apt to speak back boldly in Jesus' name, gaining authority over the enemy's lies. Often the antidote after attack is to stop several times a day and simply say the name of Jesus, ask for strength to refocus, and receive healing in our broken framing of things.

Today I will remember:
• God commands His angels to care for me.
• God's angels keep me in all my ways.
• Though I can't see them, they hold me and protect me.

Lord, thank You for giving me wisdom about the spiritual battle
I'm in and comfort in knowing there are angels watching over me.

---

131 Psalm 91:14.

PEACEMAKERS

Blessed are the peacemakers, for they will be called children of God.
MATTHEW 5:9

The red letters are the words of Jesus, and when we take them to heart, they challenge us to the core. Peacemaking is serious business because it confronts our need to be right or get revenge. As long as we need to be right, making peace when it's undeserved doesn't make sense. Paul spoke of this when he said, "if it is possible, as far as it depends on you, live at peace with everyone. Do not take revenge, my dear friends, but leave room for God's wrath.... On the contrary, 'if your enemy is hungry, feed him; if he is thirsty, give him something to drink.'...Do not be overcome by evil, but overcome evil with good."[132] These are holy words that are admittedly hard to swallow.

My pride and sense of justice rail against this wisdom. But then I realize that I am called to live as a daughter of God. John said, "He must become greater; I must become less."[133] There have been times when making peace was a priority, and other times when I stubbornly held on to hurt feelings. It's so important to learn that living by our emotions will not lead us to the life Jesus called us to. Feel the emotion, give the hurt and frustration to God, and then move into the freedom of living according to the teachings of Scripture. Baby steps in the right direction is how you start—trusting God completely over time takes you to the finish line.

Today I will remember:
• God has called me to peaceful living.
• I am blessed when I make the move to be a peacemaker.
• To make peace, I often have to put my "self" aside for the sake of doing things God's way.

Lord, I need Your help living in ways that will
honor You. Be increased in me daily, Jesus.

---

132 Romans 12:18-21.
133 John 3:30.

BLESSED ARE THE PERSECUTED

*Blessed are you when people insult you, persecute you
and falsely say all kinds of evil against you because of me.
Rejoice and be glad, because great is your reward in heaven.*

MATTHEW 5:11-12

We never expect to be hurt in the church. The sting hurts more coming from people you broke bread with. *Persecution* means to harass, punish, or cause to suffer because of belief. Though saints of old were martyred for faith, a punishing persecution is alive in church communities that fight over doctrine, power, and position. Unfortunately, I know.

Judgments were made because my husband helped a young pastor with a new church. We didn't recruit people to what we were doing, we just obeyed God in that season. The things spoken about us were not only false, they were unnecessary. It was hard to endure the gossip, and many tears were shed. But here's the deal—Jesus Himself knew that following Him would be misunderstood. Following God isn't a cattle call. Everyone doesn't get the memo.

I let the insults distract me from Kingdom work. Then one day as I was reading the Gospels, I realized I was actually blessed because of the gossip and lies. My reward was in heaven for following God's lead. Following Jesus will not earn you a popularity badge, and Jesus knew it. Jesus taught about what was real. If you have been persecuted in any way for your faith or for obeying God, take heart today. He sees, and your reward will be great.

Today I will remember:
- When insults come, Jesus sees.
- When false things are said, it grieves Him.
- We are blessed because God rewards us for following Him, not man.

*Lord, thank You for Your faithfulness in every season of persecution,
insult, or injury. I rejoice that You have always seen everything
and will reward the times I sought to sincerely follow Your lead.*

EVERY WORD FOR OUR GOOD

*For everything that was written in the past was written to
teach us, so that through endurance taught in the Scriptures
and the encouragement they provide we might have hope.*

ROMANS 15:4

It's easy to think the stories of the Bible are outdated and don't relate to our modern
lives. We don't eat manna or see water turn to wine. We aren't familiar with burning
bushes or parted seas. But every story in the Bible declares to us who God is and
how He works in human lives. We see personal intervention in plenty of the pages
of Scripture. If there were a *like* button on my Bible, I would definitely *like* this
particular verse. The stories are there to teach us, and in learning we will gain
endurance and hope.

The reality is, you and I will face difficult things. During those times, we can get
confused about God and His care for us. We start asking a lot of whys. Why does
God allow bad things to happen? Why is there so much evil? If He loves me, then
why am I suffering? The stories in Scripture help us put things in our own lives into
perspective. Remember, "All Scripture is God-breathed and is useful for teaching,
rebuking, correcting and training in righteousness, so that the servant of God may
be thoroughly equipped for every good work."[134] God uses all of Scripture to teach
us and train us.

Today I will remember:
• Every story in the Bible is there to teach me.
• Scripture is to encourage me and impart courage.
• When we are hopeless, we can find hope in God's Word.

*Lord, may I never take Your Word for granted, but rather
embrace it as the life-giving training tool that it is.
Thank You for the truth within the pages of the ancient text.*

THE SPIN CYCLE

Trust in the Lord with all your heart and lean not on your own understanding;
in all your ways submit to him, and he will make your paths straight.
PROVERBS 3:5-6

To be honest, when I am faced with a problem, I don't automatically turn it over to the Lord. I begin going through a spin cycle of processing information. I am working on stopping to ask God for wisdom. Putting my trust in Him is the best thing I can do. Where are you today? God knows the details of your current situation, and He desires to see you through to the end. The Lord will make the paths straight for us as we look to Him instead of spinning in circles.

When was the last time you felt engulfed by a problem or pain? Maybe it's right now. Perhaps the emotional force is upsetting you so much that you are barely making it through the day. You spin the facts, fret over the outcome, and worry more than trust. Believe it or not, even though feeling overwhelmed seems inevitable, as if there's no other option, the truth is that there's always a choice. Oswald Chambers says, "we should battle through our moods, feelings, and emotions."[135] The opposite of being overwhelmed is to surrender the current situation to God and trust in Him.

Today I will remember:
• I am to put my trust in God.
• I am not to lean on my own understanding.
• I am to pray and acknowledge God, and He will direct me.

Lord, I look to You and choose to live trusting
rather than spinning. Help me with this.

---

135 Oswald Chambers, *My Utmost for His Highest*, November 13.

MAKING WRONGS RIGHT

If you are offering your gift at the altar and there remember that your brother or sister has something against you, leave your gift there in front of the altar. First go and be reconciled to them; then come and offer your gift.

MATTHEW 5:23-24

Have you hurt someone lately? A friend, sibling, or parent? Maybe sharp words were spoken with a coworker or flung at your child. Before going to raise your hallelujah, raise a word of apology—offering connection or understanding to the person you hurt. Pride would keep us holding grudges, unwilling to make things right. But Jesus taught love, mercy, and forgiveness. Our pride might look like anger, withholding, and unkindness. We get to choose—mean girl or Jesus girl. Jesus encourages connection, while our stubbornness encourages disconnection. Hurts given to God turn into understanding and healing.

Broken relationships can affect our relationship with God. If we have a grievance, the problem should be resolved as soon as possible. The red letters always challenge us, but, friend, these are the words of Jesus. Being accountable for how we treat people was a high priority to Him. Right after these words He said, "settle matters quickly..." And He said, "Anyone who is angry with a brother or sister will be subject to judgment,"[136] encouraging quick resolutions. Paul also taught, "In your anger do not sin: Do not let the sun go down while you are still angry, and do not give the devil a foothold."[137] None of us wants to give the devil a foothold.

Today I will remember:
- When possible, I am to resolve situations quickly with people.
- Staying angry or withholding kindness gives Satan a foothold.
- Before raising a hallelujah at church, I need to offer an apology if needed.

Lord, dealing with people is tricky. We all have our own baggage that causes us to get offended. May I be quick to forgive and quick to ask forgiveness, settling things quickly.

---

136 Matthew 5:25; 5:22.
137 Ephesians 4:26-27.

SAY WHAT YOU MEAN

All you need to say is simply "Yes" or "No";
anything beyond this comes from the evil one.
MATTHEW 5:37

Jesus emphasized telling the truth. In His day people were divorcing their wives, breaking promises, and using sacred language casually. Jesus was condemning making a vow casually or giving your word when you know you won't keep it. Keeping oaths and promises is important and builds trust in our relationships. But sometimes people make commitments they know they can't fulfill in order to please people in the moment. My people-pleasing side makes straightforward answers harder than they should be.

People pleasing makes us fickle and makes sticking to a decision hard. It also puts people above God. Isn't it amazing that Jesus addressed these kinds of things? He was the best at leading people in life skills. James, addressing the very same thing, said, "Above all, my brothers and sisters, do not swear—not by heaven or by earth or by anything else. All you need to say is a simple 'Yes' or 'No.' Otherwise you will be condemned."[138]

Say what you mean and mean what you say! If not, the consequences are pretty steep—James said you will be condemned, and Jesus said you'll be influenced by the evil one. Is anyone perking their ears up now?

Our vows and commitments are important. Are you known as a person who keeps her word? Truthfulness is so uncommon that we feel we must close a statement with, "I promise." But if we always tell the truth, we will have less pressure to back it up with an oath or promise.

Today I will remember:
- I am to be truthful and stick to what I say.
- Being fickle in my decisions and speech is from the enemy.
- People pleasing is a trap that breeds indecisiveness.

Lord, may I tell the truth and stand by the truth. Help me to make
decisions and be bold enough to own my own decisions and stick to them.

PRAYER ROOM

But when you pray, go into your room, close the door and pray to your Father,
who is unseen. Then your Father, who sees what is done in secret, will reward you.

MATTHEW 6:6

Things changed in my life when I got serious about prayer. Before I would say, "I'm praying for you!" with regularity, but truth be told, I only thought about praying. Good intentions, right? It's like using the praying hand emoji when you don't know what else to say. But when we decide that we are going to be women who really pray and not just talk about praying, everything will change in our life because of the intimate time we spend with the Father.

Jesus invites us into a secret place with Him. I have had several designated spots for prayer over the years, and I have known mothers who retreat to the bathroom for five minutes just to pray uninterrupted. Women need to know about the power of secret prayer amidst the craziness of life. In this place of private prayer, no one sees— it's just you and your Father. The sweet spot comes when we enter into the secret place where all our cares and heartaches can be heard and expressed, a place alone with God where we can pray for those we love with abandon and detail without fear of offending. God honors those prayers behind closed doors. He already knows what we need, but it sure feels good to lay our hearts before Him.

Today I will remember:
- Jesus invites me to a secret place of prayer with Him.
- He knows what I need before I ask.
- He is intent on His Kingdom reigning in my life.

Father, thank You for inviting me into intimacy with You through
daily prayer. May I find time and space to be with You, praying
on ordinary days and watching extraordinary things happen.

WORRY SUBTRACTS FROM THE BEST

Can any one of you by worrying add a single hour to your life?
MATTHEW 6:27

Worry is as common as fireworks on the Fourth of July. This familiar habit comes naturally and can cause us to lead with fear and anxiety. Apparently it's always been a problem, because Jesus addressed it with His followers thousands of years ago: "I tell you, do not worry about your life, what you will eat or drink; or about your body, what you will wear. Is not life more than food, and the body more than clothes? Look at the birds of the air; they do not sow or reap or store away in barns, and yet your heavenly Father feeds them. Are you not much more valuable than they?"[139] Jesus went on to point out that the pagans or unbelievers run after all those things, but that we don't need to because we have a heavenly Father, and He knows us and everything we need.

These red-letter words are crucial for us as women to understand and to apply to our lives. Jesus knows our need. Our God values us and desires to provide all we need, and because of this we no longer have to be stressed out about All. The. Things. All this worry is not adding anything positive to our lives. So let's do this—"Cast all your anxiety on him because he cares for you."[140]

Today I will remember:
• Worrying does not add value to my life—it subtracts value.
• People worry when they feel insecure about things.
• I can have complete security in a God who will provide all that I need today.

Father, forgive me for my times of spinning in the worry cycle.
Thank You for the assurance that You will provide every
little thing I need without me worrying about it.

---

139 Matthew 6:25-26.
140 1 Peter 5:7.

ONE DAY AT A TIME

Therefore do not worry about tomorrow, for tomorrow will
worry about itself. Each day has enough trouble of its own.

MATTHEW 6:34

Over the years, women have told me that "worry" was a family trait. They say because Grandma, Mom, and Aunt Sue worried, that they are worriers too—they say it's in the genes. If there weren't anything we could do about it, Jesus would not have addressed it. We can win over worry and not live in the anxiety of our upbringing or past.

Whenever there is a "therefore," it's important to back up to see what came before it. We have just looked at Jesus explaining that He provides for the birds, the fields, and the lilies of the field. He said that He already knows what we need and will take care of us, too. So—because of this—we no longer have to be concerned or worried over our future. God goes before us, and the future will take care of itself. This doesn't mean that we don't plan or prepare, but that we refuse worry when it tries to creep up on us.

This date on the calendar only comes by once in your life. How sad that we waste the days with worry about tomorrow instead of living well today. Take these precious red letters to heart—allowing the truth of His care for you to fill your mind, strengthen your soul, and change your story to one of trust instead of worry.

Today I will remember:
• Worrying about the future only causes anxiety.
• Jesus goes before me every step of the way, and I can trust Him.
• I only have one shot at this day—and worrying will rob today of its joy.

Father, thank You for caring for me, providing for me,
and giving me every reason not to worry. I place my
life and days in Your hands once again today.

DOUBLE STANDARDS

Do not judge, or you too will be judged.
MATTHEW 7:1

Double standards say I can be critical of you but upset when you criticize me. Jesus called out this double standard. He didn't just call it out, He attached consequences when He said, "For in the same way you judge others, you will be judged, and with the measure you use, it will be measured to you."[141] We can make all the excuses we want, but being critical and judgmental is not God's best for us as Christ followers. Jesus said, "Let any one of you who is without sin be the first to throw a stone at her."[142] The last time I checked, I was certainly not sinless, yet as I searched my heart, I can recall hectic stone-throwing days. Yes, the double standard.

Judgments may have taken place only in my mind, but that didn't make them any less real or any less harmful. When I judge others, I am walking farther away from living like Jesus and drawing closer to doing things my way. A critical spirit can keep us stuck, and when we are filled with negativity, there isn't much room for the positive. Judgment and criticism are not a way of agape and not the way to follow after Christ. As Dale Carnegie wrote, "Any fool can criticize, condemn and complain... but it takes character and self-control to be understanding and forgiving."[143]

Today I will remember:
• Jesus instructs me to put away judging others.
• When I judge, it will be measured back to me.
• It's time to lay down the stones and love instead.

*Father, I am sorry for all the stones I've thrown and my
critical attitudes. Today I want to lay down the stones
and open my heart to loving people without judgment.*

---

141 Matthew 7:2.

142 John 8:7.

143 Dale Carnegie, *How to Win Friends and Influence People* (New York: Simon & Schuster, 2009), 14.

ASK. SEEK. KNOCK

Ask and it will be given to you; seek and you
will find; knock and the door will be opened to you.

MATTHEW 7:7

Have you ever been troubled by your prayers not being answered? I have. My inner dialogue with the Lord went, "Why? I am sincerely trying to follow Your Word... asking instead of worrying, knocking with trust on Your door. So why?" My perspective was rocked as I read God's answer to that prayer: "Which of you, if your son asks for bread, will give him a stone? Or if he asks for a fish, will give him a snake? If you, then, though you are evil, know how to give good gifts to your children, how much more will your Father in heaven good give good gifts to those who ask him!"[144]

He is answering, it just might look different than I was expecting.

What about you? Could the yet unanswered prayer be about timing? Maybe Jesus is baking the bread instead of giving you a stone. Stand today in the truth that God gives good gifts. God gives bread, not a stone, and your prayers will be answered because your good God has heard every single one. Doors knocked on will be opened, but only when it's safe to open them and only when it's time for you to receive what is behind the door. God is good. You have a God who loves you more than anyone has ever loved you—and He is preparing the best answer to those prayers!

Today I will remember:
- I am to Ask God for my needs, desires, and wants.
- I am to Seek God for His will in my life and yield to that.
- I am to Knock on the door in persevering prayer until the door opens.

Lord, forgive me for the times of doubt. I am so grateful that You hear
my prayers and want only what is best for me—in Your time.

THE GOLDEN RULE

So in everything, do to others what you would have them do to you.

MATTHEW 7:12

This has been called the Golden Rule, but these words are the words of Christ. How we treat others is a reflection of how we value God's principles. Do our actions demonstrate that God is unkind or uncaring—hot and cold? Or do our actions reflect the deep well of God's love within us? It was Jesus who taught, "But to you who are listening I say: Love your enemies, do good to those who hate you, bless those who curse you, pray for those who mistreat you."[145] Really? I mean, excuse me, Jesus, but when someone is hating me, the last thing I want is to do good to them! Fortunately, Jesus understands us. He knew we would need to be taught and then reminded about things like this—if that were not so, it wouldn't be in His powerful teachings that we find in the red letters.

Jesus taught this "Golden Rule" as a foundation for living, "Do to others what you would have them do to you, for this sums up the Law and the Prophets."[146] How we treat others is important to Jesus.

How do you want to be treated? Get clear on that answer, and then remember the teachings of Jesus. The way we treat others is not a reflection of who they are—it's a reflection of who we are.

Today I will remember:
- I am to treat others how I want to be treated.
- I am a representative of Christ on earth.
- I haven't been given a menu of options, but am to do good to all people.

Lord, thank You for knowing me and understanding that doing good to all people, all the time, is hard. Lead me to walk in Your Spirit, with the greatest aim to walk as You walked—in love.

---

145 Luke 6:27-28.
146 Matthew 7:12.

IT'S ALL ABOUT THE HEART

For the mouth speaks what the heart is full of.
MATTHEW 12:34

I have a friend who would regularly ask me, "how's your heart?" No one had ever asked me that question before. But she always cut to the chase and went deep, wanting to know how I really was, not who I was presenting myself to be. All of life flows from our heart. So if my heart is divided, I will live a divided life. If my heart is filled with unhealed hurt, I will end up hurting people. But when my heart is filled with the richness of God, it will come out in the things I do and the words I speak. I will overflow from whatever is in my heart, and so will you.

The most wonderful thing is, Jesus is not upset at us if our heart is hurting, broken, bitter, or in need of some repair. He is the greatest healer—able to touch the parts of our heart that need help and healing. He makes us new. So don't be afraid to give Him your heart, the deepest part of you—paying attention to health on the inside, where your emotions are churning and processing. Aim for health at your very center so that what comes out of you will be the best of Him and the best of you.

"I will give you a new heart and put a new spirit in you; I will remove from you your heart of stone and give you a heart of flesh."[147]

Today I will remember:
• Everything I say is an overflow of my heart.
• If my heart is filled with ugliness, that will spill out of me.
• If my heart is filled with beauty, that will be my overflow.

Lord, thank You for being my healer—heart, soul, strength, and mind.
May my heart be filled with You and my words bring You glory.

---

147 Ezekiel 36:26.

WHAT DO YOU WANT?

Jesus stopped and called them.
"What do you want me to do for you?" he asked.
MATTHEW 20:32

Jesus and His disciples were tired, most likely dusty, and probably in need of a break from the masses. Leaving Jericho, large crowds followed them and two blind men on the side of the road called out to Jesus. "Lord, Son of David, have mercy on us."[148] The people got upset, telling the blind men to be quiet, but they kept shouting to Jesus. Picture this—a tired Jesus, trying to get out of town, surrounded by crowds pushing in, and people yelling. He didn't turn a deaf ear. Instead, He stopped and asked the blind men what they wanted from Him. The answer was obvious—they wanted their sight. Jesus, moved with compassion, got laser focused on them, touched them, and restored their sight.

Their blindness was obvious, but Jesus still asked what they wanted. Sometimes this is how it is with us, too. What we need from God might be obvious, but He still wants us to ask Him—to say it. We can be comforted by this story because Jesus is a God of compassion, personally interested in us and wanting us to tell Him what we need. Jesus—I want my prodigal kid back. Jesus—I want to be healed of cancer. Jesus—I want to be freed from the effects childhood trauma. Jesus—I need rent money. There is nothing too small for Him to care about, and nothing too big for Him to handle.

He asking you this today—*Beloved, what do you want me to do for you?*

Today I will remember:
- Jesus has compassion on me—He is never too busy.
- Jesus invites me to ask Him for the things I need.
- Jesus is a healer—every part of me can be touched by God.

Lord, thank You for caring enough
to stop and tend to me. I want more of You.

TAKE THIS CUP FROM ME

*My Father, if it is possible, may this cup be taken
from me. Yet not as I will, but as you will.*

MATTHEW 26:39

Jesus knew the suffering that was coming, and He was in great anguish. He and His disciples came to the Garden of Gethsemane, and there He agonized and cried out to God—asking if the cup of suffering could be postponed or removed. Then, despite His wish to cancel the current suffering, He asked for God's will above His own, even if it meant the circumstances wouldn't be changed.

These red-lettered words of Jesus teach us something important. Jesus understands the human condition of weakness, pain, and suffering. We might not be sweating drops of blood in a garden, but our suffering is important to God. Jesus cried out and asked for the situation to change. We, too, can cry out to God and ask for the cup of our suffering to be taken from us. The greatest example is that despite His anguish, He circled back around to *not my will but Your will be done.*

"Jesus understands every weakness of ours, because he was tempted in every way that we are. But he did not sin! So whenever we are in need, we should come bravely before the throne of our merciful God. There we will be treated with undeserved grace, and we will find help."[149]

Today I will remember:
- Jesus understands my suffering.
- I can cry out to God and express my need.
- In the end, God's will is the most important thing.

*Lord, in my times of suffering, may I remain close to
You, and with freedom, cry out in my need.*

THE PLACE OF REST

Come with me by yourselves to a quiet place and get some rest.
MARK 6:31

Very little value is assigned to rest. People ask, *What are you doing?* Certainly not, *How are you resting?* Jesus was committed to the mission before Him, but He knew that rest and refueling are important. Jesus invited the disciples out of their hectic pace, to "come" away with Him—which literally meant to go with Him and to follow Him—alone. It echoes when Jesus said, "Come to me, all you who are weary and burdened, and I will give you rest."[150] The word *rest* here means to cease from labor in order to recover and collect strength. When we take that pivotal step in His direction, He will cause us to collect strength again.

What do you think of when you hear the phrase "quiet place"? Maybe a spa day, a no-kids day, a beach day? Here in the original language, *quiet place* meant secluded, lonesome, desert, solitary. For this extrovert, that sounds awful. Yet despite our personality type, there is rich meaning here. If we are going to hear God and gather strength from Him, we can't always be with people. Time alone is necessary. For some of us, the resting place might be forced upon us through circumstances. The next time you are in a desert place in life, remember that it is in these times that Jesus invites us to be with Him. If you are intentionally coming away for rest, pray and ask God what in this season would be the most important step of rest for you.

Today I will remember:
• Jesus values rest and invites me into that place.
• Activity leads to weariness if I am not making room for rest.
• The invitation is to be with Jesus—to get alone to refuel.

Lord, thank You for inviting me to
stillness when my body and soul need it.

---

150 Matthew 11:28.

FAITH IS BELIEVING

Daughter, your faith has healed you.
Go in peace and be freed from your suffering.

MARK 5:34

Jesus felt a tug on His cloak. Desperate and exhausted from years of bleeding, a woman who had heard about Him pushed her way through the crowds. Feeling the power that had gone out from Him, Jesus asked, "Who touched my clothes?"[151] She came and fell at His feet with fear, telling Him her story and why she touched Him. Jesus wasn't annoyed with her. Although the woman was healed as she touched Him, Jesus told her it was *her* faith that caused the cure. Faith must be put into action. She had the courage or maybe the desperation to brave the crowds, believing a touch could heal her.

Faith is believing. Don't be discouraged if your faith seems small. Jesus said it only takes faith the size of a mustard seed to move a mountain.[152] This woman didn't know religious jargon, but she heard He was the Messiah and a healer. That was enough faith to lead her into the crowds. And it was her act of faith that made the difference. I often forget to ask God to heal me. I go to medical offices expecting to be healed, but not to Jesus. While God uses medicine to heal us, He still encourages us to touch the hem of His garment and carry that mustard-seed faith. What do you need healing for today? Jesus is the same today as He was then— a compassionate healer.

Today I will remember:
• Faith requires action steps.
• I only need a seed of faith to move the mountain.
• Jesus still heals in response to our faith.

Lord, forgive me for the times I haven't trusted You for healing,
the times my faith was too small. Remind me
to come to You, by faith, for everything.

---

151 Mark 5:30.
152 Matthew 17:20.

JESUS PRAYS

I pray for them. I am not praying for the world,
but for those you have given me, for they are yours.

JOHN 17:9

Jesus prayed for His disciples. How He prayed for them demonstrates His heart toward His disciples today. First, He established the identity of those He was praying for— calling us *His*. Then He says that all glory will come to Him through us as His vessels in this world. Later He prayed, "Holy Father protect them by the power of your name...that they may have the full measure of my joy within them"[153] Finally, He prayed we would be kept safe from the evil one. Remember, he called Satan a thief,[154] and now He prays this thief will not steal from us anymore. He wraps it up by asking that we be set apart—sanctified—by the truth of His Word.

The Bible is clear that Jesus speaks to the Father on our behalf. Romans 8:34 says, "Jesus...is at the right hand of God and is also interceding for us." We may wonder why any of us struggle. But in this world we will face real problems. The good news is we can be assured that we aren't alone. God will never abandon us. Jesus shares our struggles and defeats the powers that are too strong for us to conquer. He still walks on water, and He still prays for those who are His. Let this give you courage today as you navigate life. In the hard, God is creating holy—more of Himself— within you.

Today I will remember:
• Jesus is interceding for me.
• He prays for my protection, joy, and sanctification.
• I can trust that I am never alone and always covered.

Lord, thank You for interceding on my behalf and covering me.

---

153 John 17:11, 13.
154 John 10:10.

WATCH AND PRAY

Watch and pray so that you will not fall into temptation.
The spirit is willing, but the flesh is weak.
MARK 14:38

There are days when I am tired and vulnerable, and temptation is knocking at my door. Can you relate? I know strength and weakness. Jesus using examples such as this helps me understand the very real battle that goes on just to get through a day. In times of difficulty, we are vulnerable to temptation—to desire something that isn't good for us or to be enticed by the devil. Jesus gave us an example in the garden of how to resist—prayer, support, and focus.

When vulnerable, Jesus prayed, "Abba, Father...everything is possible for you."[155] When we pray, we are to focus on how mighty God is and that He does have a plan in all things. Jesus also sought support from His disciples, saying to them, "Stay here and keep watch"[156] Pride keeps us from asking for prayer or help. But Jesus asked, so we can too. Finally, He gives us the example of staying focused on God's will and the purpose placed before us. This brings to mind, Colossians 3:1-2, "Since, then, you have been raised with Christ, set your hearts on things above, where Christ is, seated at the right hand of God. Set your minds on things above, not on earthly things."

To watch and pray is to be vigilant and awake so that we can be women of prayer and focus who resist the enemy on a daily basis. Remember, even though we are weak, the spirit within is willing.

Today I will remember:
- I am to be watchful in prayer.
- I am to ask support from friends.
- I am to focus on the bigger picture.

Lord, when I am weak, may I come to You to resist temptation
and stay focused on what You have called me to.

---

155 Mark 14:36.
156 Mark 14:34.

GOD WILL NOT FORSAKE US

My God, my God, why have your forsaken me?
MARK 15:34

The doorbell rang, and two policemen delivered the news of the accident. Before she could gather her thoughts, she was out the door en route to identify her precious twenty-three-year-old. She was given a bracelet her daughter was wearing when she died. Having never seen it before, she was puzzled by its meaning—a shiny heart engraved with one word: *His*. Had Lucy met someone? At the memorial, she asked her daughter's friends and found out it was Jesus she had met, a month earlier at a retreat. Lucy was coming home to introduce her mother to Jesus when the accident happened.

A few years later, I met this grieving mother at a retreat I was speaking at. As she was leaving, she asked for a picture together, then hugged me tightly. Realizing this was more than a picture, I leaned back and looked into her eyes. She pulled the bracelet from her pocket—it was a treasure she carried every day. She told me of her daughter, who was in heaven because she had been to a retreat like this. "I think you may have been the speaker." With tears, she committed the rest of her life to Christ. Now Lucy's prayers had been answered, as her mom had met Jesus too. Had she felt forsaken? Yes. But over time she saw God's hand in the story. God will never forsake us, and Mom and daughter will be reunited one day.

It was said by Shauna Niequist "I believe that loss and emptiness and confusion often give way to a new fullness and wisdom." [157]

Today I will remember:
• Even Jesus felt forsaken by God in suffering.
• God will never forsake us.
• God is with us in our hard stories.

Lord, in the times I feel You have left me,
may I stop and remember that You never will.

---

157 Shauna Niequist, *Bittersweet: Thoughts on Change, Grace, and Learning the Hard Way* (Grand Rapids: Zondervan, 2010), 17.

THE IMPORTANCE OF FOLLOWING

Why do you call me "Lord, Lord," and do not do what I say?
LUKE 6:46

We want to get our way. We might mask it with being nice or become a master manipulator, but the constant drive to have things our way is a habit that is hard to break and must be addressed. Part of the sacred journey of walking with Jesus is the path of walking less in self-life and more in spirit-life. We do this by hearing what God says and practicing following Him in that direction even when it's not what we want to do. All of Scripture will confront that "self" side of us. When we disagree or find what we read too hard, it's likely to get disregarded. But here Jesus was asking an important question—*Will you do what I say?*

Life is all about foundations. When life is calm, our foundations don't seem to matter. But when a crisis comes, our foundations are tested. When the storms come, will you be left standing or will you collapse? Jesus was asking, *Why are you building your life on sand—doing things your own way—rather than building on solid rock by doing the things that I tell you?* The one who builds on a strong foundation will be able to weather the storms and calamities of life, while the one who builds on the sand of their own ways and reasoning will collapse when the storms come.

What foundation are you laying today?

Beth Moore insightfully shares "The giant step in the walk of faith is the one we take when we decide God no longer is a part of our lives. He is our life."[158]

Today I will remember:
- Every day I choose who I will follow.
- If I follow God's way, a strong foundation will be built under me.
- If I follow my own way, an unstable foundation is formed.

Lord, may I listen to Your voice, through Your Word, and obey You.

---

158 Beth Moore, *Praying God's Word Day by Day* (Nashville: Broadman & Holman, 2006), January 1.

SIT AND LEARN

*"Martha, Martha," the Lord answered, "you are worried and upset
about many things, but few things are needed—or indeed only one."*

LUKE 10:41-42

If Jesus were coming to dinner, do you think any of us would be slacking? Of course not! Maybe Jesus wasn't suggesting that Martha's service was unacceptable, but more that her anxiety over everything was. Martha was distracted, which means to be driven and over-occupied, pulled in different directions. Martha's distraction led to a sense of self-righteousness and self-focus. She became defensive— "Don't you care that my sister has left me to do the work by myself?" and demanding—"Tell her to help me!"[159] Instead of rebuking Martha's sister, Jesus affirms Mary.

Sitting at a rabbi's feet was customary for a disciple in those days. Mary, though she was a woman in a male-dominated world, was a disciple. This is scandalous and profound. Jesus' affirmation of Mary's posture reveals His acceptance of Mary as a disciple. Jesus welcomes women to learn. We assume this story is about Mary versus Martha, but disciples are not called to either sit or serve—we are called to *both*. We are called to abide *and* bear fruit. Serving Jesus with all we have can easily leave us overcommitted in a culture that says we can multitask and do it all. We have a teacher who invites us to learn His way and His priorities. He invites us to drop the expectations we put on ourselves and make time to sit and learn as His disciple. When we do that, we will have all we need to serve.

Today I will remember:
• When I am overcommitted, I can lose focus and become defensive and demanding.
• When I sit and abide, I will eventually bear much fruit in my service.
• God has called me to both sit and serve.

*Lord, thank You for calling me to be Your disciple, inviting me
to learn from You while serving You through serving others.*

---

159 Luke 10:40.

THE DESTRUCTION OF DIVISION

Any kingdom divided against itself will be ruined,
and a house divided against itself will fall.

LUKE 11:17

Ken and Cheryl are sports fans with loyalties to opposing teams. They thought it was funny when they hung a sign in their entry that read, "a house divided." Though sports rivalries in a household can be joked about, the origins of this phrase are biblical. When left unchecked, division causes disaster. It starts small, with seeds of discontent or offense. When we fail to address those, it can grow to a full-blown war between people. Division takes root, and before long, the house crumbles or the church, organization, or workplace is in ruins because division is a tool that the enemy uses to destroy.

In the real world, we will have differing opinions. When our opinions become our god, problems begin and division takes root. Pride causes us to believe our opinion is the right one. There will always be things to divide us. We are not required to process things the same or agree on everything, but we are called to be of one mind—that being focus on the eternal and having our thoughts set on Jesus. With that in mind, Jesus taught us to treat others how we want to be treated, turn the other cheek, and bless those who curse us. And He told us not to allow the enemy into the mix, causing division and distraction. There are three sides to every story—ours, theirs, and God's.

As Abraham Lincoln famously said, "My concern is not whether God is on our side; my greatest concern is to be on God's side, for God is always right."

Today I will remember:
- Division brings ruin.
- A house divided will not be able to stand.
- An attitude of love and forgiveness prevents divisions.

Lord, forgive me for not considering others and for the times
I have participated in dividing conversations and attitudes.

—⚬§ ⟨❖⟩ ⟨⟩ ⟨❖⟩ ₂⚬—

THE TRAP OF GREED

Watch out! Be on your guard against all kinds of greed;
life does not consist in an abundance of possessions.

LUKE 12:15

Right before the pandemic, we had just moved to a new house that needed furnishing. I was excited to find what we needed, but all the stores shut down—and my shopping was put on an indefinite hold. With life stopped, I filled my time watching HGTV—and wanted even more things. Before long, I dreamt of changing and remodeling everything in our new "dream house." Greed isn't about the things we need, but an intense desire for more than we need. In the original language greed is covetousness—wanting what we don't have. Jesus warns against this constant need for more and better. I had to ask myself, When will enough be enough? When will life and contentment no longer be dependent on what I have?

I am reminded of my cousin who died unexpectedly in her late thirties. My sister and I were her only relatives. When we went to her condo to clear it out, it was devastating to toss things she loved. Except for giving keepsakes to her closest friends, all she had got donated or trashed. The visual of the large trash bin filled with her stuff haunted me for years. I don't remember her by what she had, but by who she was—and sadly now by all that was tossed. Jesus taught that life isn't about what a person has, because we don't take anything with us.

Today I will remember:
- I am to guard against greed of any kind.
- Life doesn't consist of what I have.
- Life is a beautiful gift to be lived in gratefulness, not greed.

Lord, may I find joy every day in the things You have provided and
in the security that what I have is enough because I have You.

SEEK HIM

Seek his kingdom, and these things will be given to you as well.
LUKE 12:31

Most Christians have heard this verse and possibly even sung it in worship songs at church. We often sing and repeat the words without understanding the meaning intended. Reading the teaching of Jesus in context, we see that the verses before are about the worry, anxiety, and temptations most of us face. Jesus warned His disciples about their worldly concerns often, and He taught how to counter them by seeking God and His righteousness. Our Father, who knows what we need, encourages us to keep an eternal perspective even while crossing things off our lists and calendar. Jesus then wraps up this teaching about the worries of this world with a promise—when we seek Him first, He gives us exactly what we need. We can trust Him.

Friend, when you are worried, run to the Father. He is trustworthy. Above all else, seek God and His Kingdom's rule over your life. Always remember that God is good. You can seek God's Kingdom in several ways, including through prayer, Bible reading, worship, repentance, and gratitude. As you shift your focus from worry to God's faithfulness, you will experience all you need and more—with everything in between being added to you as well.

Jeremy Treat reminds us "We do not build the kingdom for God, we receive the kingdom from God. The sign of Christianity is not a ladder; it's a cross."[160]

Today I will remember:
• When I am prone to worry, God calls me to seek Him.
• God promises to provide all the things I need.
• I am of value to God and trust His Kingdom rule over my life.

Lord, worry is easy, but worship takes intentionality.
May intentionally seeking Your Kingdom be my heart default.

---

160   Jeremy Treat, *Seek First: How the Kingdom of God Changes Everything* (Grand Rapids: Zondervan, 2019), 175.

October

LIVING COURAGEOUSLY

"Courage is contagious. When a brave man takes a stand,
the spines of others are often stiffened."
Billy Graham[161]

---

161 Billy Graham, "A Time for Moral Courage," *Reader's Digest* (July 1964).

STANDING FIRM

Stay alert! Watch out for your great enemy, the devil. He prowls around like a roaring lion, looking for someone to devour. Stand firm against him, and be strong in your faith.

1 PETER 5:8-9, NLT

A few years ago, we moved into a new house. The previous owners, knowing we had grandchildren, left some large, lifelike stuffed animals for us. One was a giant tiger. Since our two small dogs were afraid of the tiger, we decided to place it at the top of the basement stairs to keep them from going down. It was funny to watch them see the tiger and get freaked out. The stuffed tiger was just a prop and couldn't really hurt them. Though they thought it was real, it was just a big stuffed animal!

My friends, this is how it is with us. The enemy tries to scare us. He props himself up and mocks us by causing fear and anxiety. But, like the stuffed animal, the enemy is only taunting us to keep us from trusting God. Though he tries to bring us down, we have the power and authority to stand firm. Let's not fall for fear. Standing firm against the enemy is the way we live with courage in this life. Satan isn't going away, but in Christ we have the victory.

Today I will remember:
- I have an enemy whose job is to divert me from faith and courage.
- He looks for ways to devour me, which can be as simple as a trigger from my past.
- I can choose this day to stand firm in faith regardless of circumstances.

Lord, thank You for the victory of the cross. Forgive me for falling for the taunts of the enemy and forgetting the victory I have in You. Help me, Lord, to live with courageous faith.

SET YOUR FOCUS

Be strong and very courageous. Be careful to obey all the law
my servant Moses gave you; do not turn from it to the right
or to the left, that you may be successful wherever you go.

JOSHUA 1:7

What trips you up and causes you to lose courage? A friend taught me about courage through focusing on God's strength in her weakness. I never knew her circumstances, but I knew she was standing courageously and trusting God. She repeatedly said, "I'm not turning to the right or the left, just staying the course in front of me." I had no clue what that meant, but I learned it came from Isaiah: "because the Sovereign LORD helps me, I will not be disgraced. Therefore I have set my face like a flint, and I know I will not be put to shame."[162] My mentor held on to this too, so now I was even more intrigued.

A flint is a very hard rock and is used figuratively in the Bible to express the toughness of unwavering determination in the face of an impossible task. My friend's determination to walk with Jesus in the hard gave her a fierce focus. Each time she repeated this Scripture, it was as if she once again refocused on the bigger picture, and this gave her extreme faith and courage.

It would be many years before I needed that kind of courage, but God used her to plant seeds of truth in me that have helped me walk through many things—and still help me to this day. In today's verse, Joshua had instructions, and he was to stay laser focused on those, not turning to the right or left but going straight toward God's call and plan. Having this focus will give us courage.

Today I will remember:
- God has called me to be strong and have courage.
- Whatever God has called me to, He will equip me for.
- My focus on God's faithfulness in the past will give me courage today.

Lord, as I focus on your faithfulness, may I find new strength
and courage to live the life You have placed before me.

THE THIEF

The thief comes only to steal and kill and destroy.
JOHN 10:10

Yesterday morning our neighbors were held up at gunpoint. They opened the door for a fake delivery man. The house was ransacked in front of them, but they weren't hurt. We live in a safe neighborhood dotted with lakes, geese, and beautiful paths. I'm sure it never occurred to them that answering the door midday would be a problem. In the same way, we may be oblivious that spiritually we have a thief knocking at our door. He comes in as a fake—disguised just like the delivery man. His goal is to take from us, kill our hope, and destroy us.

When I try to type in the word *destroy*, my screen keeps trying to type destory. Isn't that interesting? The thief comes to de-story us—trying to rob the hope that our Good Shepherd has plans for a beautiful story to be played out in our lives through redemption and restoration—turning ugly things beautiful and causing broken hearts to beat again.

What is the thief trying to steal from you? What aspect of your life is he actively trying to de-story? Let's join today standing firm against the enemy's attempt to defeat, discourage, or confuse us. Let's find strength in knowing that Jesus came to destroy the work of the devil.[163]

Today I will remember:
- I have an enemy whose only job is to steal from me.
- This unseen thief wants to ransack my life with fear and unbelief.
- Jesus wins—the Good Shepherd is the victor of the story.

*Lord, may I continually trust that it is Your heart to lead me
into abundant life—while being equally aware that in this life,
I do have an enemy and You have already won the battle.*

---

163 1 John 3:8.

COURAGE TO BE SET APART

*My prayer is not that you take them out of the world but that you
protect them from the evil one. They are not of the world, even as
I am not of it. Sanctify them by the truth; your word is truth.*

JOHN 17:15-17

Jesus didn't ask God to give His disciples blessing and untroubled lives. Instead, He prayed that that they would be protected from evil. The evil one is said to be the prince of this world, the thief of all good, the father of lies, and the accuser of the brethren. This is what Jesus prayed for His disciples to be protected from—and now this prayer is for us. It's a prayer for courageous lives.

Evil is all around us. It's easy to live in fear, but that is not God's best for us. Maybe you, like me, have backed away from this kind of prayer because getting near the subject of evil is uncomfortable. And yet, as Jesus' disciples we can stand in solidarity in the power of this prayer against evil. He prays for our safety because He knows that though we are not of this world, we are affected by the things of this world. He prayed to the father that we would be sanctified—holy and set apart—by the truth of His Word.

Today I will remember:
- Jesus prayed a specific prayer that applies to me today.
- While I am in this world, Jesus asked the Father to protect me from the evil one.
- Satan—the evil one—has no power or place in my life because I am set apart for God's purposes.

*Lord, thank You for Your heart of safety, sanctification,
and covering for Your people. Help me to believe this
and trust You when life seems hard and dark.*

CONFIDENT THAT GOD IS WORKING

*Being confident of this, that he who began a good work in
you will carry it on to completion until the day of Christ Jesus.*

PHILIPPIANS 1:6

Many women I know are trying to find their place in business or ministry. The new pressure to be influencers, gain followers, and increase social media platforms is making it hard to have the courage to try. There are so many things that can eat away at our confidence. Feelings of not being good enough can tempt us to quit moving forward and thwart us when we dream of doing something that we have never tried before. But there is one thing we can remain confident in: regardless of circumstances, personal ability, or the seasons of life, God is always at work in us.

The apostle Paul calls us to a place of confidence. Be confident in this—God will complete the work that He began in you. I take great comfort in this truth. Not only will God finish the work, He will carry it to the finish line. Do you hear that? He will carry us to the finish line. He will not place us down and forget about us, but instead will continue working in and through us until our very last breath. If we ever had reason to hope, this is it.

Today I will remember:
- I can live in confidence because of God's promise to complete me.
- He is always working in me.
- Until my last breath, I am carried and led by the God who made me.

*Lord, today I declare that You are at work in me. Despite what I can or cannot
see, I will stand in this truth and live in confidence because You are writing my
story, completing Your plan, and carrying me along the way. Thank You.*

HOLD THINGS LOOSELY

Many are the plans in a person's heart,
but it is the LORD's purpose that prevails.
PROVERBS 19:21

I was counting down the days until our out-of-state kids and grandkids would come to visit. I was planning for their stay, purchasing tickets, making reservations, and ensuring everything was set. But they got sick. They couldn't come when planned, and some plans had to change. Naturally, I felt bad they were sick—and I was disappointed that my plans were for naught. I quickly felt a nudge to hold my plans loosely, choosing to love my kids over and above my own plans and desires. I chose kindness, care, and peace instead of disappointment.

There is nothing wrong with having a plan, but all of our plans must ultimately be held loosely because things can change them. When I was younger, a change in my expectations rocked me. I could not adjust to such disappointment. But over the years, I have learned to hold my plans loosely and openhanded before God. As I commit all things to Him, I learn more and more how to have joy not in circumstance alone, but in trusting the purposes of His heart. We don't know why things happen, but we can trust the God who is with us in the middle of each happening.

Today I will remember:
- I make lots of plans, but plans can be changed by circumstances out of my control.
- My heart must yield to the Lord's plans.
- As I look to God, I can learn to trust the purposes of God's heart over my plan.

Lord, thank You for teaching me the importance
of holding loosely my plans and expectations. Lead me daily
on the path of trusting You with all things, big and small.

THE COURAGE OF MIND SHIFTING

Set your minds on things above, not on earthly things.
COLOSSIANS 3:2

To *set* something is to move it or position it in place. I love to decorate. Part of the process is setting decor items in just the right spot. I move things to different places, intentionally setting things in the place that best complements the room. I have the ability to do this with common things like vases, pictures, and plants. I also have the ability to do this with my mind and thoughts. So do you. Paul was teaching the early Christians to move their minds to a different place. Imagine taking your mind and placing it on something solid. Where you place it will determine how well it is supported. When we place our thoughts and minds on the solid foundation of God's Word and the bigger picture of God's plan, we are secure, solid, and able to live from a place of truth and peace.

Our minds are powerful. When we think repeated thoughts, research tell us that our brain forms neural pathways. The apostle Paul was teaching that because we have been risen with Christ, what we set our minds on is important. It takes courage to let go of values and habits that don't agree with God's will and adopt a new mindset built upon truth from Scripture. The choice is ours—biblical view of life or carnal view of life.

Today I will remember
- Where I set my mind is important.
- Setting my mind on worldly things will make the desire for the world stronger.
- Setting my mind on things above will make my desire for Jesus stronger.

Lord, it is so easy for me to get caught up in social media
scrolling and all the latest news events. May I set my
mind on things above and find new strength in doing so.

HE IS OVER ALL THINGS IN MY LIFE

Guard my life, for I am faithful to you; save your
servant who trusts in you. You are my God.

PSALM 86:2

A custody case accusing me of things I never did caught me off guard and sent me spinning. I had never been in a situation like this before and didn't know what to do—cry, scream, resist—all the negative emotions flooded me with frustration and fear. Tenderly God spoke to my heart that He was with me, and He knew the truth. As I went through the motions of a humiliating psychological evaluation, He kept reminding me that He was with me. I had a simple prayer on repeat: "You are my God, and I trust You."

The day the court evaluator cleared me in front of the courtroom with glowing remarks of all the good she discovered about me and my children during the evaluation, my heart leaped for joy. Yes, I wanted to be vindicated, but it was more than that. My heart swelled inside with a knowledge that it was God who protected me, guarded my mental stability through such a crazy ordeal, and kept me from lashing out to hurt the one who was viciously trying to hurt me.

Where in your life do you need to know that God has you? Things might look crazy on the surface, but underneath it all God is working on your behalf as you continue to stay devoted to Him and continue to trust Him. He is a God who saves. Be encouraged.

Today I will remember:
• God guards my life—He watches over me in order to protect me.
• I am to remain devoted to Him—loyal.
• He is a God who saves.

Lord, throughout the years I have watched You take hard things and make
them holy places of remembering Your faithfulness. My greatest desire is to
remain loyal to You and trust You to guard me every step of the journey.

COURAGEOUS FAITH IN BAD NEWS

Even though I walk through the darkest valley, I will fear no evil.
PSALM 23:4

It happened so fast, as bad things often do. A high fever led to a trip to the emergency room, which led to my husband being hospitalized. The man who never gets sick—ever—spent five long days sicker than I've ever seen anyone. After initial tests were run, the words lung tumor kept rising to the surface. Since both our fathers died of lung cancer, the thought of history repeating itself was terrifying to me. But it wasn't terrifying to him. He kept repeating, "I am a man of faith. If I can't have faith in the hard times, then I have had no faith at all." He meant every word.

How do we have courageous faith in hard situations? Simplistically we read in Hebrews that "faith is confidence in what we hope for and assurance about what we do not see."[164] It's not confidence in what we see in front of us, because frankly oftentimes what is before us can be alarming, unwelcome, and confusing. Faith is being assured that God is able beyond what we see. It is being confident that God is able, God is willing, and God is working.

Within a few days, the diagnosis was lung cancer. It's surreal hearing that word related to you or someone you love. But courageous faith informed my sweet man that it was just a word, and that God was bigger. As I write this, tears are close because for reasons unknown to the doctors, the tumor has been shrinking without any treatment. So we wait for scans in a few months. Nothing has changed for my husband—he had courage when this started and has courage as he waits. He is learning to fear no evil, despite trial and diagnosis. I am gaining courage daily because of his example. How can you begin walking in courage today? What hard thing can you trust God has even if it looks bad in the present?

Today I will remember:
• God is with me in each dark valley.
• I will not fear, because He will never leave me.
• Faith is confidence in a God who is near and able to move mountains.

Lord, I want to have the kind of faith that gives me courage in every situation—
A faith so confident in Your power and care that I lose my cares in trusting You.

---

164 Hebrews 11:1.

COURAGE TO LIVE WHAT WE BELIEVE

Only let us live up to what we have already attained.
PHILIPPIANS 3:16

We can believe things in our heads but have no idea how to practically walk them out in real life. Believing is the head knowing truth, while living it out is putting feet and steps to the truths we have carried around with us. Personally, I find it is easy to "believe" and have theories based on that belief system. I find it much harder to have the courage to walk the truth out when the rubber meets the road in my life and things are much harder than I ever anticipated.

How do we walk out the truths God has shown us? Do we fake it? Do we stuff our feelings and problems? No, in Christ we are free to bring all of our cares and needs to Jesus, and He promises to care about every single one.

1 Peter 5:7 tells us "Cast all your anxiety on him because he cares for you."

This instruction from Scripture is a good place to begin the practice of walking out truth in real life. Are you troubled? Take that trouble to God. Are you doubting His care for you? Claim this truth—He cares for me!

Today I will remember:
- It takes courage to walk out the truths I believe.
- God invites me to throw all my cares His way.
- Confident faith is developed one truth, one step, at a time.

Lord, May I remember the things You have shown me and live my life accordingly. Thank You for inviting me to give all that troubles me to You and to believe that You care about every detail.

RESTORING LOVE

*He restores my soul; He leads me in
the paths of righteousness for His name's sake.*
PSALM 23:3, NKJV

I get distracted. Often whatever is distracting me leads me down a path away from not only God, but also whatever is most important in life. Caught up in my own problems, or sometimes even successes, leaves me exhausted and in need of restoration. Psalm 23 contains just six verses, but they are powerhouse promises. *Restore* here in the original Hebrew means to return or bring back, while *soul* in the original can mean mind, emotions, heart, body, desire, or appetites. We often think of our soul as the spiritual side of us and might not have connected with this verse as the powerful promise that it is. God restores us—mind, will, and emotions—where it counts!

God brings us back to His original design. He brings about a return to what He had planned from the beginning. Restoration is an ongoing work of God's Spirit in our lives When I have restored old furniture, it didn't happen overnight but over time. It wasn't easy. It took work and intention. In soul restoration, it is God's work and intention—one step at a time.

Psalm 23 is a reminder that God is working. He makes me, leads me, restores me, and guides me. He is with me, comforting me, anointing my head, and following me all the days of my life. I agree with the psalmist—my cup overflows.

Today I will remember:
• God is working in me to bring me back to His design for me.
• He returns my mind back to health.
• He guides me in healing paths.

*Lord, thank You for being my Shepherd, the One who is always
working to bring me health in every area. May I believe the power
of Your ability to restore my life and guide me on right paths.*

—⸱§⸱⟨⟩⸱3⸱—

HIS FAITHFUL PROVISION

For the word of the LORD is right
and true; he is faithful in all he does.
PSALM 33:4

A friend's husband traveled every month. Though not prone to fear, one night she heard noises that freaked her out. The next day she decided she needed a dog. After praying and then making a list of what she wanted, she headed off to the local animal shelter. On the way she even named her dog. She just knew that God was going to provide. At the kennel, the staff laughed at her list and said it would not be possible to find all the things she listed at an animal shelter. Another employee looked at her list and said, "Hey, we do have a new dog that was dropped off named Isabel that matches this." What they didn't know is that Isabel was the name my friend had already picked. It was her mother's name—Bella for short.

Within one hour my friend and Bella were on their way home, where she has slept at the foot of the bed every night since. She barks when appropriate and cuddles all the time. God knew exactly what my friend needed.

God is faithful in all He does—not just in some things, but in all things. The verse before this says, "It is fitting...to praise him."[165] What do you have on your list of needs today? God knows exactly what you need and will give you what is best. Start by praising Him and then praying—giving Him all the details. Either your desires and detailed wish list will shift or you will be given a Bella too.

Today I will remember:
- God is always faithful.
- I can go to Him with every need.
- His Word is true, and He delights in giving good gifts.

Lord, thank You for caring about the details of my life.
May I trust You to be faithful in all things.

---

165 Psalm 33:1.

FINISH THE COURSE

*I want to know Christ—yes, to know the power of his resurrection and
participation in his sufferings, becoming like him in his death...Not that
I have already obtained all this, or have arrived at my goal, but I press on.*

PHILIPPIANS 3:10, 12

Sometimes we need a road map for living with courage. It's hard to wait for things to get better, for life to fall into place, or for grief to subside. Being spiritually focused is especially important in these times. Looking to God will change the way you go through the circumstance. The apostle Paul didn't only want to know the upside of following Christ, but also the suffering side. Does this mean he wished for sufferings? Surely not. But in his sufferings, he wanted to walk the way that Jesus did—"he humbled himself in obedience to God."[166]

Paul taught the church to not only look after themselves, but to take an interest in others, too. To humble themselves before God and go where He leads. To take courage that God is working. And to live in moments of difficulty without complaining or arguing—pouring out their lives like an offering to God.[167]

When we realize that in the daily battle we can be obedient and pour out our lives before God, we live differently. Ask yourself, Do I quit? Or do I finish the course, believing I am really going to be OK?

Today I will remember:
- It takes courage to trust God is at work in hard things.
- I can grow to know Christ more in my sufferings.
- When I pour out my life before Him, my focus changes.

*Lord, I want to know You more intimately. I humble myself
before You in this current challenge, trusting You to
help me to die to myself so I can be more alive in You.*

---

166   Philippians 2:8, NLT.
167   Philippians 2:4, 8, 13, 17.

LIVING EMPOWERED

Be on your guard; stand firm in the faith; be courageous; be strong.
1 CORINTHIANS 16:13

I have ten grandchildren, and six are boys. Shields, swords, and other forms of battle are a regular thing when they are together. It's fun to see how engaged little boys get in a good old-fashioned sword fight. They watch their opponent's every move, strong and on guard. A few minutes later they are laughing and loving each other. We can learn a lot from watching children and their natural play.

In Paul's final instructions for the church in Corinth, he told them to stay awake, be vigilant, and have full assurance in Christ—to live empowered. Then, in the next breath he said, "Do everything with love."[168] Those seem like contradictory commands, but they coexisted in Paul's ministry just as they coexist in my grandsons' play. Paul had the courage to not only stand strong in Christ, but also to stay committed to loving others. Am I living this out in how I treat others? Do they sense God's love in my actions and attitudes? When I focus on others, I find myself staying alert, being firm, and living empowered in the Lord. It takes courage to be less self-focused.

Today I will remember:
- I am to stand guard—to be awake and vigilant.
- I am to be firm in faith—assured of Christ and His faithfulness.
- I am to live empowered—with strength and courage.

Lord, may I live by this wisdom that Paul left
with the church—remaining alert and focused.

GOD IS NOT FINISHED YET

So do not throw away your confidence; it will be richly rewarded.
HEBREWS 10:35

Have you ever been so discouraged that you wanted to give up? Me too. I felt God's call at nineteen. Fifteen years later, I wanted to give up. I had tried living pretty, perfect, and polished for Jesus—and it left me a divorced pastor's wife with my dreams unraveled. In my mind, I was a disqualified loser. At a going away party, the women I worked with presented me with gifts of money and a large envelope containing all I had written for Design4Living, the women's ministry. I insisted it was their ministry, not mine. They insisted God was going to use it again, and He would do it through me. That night, in tears, I tossed the envelope in the trash. I was sure God was done with me. Fast-forward seventeen years and much healing later, the first Design4Living conference was sold out within days of the tickets going public. As I met Amy Grant in the green room, I felt like I was in a dream. Only God could have done it.

As I looked at a gathering of over 1,500 women that weekend, I thought of the brokenhearted, rejected pastor's wife who was confident of only two things—that I was unloved and that God was done with me. I had thrown away my confidence, but God kept coming after me to restore and rebuild me on a new foundation of His love. No more pretty, perfect, and polished. Life on love's foundation was about three different P's—position, passion, and purpose. As I began to heal and know my position as His, I began growing in passion to serve Him and became convinced He has a purpose for me.

Friend, turn to Jesus with all of who you are and watch Him make more through you than you could imagine. He is the God who restores and rebuilds.

Today I will remember:
- God invites me into courageous living.
- My confidence needs to shift away from me and on to God.
- Confidence in God is rewarded.

Lord, thank You for Your faithfulness. May my confidence
and expectation always be in You and Your love.

NEW VISION

Let us fix our eyes on Jesus, the author and perfecter of our faith, who for the joy set before him endured the cross...Consider him who endured such opposition...so that you will not grow weary and lose heart.

HEBREWS 12:2-3, NIV 1984

I have worn corrective lenses since my early 20s. I'm amazed how much my vision can mess me up when my contacts are clouded, or when a lens is scratched or dirty. If my lens isn't right, I see things differently. When I'm not seeing correctly, I get headaches and feel off all day long. Our vision is extremely important to our physical well-being. In the same way, our spiritual and emotional vision is important to our spiritual and emotional well-being. I think we can all agree that our eyes, our focus, and our attention are often in need of adjustment. We scatter our focus every which way, when what we need is to focus on Jesus and His faithfulness. When our focus is off, we walk around blind instead of living with the gift of sight.

To fix our eyes means to put in order, adjust, or arrange—or to hold the eye's attention in one place. We need to learn how to fix our eyes on Jesus, holding our attention on faith in Him and His ways. Attention fixed on Jesus gives us courage. When we have courage, we live differently.

Oswald Chambers has said "Being born of the spirit means much more than we usually think. It gives us new vision and keeps us absolutely fresh for everything through the never-ending supply of the life of God."[169]

Today I will remember:
- My attention and focus are to be on Jesus.
- When my attention is rightly focused, I have courage.
- When my focus is off, everything is off, and I lose heart.

Lord, may I fix my eyes on You, giving attention to Your presence around me.

---

169 Oswald Chambers, *My Utmost for His Highest*, January 20.

TRIUMPHING OVER FEAR

They will have no fear of bad news;
their hearts are steadfast, trusting in the LORD.

PSALM 112:7

Ten years ago, I was having breast cancer surgery. I remember all the details leading up to the diagnosis like it was yesterday. The trickling waterfall and instrumental music quietly filling the pretty, pink, spa-like room where women waited to have a needle driven into their breast. Then the agonizing week waiting for results. Then the call. It was surreal then, and it's surreal now. Yet despite the fear, God was with me.

The waiting is always the hardest part of any trial. It's in the waiting that we must find the courage to stand firm in who He is and how He loves. Imagine having no fear of bad news because we know the good news. Scripture tells us, "The steadfast love of the LORD never ceases; his mercies never come to an end; they are new every morning; great is your faithfulness."[170] That word *steadfast* is key, because it means fixed, firm, and unchanging. Though we go through difficult things in this life, we can remain fixed on the truth of God's faithfulness, firm in the belief that He is good even if life is hard, and unchanging in our conviction that we can trust His love covering us.

As Nelson Mandela once said, "I learned that courage was not the absence of fear, but the triumph over it. The brave man is not he who does not feel afraid, but he who conquers that fear."[171]

Today I will remember:
- It is possible to live trusting God's love.
- Courage looks to God instead of fear.
- Regardless of circumstances, I can be courageous if I trust the Lord.

Lord, Your love is so great that it's hard to comprehend.
I trust Your love and ask You to give me a mind that remembers
the reality of Your love—especially in waiting seasons.

---

170 Lamentations 3:22-23, ESV.
171 CNN, "Mandela in His Own Words," https://edition.cnn.com/2008/WORLD/africa/06/24/mandela.quotes/.

TURBULENCE CALMED

Peace I leave with you; my peace I give you. I do not give to you as the world gives. Do not let your hearts be troubled and do not be afraid.

JOHN 14:27

Have you had seasons when everything hit you all at once? Just when you think the last crisis was the worst, the bomb of circumstance comes hurtling your way again. In our humanness, it would be impossible to have peace in some of the turbulence we find ourselves in. But when we are turned toward Christ, He speaks peace to our spirits. "The Spirit gives life; the flesh counts for nothing. The words I have spoken to you—they are full of the Spirit and life."172

When we are not right with God, our mind turns toward ourselves when things are hard—and there is no peace there. We can become easily troubled when we don't take His faithfulness into account. But when we are looking to Jesus, we can receive His peace and make a choice to turn from the churning of troubling thoughts that bring fear. We must remember that Jesus gave us His peace as a gift.

Will we have the courage to open the gift and receive His peace? Can we turn away from our obsessive thoughts and look into the face of the One who gives us courage? Friends, it's possible, because Jesus said, "Do not let your hearts be troubled and do not be afraid." We can choose Him.

Today I will remember:
- Jesus gives peace.
- The world gives confusion and fear.
- I can choose to look to Jesus, receiving His peace.

Lord, forgive me for the times I am self-focused and filled with doubts and fears. May I learn to receive from You the wonderful peace that You have left for us. I choose You today.

EVERY THOUGHT CAPTIVE

The weapons we fight with are not the weapons of the world.
2 CORINTHIANS 10:4

We have developed habitual ways of dealing with life. Most of us didn't grow up learning about demolishing strongholds and have learned to fight battles according to the wisdom of this world. The problem is, we are in a spiritual battle—and spiritual battles must be fought with spiritual weapons. "For though we live in the world, we do not wage war as the world does."[173] Paul goes on to talk about the battle being waged in our minds: "We take captive every thought to make it obedient to Christ."[174]

How do we demolish the strongholds in our thinking? We do this by making our thoughts obedient to Christ. This means aligning our thoughts with the truths in God's Word. When truth is appropriated, it touches every aspect of the heart and we are emotionally transformed.

The psalmist said, "May my meditation be pleasing to him."[175] Meditation is simply focused thinking. If you know how to worry, you know how to focus your thoughts. Our thought life is shaped less by external events in life and more by how we perceive them. In other words, when the battle is causing us to doubt and lose courage, or when we are spinning with negative thoughts, do we keep them spinning or stomp their fire out with truth from Scripture? It's our choice. Unchallenged thoughts are part of the reason we are discouraged rather than living in courage.

Today I will remember:
• I am not of the world, and my battles aren't either.
• The enemy is after my thoughts to discourage me.
• Focusing my mind on the truths in God's Word is a battle-winning strategy.

Lord, may I challenge every thought that does not align with truth,
bringing my mind and focus into agreement with the Scriptures.

---

173 2 Corinthians 10:3.
174 2 Corinthians 10:5.
175 Psalm 104:34.

THE COURAGE TO LIVE IN PEACE

If it is possible, as far as it depends on you, live at peace with everyone.
ROMANS 12:18

I have lived through in-laws, out-laws, and ex-laws. I have been divorced and remarried and in court more times than I want to remember. I usually assume it's just not possible to be at peace with people who are not reasonable, don't agree with me, or choose to be against me.

What if I am not the one creating the problem? What if the other party is unreasonable or unkind? Are they still included in this "everyone" clause? Yep, I am afraid so. It's not about them. The Scripture is talking to me about *my* responsibility. Ugh! This word *possible* can mean if you are able, if you could, or if you are strong. Look at yourself as being the one who stays in a position of peace.

Jesus, when He was talking about the rich entering heaven, used the illustration of a camel going through the eye of a needle and said, "With man this is impossible, but with God all things are possible."[176] The same is true in our relationships. Somethings seem impossible, but with God all things—including living at peace—are possible. All. Things. Are. Possible.

Today I will remember:
- I am to be more concerned of my response to situations than the situation itself.
- As I take my part and depend on God, all things are possible.
- It is God's best for me to learn to live at peace with everyone.

Lord, I look to You and depend on You to show me how to pay attention
to my responses more than the other party when there are problems.
Show me in each situation what I can do to promote peace.

---

176 Matthew 19:26.

COURAGEOUS HUMILITY

Confess your sins to each other and pray for each other so that you may be healed. The prayer of a righteous person is powerful and effective.

JAMES 5:16

We were made for relationship. Part of honest relationship is being able to admit when we are wrong, ask for help when we are struggling, and pray for each other. But because we live in a world that shines the light on filtered pictures, curated moments, and notable accomplishments, it's hard to be eager to share our faults or areas of brokenness.

To confess is to disclose our faults or admit something that might seem damaging about ourselves. It is making it known that we do not have it all together. Obviously this isn't safe to do with people we aren't in relationship with, but when we are, confession, prayer, and healing should be part of the package.

That in turn brings us to humility. It's hard for a proud person to admit they have been wrong. Scripture tells us clearly that God opposes the proud but gives grace to the humble.[177] I don't want to be at arm's length from God because of my pride. Today is the day to decide to walk toward more humility of heart and deeper connection with others.

Today I will remember:
- I am to admit my sins and shortcomings.
- I am to ask for prayer and pray for others.
- Healing comes when I pray and live in relationship and community.

Lord, forgive me for the walls that I put up and the fronts I create that keep people at arm's length and prevent them from truly knowing me. In a world of perfect photos and curated images, may I walk in humble honesty before You and the people in my life.

THE COURAGE TO ADMIT I CAN'T

For we have no power to face this vast army that is attacking us.
We do not know what to do, but our eyes are on you.

2 CHRONICLES 20:12

I was driving in downtown Pleasanton, California when a distressing call came. Alarmed, I pulled to the side of the road and told myself to breathe. The truth was, there was nothing I could do to fix things. The lack of control caused my anxiety to rise to new levels. Remembering the story of King Jehoshaphat brought focus to my frantic feelings. Jehoshaphat was alarmed by his problem and prayed to God, admitting his weakness. He admitted he had no power to face the problem.

It takes courage to admit that we don't have the power face some things. We like ourselves to strong, but let's face it, under some pressures we are weak. The best we can do is echo these words: "I don't know what to do, but my eyes are upon You."

That day I began praying today's verse. I repeatedly said, "I don't know what to do, but my eyes are on you." I wanted to meddle, but my hands in the mix would only make it worse. So instead, I focused on what I could do—put my eyes on God. Every time the twinge of anxiety came, I put my eyes on God. The problem came and went, as problems usually do. But I had taken a stand of courage to truly trust God would handle the situation without my fingerprints on it. I learned a lot about my weakness, God's strength, and the courage to trust God until the storm passed.

Today I will remember:
• It takes courage to admit I am powerless.
• Life's problems sometimes feel like an attack.
• When we don't know what to do, we can put our eyes on Jesus.

Lord, grant me the courage to quickly fix my eyes on You
when life hits hard and my emotions are shaken.

THE BATTLE IS THE LORD'S

*Do not be afraid or discouraged because of this vast
army. For the battle is not yours, but God's.*
2 CHRONICLES 20:15

Wherever we go, we leave imprints—on doorknobs, dishes, and books. But leaving our imprint where it's not supposed to be invites trouble. God clearly told King Jehoshaphat that the battle was not his. His words were part tender—don't be afraid or discouraged—and part corrective—it's not your battle. God was giving a charge to take up courage and let fear drop to the side because He had a plan for rescue. Why is it so hard to receive this encouragement from God? Do you ever find yourself responding, "Oh, thanks, Lord, but I've got it"?

Why on earth do we want to fight the battle? It takes courage to drop the fear of having to do it all and choose to let God be God and fight the battle for us. The thing King Jehoshaphat had to do was to take his position and stand firm.[178] What does that mean for us in our battles? Taking our position is standing in our position as God's beloved. In that place of identity we stand, trusting in our deliverer because He takes care of those He loves. He fights our battles. We just have to take that position and stand firm. Not having the answers and still standing firm takes courageous faith. It's faith in a God we cannot see, believing He can do what we can't do.

Today I will remember:
- The battle is God's, not mine.
- I am not to be afraid, because He has me.
- I am to take up courage and stand firm in my position as His beloved.

*Lord, may I learn to let go of the reins quickly
and trust that You are battling for me.*

---

178 2 Chronicles 20:17-22.

THE COURAGE TO LET IT GO

Without wood a fire goes out;
without a gossip a quarrel dies down.
PROVERBS 26:20

Have you ever had a friend or relative who loved to stoke a fire, playing with it to keep it burning? There's a name for that—pyromaniac. They love starting fires and keeping them going. Solomon speaks of keeping the flames of a quarrel hot by adding wood and fanning the flame. In the moment we don't realize that having to have the last word is adding fuel to the fire. Nor do we give much thought to how our reckless conversations that turn into gossip are actually building a bonfire that is going to burn someone or something up. Some people are skilled at both arguing and gossiping and don't realize that what they are doing is hurting rather than helping.

It takes courage to stop. This is where biblical wisdom comes in. God's Word directs us into what will work for us and what won't. But it takes courage to admit that God knows best and heed the warning of Scripture. If no wood is added, the fire dies out.

Let's be women who are courageous enough to not fall prey to gossip, idle talking, or arguing. Walk away, don't text back in the heat of the moment, don't put yourself in a position of telling tales and spreading gossip. If we heed God's Word, we won't be burning down lives, marriages, families, friendships, and churches. Quarrels don't happen on their own; there needs to be someone bringing the wood and adding it to the smoldering heap.

Today I will remember:
- I can be part of the problem.
- It takes courage to let a fire go out.
- It takes courage to turn away from gossiping.

Lord, may I listen to wisdom and have the courage to back
away from anything that will add fuel to a relational fire.

—⟨⟩—

COURAGE TO FACE THE PAST

*But Moses said to God, "Who am I that I should go to Pharaoh and bring
the Israelites out of Egypt?"And God said, "I will be with you. And this will
be the sign to you that it is I who have sent you: When you have brought
the people out of Egypt, you will worship God on this mountain."*

EXODUS 3:11-12

Moses was a leader, but he still had insecurities and fears. He faced his insecurity by
responding to God's call to go back to Egypt where his fears began. What motivated
him was the vision of God working through him to save his people, the Jews, from
the suffering they were experiencing. It took courage for Moses to trust God in this.
But God promised that He would be with him through the journey. In turn, Moses
bravely inspired the Jews to follow his lead through the parting of the Red Sea to
escape the Egyptians. His courage gave others courage.

My friend Noel had spent years distanced from family. God was leading him
to return to a troubled family relationship that he had spent years running from.
He knew that God would be with him. After years of distance, he went back and
apologized for how he chose to be bitter instead of resolving the issues that were
separating the family. The conversation went well, and as a result there was healing.
It took courage to face past hurts, but without the courage to face it down, there
would never have been repair. What are some unresolved things that you have
avoided? How has the fear of rejection or insecurity held you back?

Today I will remember:
- Insecurity can keep us from answering God's call.
- God calls us to do things that make us face our fears.
- God will be with us as we follow His lead.

*Lord, grant me the courage to follow wherever
You lead, regardless of my insecurities or fears.*

THE COURAGE TO FACE THE IMPOSSIBLE

*[David replied,] "The LORD who rescued me from the paw of the lion and
the paw of the bear will rescue me from the hand of this Philistine."*
1 SAMUEL 17:37

Publishing a book is nearly impossible. So it seemed, twenty years ago. I wrote a Bible study for the women at our church that was wildly fruitful. We started with 50 copies and printed 700 in the first month. The women wanted to see it published. But I didn't know if a publisher would be interested. It turned out they weren't. Every manuscript was returned to me.

A year later I got a call—a publisher wanted it! But after a feasibility study, they had second thoughts. I had no platform, no famous friends, and no endorsers. Our women prayed. In the end, a contract was signed. It felt very much like I was David going up with my little slingshot to the impossible giant of the publishing industry. Though Christian publishing was not an enemy to fight, it was an obstacle too big for me. Yet God did it. That contract ended up being the first of many.

David had courage because God protected him from danger countless times. He acted on faith to fight Goliath with a slingshot, and God gave him victory. As a result, the whole army fought at his side, and with God's help they won a great battle that day.

What battles could be won in your life if you walked courageously into them with God? What are you afraid to tackle because you believe it would be impossible?

Today I will remember:
- I might be small, but God is big.
- I might feel like nobody, but God is somebody.
- God can do through me what I could never do by myself.

*Lord, may I trust You to work the impossible in and
through my life and trust You for the outcome.*

THE COURAGE TO TAKE RISKS

Go, gather together all the Jews who are in Susa, and fast for me. Do not eat or drink for three days, night or day. I and my attendants will fast as you do. When this is done, I will go to the king, even though it is against the law. And if I perish, I perish.

ESTHER 4:16

Esther risked her life to persuade her husband, King Xerxes, to foil the plans of Haman to annihilate the Jews in their country. She was motivated by the faith her Uncle Mordecai taught her. She would be fulfilling the call to save God's people through her. Esther prayed and fasted, putting her trust in God for courage to plead with King Xerxes to protect her people. Her faithful sacrifice paved the way for the Jews in her country to stand up against attacks on them and fight back to protect one another. God brought about a great victory for them that day.

I have a friend, Eileen, who has been like a Mordecai to me. She encourages me to stay true to God and align my life with His Word. She's helped me navigate so many things, especially female feelings of insecurity and hurt when I was rejected and cast aside by friends. Some of the risks I have dared to take have been because of the courage she imparted to me.

Who are people that God has placed in your life to help you live according to His Word, like Mordecai did for Esther? In the difficult situations in your life, have you prayed and fasted to put your trust in God's plan?

Today I will remember:
- God directs His people to take risks.
- Where God leads, He will provide.
- Without faith, it's impossible to please God.

Lord, may I follow You even if it's risky or
I feel unsure. Teach me to trust Your faithfulness.

THE COURAGE TO NOT GIVE IN

When Daniel knew that the document had been signed, he went to his house where he had windows in his upper chamber open towards Jerusalem. He got down on his knees three times a day and prayed and gave thanks before his God, as he had done previously.

DANIEL 6:10, ESV

Christians have always faced the battle to remain faithful to God despite the oppression around them. Twenty-five centuries ago, Daniel could have lost all courage. He found himself facing politically motivated administrators who tried to trap Daniel by manipulating King Darius to sign into law a regulation that would put to death anyone who worshipped any God other than him. Daniel stood on his conviction to pray to God only, in spite of the consequence of being thrown into a den of lions as punishment.

Daniel's courage grew through praying three times a day even though it was against the law. He made no attempt to hide his daily prayer routine from his enemies in the government. Once discovered, he was thrown into the lion's den, with the King saying, "May your God, whom you serve continually, rescue you."[179]

The next day the king found Daniel rescued from the lions. Daniel testified, "My God sent his angel, and he shut the mouths of the lions. They have not hurt me, because I was found innocent in his sight."[180] His devotion to God inspired King Darius, a foreign king, to write to all nations to fear and revere the God Daniel worshipped.

Today I will remember:
• God calls us to stand firm in opposition.
• When faced with fear of consequence, God directs us to trust Him.
• God will protect us when what we are doing is to honor Him.

Lord, may I have the courage of Daniel and the faith of one who knows that You are the One true God.

---

179 Daniel 6:16.
180 Daniel 6:22.

THE COURAGE TO BELIEVE

But to Hannah he gave a double portion because he loved her, and the
Lord had closed her womb...Her rival kept provoking her in order to
irritate her...Her rival provoked her till she wept and would not eat.

1 SAMUEL 1:5-7

All Hannah wanted was baby, but the Lord had closed her womb. One day, Hannah went to the Temple and cried out to the Lord. Eli the priest saw her, and, thinking she was drunk, he rebuked her. Hannah told him that she wasn't drunk, but she was praying. Despite what Eli or anyone thought about her, she sought the Lord and poured out her heart to Him. Hannah wasn't afraid to go before the Lord with her petition, and we can't be either. Hannah is an excellent example of persistence in prayer. Scripture tells us, "In the course of time Hannah became pregnant and gave birth to a son. She named him Samuel, saying, 'Because I asked the Lord for him.'"[181]

It took almost five years and two miscarriages to finally have my first child. When you are young, you plan the age you'd like to start a family and it happens. But for some with fertility issues like myself, the courage to believe for a child was a long road of monthly disappointment.

We are encouraged to approach the throne of grace boldly. Stop what you're doing right now and offer up your petition. Tell the Lord boldly, yet reverently, your heart's desire and believe by faith that He will answer your prayer in His perfect timing.

Today I will remember:
- The Lord remembers me and sees my desires.
- Persistent prayer honors God.
- It takes courage to believe in the face of disappointment.

Lord, give me courage to believe You for everything I need
in this life and a heart that seeks You though disappointment.

---

181 1 Samuel 1:20.

COURAGE TO LEAVE THE FAMILIAR

The LORD had said to Abram, "Go from your country,
your people and your father's household to the land I will show you."
GENESIS 12:1

God's plans are sometimes hard to understand. And yet, when we follow Him into unknown or uncomfortable territory, He never leaves us there alone—He is with us. His plan is being worked out in and around us at all times. I have only moved three times in my life, but each time was hard. Leaving behind those you did life with takes a toll, and rebuilding takes time. It takes courage to leave the familiar and have faith that God is leading.

Abram knew that kind of courage. Imagine living with your family and friends, and suddenly hearing the Lord tell you to leave it all behind to move to an unnamed, unfamiliar place. That's precisely what happened to Abram, later named Abraham, when the Lord told him to leave his country, his relatives, and his father's house. Abraham obeyed the Lord's voice and became the father of a great nation. "I will make you into a great nation, and I will bless you; I will make your name great, and you will be a blessing. I will bless those who bless you, and whoever curses you I will curse; and all peoples on earth will be blessed through you."[182]

We, too, are called by God. We are called to do great things for the Kingdom of God. We are called to leave what's familiar to embark upon a journey with the Lord. When we obey God, He uses us in surprising ways, and we can be a blessing to many people.

Today I will remember:
- I am to be more attached to following God than my plans.
- God leads us away from the familiar into a new assignment.
- God blesses those who listen and follow Him.

Lord, may I have courage to follow You into the unfamiliar.

182 Genesis 12:2-3.

COURAGE TO BELIEVE GOD HAS A PLAN

Joseph's master took him and put him in prison...But while Joseph was there in the prison, the Lord was with him; he showed him kindness and granted him favor in the eyes of the prison warden.

GENESIS 39:20-21

I like to know there is a plan. The in-between times or meantimes are some of the hardest to get through. If I think the meantimes are just mean and have no real value, then I get discouraged and feel sorry for myself. But if I believe that all the challenges I have faced have redeeming value for spiritual growth and development, I have courage.

When I think of plans that don't make sense, Joseph comes to mind. God's plan was to make him the ruler of Egypt, but in the meantime, he went through all kinds of crazy things get there. God's Ruler of Egypt course outline might have looked like this:[183]

STEP 1: Use your gifts, get mocked and ridiculed by your family.
STEP 2: Obey your father, get beat up by your brothers.
STEP 3: Get sold into slavery, spend 13 years as a slave.
STEP 4: Resist temptation, go to jail.
STEP 5: Use your gifts, spend an extra two years in jail.
STEP 6: Become the Ruler of Egypt.

We know the end of the story. But when you are in the story, it's easy to think that God has forgotten you or something has gone wrong. We must remember that God has His own timing; He is not on our schedule. God always has a plan, even when we can't understand it or we don't agree with it, and God is always working—and His plan will be accomplished.

Today I will remember:
• God has a plan.
• I might not understand the plan.
• In the end, His plan will be accomplished.

Lord, give me faith to believe in the bigger picture and trust in Your greater plan.

---

183   Bob Cull, "Some Things I have Learned about God from the Life of Joseph" (Earthen Vessel Productions, 1997), 4.

November

LIVING GRATEFULLY

"Eucharisteo—thanksgiving—always precedes the miracle."
Ann Voskamp[184]

184 Ann Voskamp, *One Thousand Gifts: A Dare to Life Fully Right Where You Are* (Grand
    Rapids: Zondervan, 2010), 35.

IN ALL THINGS

Rejoice always, pray continually, give thanks in all circumstances.
1 THESSALONIANS 5:16-18

The apostle Paul didn't say to give thanks in *some* circumstances, but in *all* circumstances. It sounds easy—find joy, pray, and thank God. But in real everyday life these words are not so simple. There are circumstances that are not praiseworthy. Much of what we find ourselves "in" is something we would never choose and seems unfair. Giving thanks is not always easy.

How we handle the everyday stuff reveals a lot about who we are and what we believe. Often the heat is turned up so we can be refined and transformed. It helps if we remember that though all things are not good, God is always good—and therefore we can always give thanks. It also helps if we focus on the truth that there is purpose in all things, and in all things, God is with us. We can thank God when we are reminded that Jesus is working in us through all circumstances.

The next time you are in a hard spot, pray. Then remember that Jesus is over you, covering you. Finally, give thanks in the middle of each and every situation, because by giving thanks you are saying, "God, I trust you." By doing these three things, we are aligning our hearts, minds, and lives with the Word of God that tells us these three things are important.

Today I will remember:
• Pray always.
• Find joy when looking up.
• Give thanks in everything.

Lord, thanking You in all things does not come naturally. I can praise You in the good but often grumble in the challenges. My life would be different if I focused on living by these three things. Give me the grace to make that change.

GOD'S WILL

Give thanks in all circumstances, for this is God's will for you in Christ Jesus.
1 THESSALONIANS 5:18

Most of us want to know God's will for us. We overthink, processing circumstances, opportunities, and facts over and over again to determine what God's will is. There is a real need for direction in life, but here we get a glimpse of the foundation of God's will. If we are open, we can understand God's will without much processing, because it's straightforward— God's will is for us to live in gratitude, thankfulness, and appreciation.

There are three keys to this verse:
• Thankful
• In all circumstances
• God's will

Thankful in all circumstances means everything—not some things, not the easy things, but all things—the good, the hard, and the ugly.

How can we do that? The ending of this verse is the reason we can thank God in all things—we belong to Christ Jesus. There is much in Scripture about belonging, being God's holy people, and being His possession. Because we are His, we are cared for and loved in the practical everyday things as well as the eternal. We give thanks, not just for heaven, but for God with us in our lives here on earth. He is with us, guiding, providing, and caring for us each step, each day—and so we are thankful in all things.

Today I will remember:
• God cares about my attitude.
• God calls me into a place of thankfulness.
• God can use all circumstances for my good—and therefore I can thank Him in all things.

Lord, I need some work in this area. Remind me to thank You,
to remember You, to be appreciative of Your love and care for me.
Teach me to view circumstances as temporary and my life as eternal.

━◦§ ◈ ◈ ◈ 3◦━

THE SAFETY OF GRATITUDE

*Rejoice in the Lord! It is no trouble for me to write
the same things to you again, and it is a safeguard for you.*

PHILIPPIANS 3:1

There is nothing new. Similar problems to those we faced yesterday will be repeated another day. The apostle Paul was teaching people like us who needed to hear repeated instructions. He didn't mind repetition because it was for their good. So it is no surprise that he is telling them over and over again to rejoice—or find joy—in their circumstances.

Thanking God redirects our thoughts even when we don't like our current circumstances. Rejoicing is a choice. It is something that we can practice and lean into more over time. And, just like Paul repeated this instruction to the early church, we too need to be reminded to rejoice in the Lord and find safety in trusting in His covering over the details of our lives. When faced with hard things, our response can be straight from Scripture: "Power and might are in your hand. I don't know what to do, but my eyes are on you."[185]

When the day is long and your life feels hard—turn to Jesus. When the day is awesome and you are grateful—turn to Jesus. Turning to Jesus and tuning our hearts to Him are a safety latch for our mind. I don't know about you, but I need a safety latch from wayward worrisome thoughts.

Today I will remember:
- Rejoicing in the Lord is to be part of my daily life.
- Finding joy by trusting God is something that will give me stability.
- Praising God puts a safety latch on my thoughts.

*Lord, remind me to rejoice in You—over and
over again. Protect my mind and secure my heart.*

---

185 See 2 Chronicles 20:12.

OVERFLOWING THANKS

All this is for your benefit, so that the grace that is reaching more and more people may cause thanksgiving to overflow to the glory of God.
2 CORINTHIANS 4:15

Just before the lockdown of 2020, we moved to a new state. Then the world turned upside down, and it would be months before we would meet people. My speaking calendar was cancelled, so I was bored. No friends, no restaurants, no shopping—nothing. It was just the two of us. But my husband had chosen a word for the year: grateful. It's the first time he joined me in this practice, and once he makes a decision, he sticks to it.

Because of his desire to remain grateful in 2020, nothing moved him. I would be down, and he would pick me up. I would complain, and he would help turn my thoughts around. The year came and went, and I was blessed to live with a grateful retired man who taught me more than he will ever know about choosing to live gratefully. I sometimes choose the opposite, but the Holy Spirit reins me in in much quicker since that year of practicing gratitude.

Our problems are actually a benefit because they teach us how to rely on God more fully.

We can be grumpy or grateful—it's our choice, but being grateful brings glory to God as it ushers grace into our relationships and environment every single time.

Today I will remember:
• Problems can benefit me as I learn something new.
• Being grateful is choosing thanks in the middle of uncertainty or unrest.
• Thanking God helps us, but it also brings glory to God and helps others redirect.

Lord, may I choose gratitude, thanking You in all the storms.

LIVES LIVED IN HIM

Just as you received Christ Jesus as Lord, continue to live your lives in him, rooted and built up in him...overflowing with thankfulness.
COLOSSIANS 2:6-7

Bubbles overflowed in the laundry room—a comical life lesson that what you put in matters. The life lesson isn't about the soap. It's all about how what we measure into ourselves will be what overflows out of us. If we put in negative, critical thoughts, that is what will come out. But if we put in gratefulness and dwell on the positive, then thankfulness and peace spill over. Ugly in—ugly out. Beauty in—beauty out.

There was a time not long ago when I watched home improvement shows every day. I liked seeing how things could be transformed. But I soon became dissatisfied with what I had and wanted to toss everything and start over. Since that wasn't an option, I realized I could be thankful or continue to pick everything apart. It took me a minute, but I chose to begin thanking God for what I had. This changed my focus and began to root me more firmly in the Lord. Over time we did a few affordable home improvement projects, but they weren't my focus—thanking God for His provision was.

We can't take things with us and eternity is forever. Overflowing in thankfulness is how we continue to live in Him.

Today I will remember:
• I received Christ, and now I must continue to choose to live in Him.
• Being thankful builds faith and causes my roots go deep in Him.
• To be overflowing with thanksgiving should be my goal—one day at a time.

Lord, may my life overflow as I remain grateful.
Remind me that what I put in is what will overflow out of me.

CALLED TO PEACE

Let the peace of Christ rule in your hearts, since as members
of one body you were called to peace. And be thankful.

COLOSSIANS 3:15

My friend thought she hung up the phone, but I could hear her after-call complaints about me. "She just doesn't have any good news!" she exclaimed to her husband in frustration. Our conversations were about world events, and since we didn't agree on the causes or solutions, the usual peace between us was not there. I was allowing my view to rule my heart, and she was doing the same. While all along God was still on the throne.

There will always be plenty of things to disagree about, but we can keep our relationships peaceful by focusing on the importance of trusting God in all things. We can choose to be thankful that God loves us all, even when we don't have the same opinions. Christianity is not a church country club or political party, it is a relationship with Jesus. And we are all at different points in our journey.

We have been called to peace. Let that sink in. We don't have to agree in order to live in peace. Our flesh insists on being right, and so we fight the peace. Can we agree to disagree? In a world of discord and drama, we have been called to something different.

The early Christians lived in turmoil, political and religious unrest, and these two things were held out to them—peace and thankfulness. Let's pay attention.

Today I will remember:
- The peace of God is to rule my heart—not the problems of the day.
- I affect others when I am negative, and we are part of each other.
- We are called to peace and thankfulness.

Lord, remind me to respect others. Turn my thoughts to good when
my emotions spiral down. You have called me to peace.
Teach me in practical ways how to walk in it.

PERSISTENT THANKFULNESS

I have not stopped giving thanks for you,
remembering you in my prayers.

EPHESIANS 1:16

I love my family and friends and pray for them when there is a need. But what if I didn't wait for a need to regularly thank God for them? The apostle Paul made it a practice to pray for people and also to thank God for them. I want to be more like that.

I began to thank God for the people in my life. I started looking forward to stopping at each name to thank God for all the good that came to mind. I practiced remembering the good in them, about them, and around them. The love God poured into me for each person was tangible.

Paul didn't stop at gratefulness. He prayed specifically: "I keep asking...God [to] give you the Spirit of wisdom and revelation, so that you may know him better."[186] There aren't always circumstantial needs to pray for. But we can still pray for the same things Paul prayed for—the Spirit of wisdom and revelation so that the people we love would know Jesus better. And we can pray those same things for ourselves too.

When we know Jesus more, many things don't seem as important because we realize that He has us and that we can trust Him in and through everything. So let's begin thanking God for the people in our lives and praying this simple prayer for them and for ourselves. It's the best gift we can give and will draw us into even more gratefulness.

Today I will remember:
• To make a practice of thanking God for people.
• To remember those I love in prayer on a regular basis.
• To ask that people would know Jesus better and be filled with wisdom.

Lord, I get distracted and unfocused and forget to pray.
Draw me into the practice of remembering the good in others and
praying for Your Spirit to work in them so they can know You better.

ALL THAT I NEED

The Lord is my shepherd, I lack nothing.
He makes me lie down in green pastures,
he leads me beside quiet waters.

PSALM 23:1-2

It was another day of waiting for things to change. My eyes and emotions focused on all the setbacks, while God was assuring me that I was His—and He had me. This Shepherd reality brings relief when I stay with the truth and reassure my shifting emotions that I am not walking this life alone, but have a good God who leads, guides, and protects me.

Sometimes Scripture can become so common to us that we don't take in the wonder of the rich promises and meaning. That is true of Psalm 23. It is recited at funerals but forgotten in the real roads of hard life. While it's easy to look around and find lack, we can turn that around to being grateful for the very promise that we do not lack anything we truly need. If we don't have it, we don't need it at this moment.

Sometimes life feels like it's on a time-out. But the truth is, the Shepherd looks after us—stalling and sometimes stopping us to provide rest or realignment. While we are accustomed to the rush of busy life, God knows that we need quiet and calming waters. So, when you find the brakes put on your life, remember that God is leading, guiding, and slowing you for your good. There is a lot to be grateful for in these two verses.

Today I will remember:
• I have a Shepherd, and He is good.
• I have all that I need in this moment.
• He leads me daily and through all things.

Lord, I trust that I will have what I need, when I need it. I trust that every
perceived stall is You letting me catch my breath and be refreshed for a moment.

CULTIVATE PEACE AND THANKFULNESS

*Let the peace of Christ keep you in tune with
each other... and cultivate thankfulness.*
COLOSSIANS 3:15, MSG

There's a lot of talk in the Bible about peace. And yet we live in situations that are troubling and in relationships that are not peaceful. Verses like this bring a question mark. I read this and think, *in a perfect world with perfect people, peace would reign. But the Bible is for real people in an imperfect world.*

Peace does not depend on all things being perfect. We can let the peace of Christ rule and reign in our hearts by cultivating thankful hearts. The peace is not dependent on circumstances. It doesn't say, when things are going well, let peace reign. In fact, there is no mention of circumstances at all—none, nada, zilch. Peace will rule our hearts in the direct proportion that we allow Christ into it. In fact, *let* means to permit to enter, to pass through, to give opportunity to, or to fail to prevent. When we live ungrateful lives, we are not permitting peace to enter. But when we lean into thankfulness daily, we are opening the doors wide for peace and the presence of Christ.

Today I will remember:
• I am to permit the peace of Christ to pass through my heart and into daily life.
• I am to allow peace to rule my relationships.
• I am to be thankful regardless of circumstances.

*Lord, today it occurs to me anew that I have a part in ushering
peace into my own mind and into the relationships I am
part of. May I let peace in and remember to be thankful
for all things and all people—regardless of circumstances.*

A CHANGE OF FOCUS

Give thanks to the Lord, for he is good; his love endures forever.
1 CHRONICLES 16:34

Gratitude is a popular subject and a media favorite. Many benefits are linked to being grateful, things like better sleep, enhanced immunity, lower blood pressure, and less anxiety, to name a few. Though being grateful is getting a lot of press, let's remember that there are many verses in the Bible about living grateful lives. This biblical wisdom has been around for thousands of years.

How does one go about being grateful in a life that is hard? This verse lets us in on a simplified route—thanking God because He is good and He loves us. Regardless of circumstances these are two truths that do not change. Life changes, people change, we grow older and everything changes—but God never changes.

Today, take these two truths and think about them, thanking God for them. What we focus on will be what we fall upon in good times as well as bad times. These two truths will give us a starting point of focus. Try starting your day with these two truths, stopping again at noon to remind yourself of them and ending each day with them. It makes sense that a God who came to give us abundant life would lead us to focus on life-giving truth more than fleeting things. When we make His goodness our focus, our imperfect lives suddenly seem perfect enough—God is good, and our lives can be viewed as good too.

Today I will remember:
- I will focus on thanking God for His goodness in my life.
- I will remember His love for me and rest in the truth of His unfailing love.
- I will thank God regardless of circumstances today.

Lord, prompt me to see Your goodness and recognize Your love. May I learn to live a life of gratitude, increasing my well-being and drawing closer to You.

GRATITUDE IS SPIRITUAL WARFARE

So do not fear, for I am with you; do not be dismayed,
for I am your God. I will strengthen you and help you;
I will uphold you with my righteous right hand.

ISAIAH 41:10

Gratitude is a weapon of spiritual warfare. Many times in Scripture we see how God's people thanked God in the most undesirable of circumstances—when in danger, afraid, or alone. We are stronger when we learn that being grateful is a spiritual discipline and a practice the enemy wants to tempt us away from. It's hard to be grateful when we have a victim mentality, assuming we are alone and without any help. But when we stand in the truth that God is our help, our strength, and the One who upholds us, we find a way through our hardest days and a way to enhance even the best ones.

Today, let's focus on these truths: God is with us, God will strengthen us, God will help us, and God upholds us. Memorize them and practice saying them throughout the day—thanking God for these truths. Thank someone for the way they helped you in a time of fear or distress. Thank God for the ways He provided tangibly when you weren't aware of His involvement in your life. Make thanks a focus of your prayers.

Today I will remember:
- I don't have to be afraid, because God is always with me
- I don't have to be discouraged; God will strengthen me.
- I am upheld by God, and He will help me—I can thank Him for His care.

Lord, I make life hard, but You lead me to a simpler life and path. Help me to
focus on the truth of Your care for me, thanking You frequently for who You are
and how You are with me. May gratefulness be my stance against the enemy.

⋄ ⚜ ⋄

THE BATTLE CRY OF GRATITUDE

*Jehoshaphat appointed men to sing to the Lord... "Give thanks
to the LORD, for his love endures forever." As they began to sing
and praise, the LORD sent ambushes against [their enemies].*

2 CHRONICLES 20:21-22

Maybe you have a battle that is too much for you—marital problems, financial troubles, a health battle, or relational turmoil. The battles are real. When facing a literal armed conflict, King Jehoshaphat did something interesting. Led by the Lord, he set up an army of worshippers to go before them into battle. The worshippers had a battle cry: "Give thanks to the LORD, for His love endures forever."

As they began to sing and praise, an ambush was set up against their enemies and they were defeated. Was God using thanks and praise as a war cry? I think it's safe to assume that giving thanks is spiritual warfare, and many times it's the best we can do in a situation.

If you don't have the energy to sing, turn on some worship music and let it fill your space. Sing out your own tune thanking God for His love. Watch as the battleground turns into a place of peace. Only God can do this, and He instructs us to take our positions, stand firm, and watch Him deliver us. It all comes back to His enduring love—thanking Him for this one foundational truth wins the battle before us.

Today I will remember:
• To thank God is an act of worship.
• I can thank God in particular for His enduring love.
• I will incorporate praise and thanks into my daily battles.

*Lord, there are so many battles in this life, and I often feel weak and unable to
face them. Thank You for this example in Scripture. Remind me to praise You in
the battle, resisting the forces of hell as I lift my thanks and praise to heaven.*

GRATITUDE PRECEDES THE MIRACLE

*Taking the five loaves and two fish and looking to
heaven, he gave thanks and broke the loaves.*

MATTHEW 14:19

There wasn't enough food to feed five thousand men—not to mention the additional women and children. All Jesus had was five loaves and two fish. With that impossibility before Him, He looked to God and gave thanks. Miraculously, all were fed and there were twelve baskets left over!

Giving thanks takes what is small and makes it large. It takes what is hard and makes it holy. It takes what is broken and provides fresh surrender. Jesus stopped and gave thanks. He broke the bread and looked to God with little, and it was purposed into much. We, too, can stop with our broken hearts or hard situations and lift them to God in remembrance of what Jesus did on the cross. Gratitude precedes the miracle.

Our strategy to rise from a discouraged state is to practice thanking God. Gratitude turns the little we have into abundance. Gratitude is more than saying thank you—it is a way of life that starts small but then changes perspective as the practice of being grateful pauses our entitlement and presses us into God's purposes for us.

Today I will remember:
- Sometimes it looks like I don't have enough, but gratitude enlarges what I have.
- I will stop and look to God, giving thanks even for the little I have.
- God provides, and gratitude precedes the miracle I am waiting for.

*Lord, I have spent a lifetime looking to things rather than looking to You.
I calculate what I can do based on my limited wisdom, not counting You in the
equation. Teach me to stop, break the bread, and look to heaven for all provision.*

GIVE THANKS AND REMEMBER

And he took bread, gave thanks and broke it, and gave it to them,
saying, "This is my body given for you; do this in remembrance of me."
LUKE 22:19

Many times we see Jesus stopping, looking to heaven, and thanking God. At the Last Supper, He left a clear message—*remember me*. Simple yet profound, and He knew it. When we give thanks, we are to offer gratitude based on who Christ is and all He has done on our behalf. Remembering Him is a pathway to gratitude. When we forget all that He is and how much He loves us, we sink into complaining and grumbling, forgetting to break open our hearts before Him as we look to heaven. It's easy to forget, and that is why we must make it a goal to develop gratitude, regularly stopping to appreciate what is in front of us—and trusting God with what is beyond.

Gratitude can have a transformative effect on our lives because it focuses us on the present and magnifies all that is good, creating a positive emotional space. Looking to God on a regular basis helps us recognize our value as one loved by Him and can increase our sense of being loved in a lonely world with many reasons for insecurity. Remember Him today by practicing being thankful.

Today I will remember:
• I will receive things in life by bringing them to God and giving thanks.
• I will stay focused by breaking my problems open before Him and asking for help.
• I will remember Jesus by thanking Him for who He is and how He loves.

Lord, it's easy to forget, but I long to remember. It's easy to grumble,
but I want to be grateful. Help me to start one step at a time and
cultivate a life of giving thanks and living in the moment.

GRATEFUL WOMEN REFLECT BEAUTY

As water reflects the face, so one's life reflects the heart.
PROVERBS 27:19

I can shine up my lips and put my hair in place and still have a heart that is filled with ungratefulness. When my heart is grateful, my countenance will show it. All of life ebbs and flows from the center core of the heart. If our heart is divided in loyalty, we will move in two directions. There will be a push and a pull to our lives, creating conflict and restricting us from living in the freedom that is ours as Christ followers.

Throughout Scripture we read about the importance of our heart condition and its centrality to everything concerning us. As we try to walk down two opposite paths, bitterness and blessing—the human side and the spiritual side of us—we will become increasingly unstable as time goes by. Rather than living a full and grateful life, we will settle for an empty life and get into the groove of living for two masters—God and self.

God has a gift for us. We can't buy it at a trendy boutique or an exclusive department store. It is more beautifying than any spa treatment or plastic surgery. And though it's free, it is the most valuable gift you will ever receive. The gift He offers is a heart renewed by gratefulness. A grateful woman reflects beauty and reliance on God.

Today I will remember:
• Water and mirrors both reflect how I look.
• My heart reflects who I am on the inside, where it counts.
• If I live in gratefulness, I will reflect beauty from a renewed heart.

Lord, when paying attention to the outside, it's easy to forget that the most important part of me is under the exterior that everyone else sees. A grateful woman is a true beauty, and that is the kind of beauty I want to reflect.

―◇―§―◈◇◈―ʒ―◇―

THE CHEERFUL HEART OF THANKSGIVING

A cheerful heart is good medicine, but a crushed spirit dries up the bones.
PROVERBS 17:22

Have you known someone who continued to be grateful despite adversity? It's inspiring to watch someone continue to praise God in the storms of life. I admit that at times I thought such cheerfulness was forced or fake. But I have since learned that thanksgiving is a lifestyle to be learned if we want to be women who are full rather than empty.

Being grateful and cheerful go hand in hand. It's hard to find a grateful woman who doesn't carry joy around with her. But for the one who is looking down instead of up, the crushing weight of life and its circumstances can take over and cause defeat.

One way to increase gratitude is reframing our experiences. This helps us focus on things to be grateful for here and now. Instead of seeing life through an empty cup, the grateful woman challenges herself to see the cup full because God Himself is her portion and cup. Oswald Chambers said, "The circumstances of a saint's life are ordained of God."[187] Think about that statement for a moment. We can find gratefulness in knowing that our lives are not haphazard. As the psalmist said, "LORD, you alone are my portion and my cup."[188]

God is the one who assigns what is portioned out to us. Remembering truth is good medicine, but when we forget, our spirit is downcast, like dried-up bones.

Today I will remember:
• When I am cheerful, it's like taking good medicine.
• When I forget God is with me, my bones dry up and I lose heart.
• God Himself is my lot in life, my portion, and He holds the cup of circumstances.

Lord, thank You for always supporting me, in the good and the hard.
May I remember You and be grateful, finding the good
soul medicine that brings cheer to my heart.

---

187 Oswald Chambers, *My Utmost for His Highest*, November 7.
188 Psalm 16:5.

SACRIFICE OF PRAISE

*Through Jesus, therefore, let us continually offer to God a sacrifice
of praise—the fruit of the lips that openly profess his name.*
HEBREWS 13:15

Has praising and thanking God ever been the very last thing you wanted to do? It's not that you quit believing, but you were down and maybe a little depressed. I have been in that place more than once. I didn't praise God or thank Him in my troubles, but rather spiraled down. I am an expert at spiraling but have learned how to be grateful even in the hard stuff.

Sometimes praising God is a sacrifice—it costs us because we don't feel like doing it. To *sacrifice* means the act of offering something precious or the surrender of something for the sake of something else. In this verse we see a few keys: through Jesus—continually offer—a sacrifice of praise.

When we don't feel like it, we do it anyway—through Jesus. Our days are to be filled with a continual offering of praise to God. When we are the furthest down it will cost us more. We willingly give up being discouraged by praising God and reclaiming the courage to continue on when circumstances aren't what we hoped in the moment.

Today I will remember:
- I am to continually offer praise to God.
- Praising God is a sacrifice when I do not feel like praising Him.
- In the times when I am not feeling like being grateful, I praise through Jesus on the basis of who He is and how He loves me.

*Lord, there are so many times that I don't want to praise You.
May this Scripture and instruction burn in my heart so that I become
convinced that praise is not an emotional feeling but a sacrifice. I want
to praise You in the highs and lows, living continually grateful.*

THE THANKS OFFERING

Sacrifice thank offerings to God.
PSALM 50:14

Growing up, Sundays were spent going to Mass with my mom. In the parking lot, she gave me money for the offering and secured my head covering, which was often a Kleenex attached with a bobby pin. I felt stupid about the Kleenex pinned to my head but proud to drop the money in the velvet bag as it passed by. Though our home life was chaotic, and we never talked about God, it felt good to give an offering, knowing that my small contribution was part of a bigger picture.

Offerings are not just our money. The psalmist spoke of thank offerings. Lifting our voices, praying, and singing are all offerings of respect and appreciation for who He is. Giving of thanks, especially in real life when we don't understand why we should, is a sacrifice of our emotions, understanding, and time. Let's not overcomplicate it—just thank God for any good that you experience or see in your life. Then thank Him for who He is and how He loves you and is a shield about you in a world filled with trouble and hardships. Sing thanks, speak thanks, pray thanks—as Nike says—just do it!

Saint Catherine of Siena once said "I offer you my life from this moment and for whenever you wish me to lay it down—for your glory."[189]

Today I will remember:
- Thanking God is to be part of my life.
- Thanking God is often sacrificial.
- Thanking God is my greatest offering.

Lord, help me to lean my life and praise continually toward You.

---

189 Wyatt North, *Prayers by Catholic Saints Volume II* (Wyatt North Publishing, 2012).

GRATEFUL FOR HIS STEADFAST LOVE

Give thanks to the LORD, for he is good; his love endures forever.
PSALM 107:1

Understanding God's love for us is at the core of building a firm foundation in which we can give thanks to Him—regardless of our circumstances. But many of us grew up believing Christianity was more about rules than embracing love. If we were good, we were loved. If we blew it, we were a disappointment. Some people grasp that a big God loves them but doubt that He really likes them. The foundation is cracked from either the homes we grew up in or the culture we've been raised in. Without an understanding of God's love, being grateful is impossible unless life is perfect. But when we understand His love, we get comfortable with our perfectly imperfect lives.

What does God's love look like to you? Remote authority figure? Critical parent? A divine crisis manager that you pray to as a last resort? If any of that sounds familiar, it's time to experience God as He truly is—your Creator, your Healer, your Champion, and your Best Friend. Contrary to anything you may have believed, God is good, and His love is steadfast—which means fixed, firm, and unchanging. When this good God with His constant love toward us is at the forefront of our minds, being grateful becomes easier and thanking Him in all things is more natural.

Today I will remember:
- God is good—always—even if my circumstances are not good.
- God's love is steadfast—unchanging even in the changes of life.
- I will thank God based on who He is, not on what I'm experiencing today.

Lord, I want to keep Your goodness in the front of my mind. Help me to continue thanking You, based on love, not on my circumstances in this fallen world.

LEARNING TO BE GRATEFUL

This is the day that the LORD has made; let us rejoice and be glad in it.

PSALM 118:24, ESV

Nothing was ever good enough. My mother complained about everything. She actually resisted being grateful. I learned from a young age that being ungrateful was an ugly trait. As she grew older and barely survived a few medical emergencies, she softened and began to see the good around her. It was like watching a flower bloom. Imagine waking up to the power of grateful living when you lived years trapped in negativity. She lived with us in her later years, and one year, we made gratitude journals together. We held each other accountable to find things to thank God for and positive things to focus on every single day. I honestly had never seen her so happy. Gratitude changed her and made her heart glad.

Being grateful is a spiritual discipline. All of us can be as grateful as we choose to be. Our circumstances might be out of our control, but our daily attitude is ours to manage. The phrase "Let us rejoice" comes from a Hebrew root phrase that means to brighten up, cheer up, or make merry. It is an active phrasing that includes choosing gladness. In order to do this, we must live in awareness of the good around us and let gratefulness and thanksgiving be our daily default. Rejoicing is not a response to circumstances, but a determined response to God.

Today I will remember:
- This is God's day, and life is a gift.
- I will count the reasons to be grateful today.
- I will allow my heart to be merry even when circumstances aren't.

Lord, may I learn to live in gratefulness and gladness because I know You and am confident that You hold my life in Your mighty hand.

CONSIDER HIM

*Be sure to fear the LORD and serve him faithfully with all
your heart; consider what great things he has done for you.*
1 SAMUEL 12:24

This past year I have had friends die suddenly. It's a wake-up call to the brevity of life. Each time I ask myself if I'm living with a grateful heart or wasting days with ungratefulness, worry, and fault-finding. Do I remember God each day, or do I say that I do while living like I don't? Fearing the Lord is giving Him respect. We do this by living surrendered to Him and mindful of all He has done. Taking time for reflection allows us to focus on God's goodness and strengthens our faith.

It's easy to take the present day for granted. It's another day, the same life with the same problems. But each day is a gift. Jesus taught us to live well today, saying, "do not worry about tomorrow, for tomorrow will worry about itself. Each day has enough trouble of its own."[190] And though each day having trouble doesn't sound encouraging, Jesus said this after telling His disciples He would take care of them as they sought the Kingdom of God above all else. Friend, He promises to care for you, too.

What are some of the ways God has shown up for you? Spend time today considering the things He has done. What are some ways you can show respect to God by the way you live? Can you be grateful today even in the ordinary places of real life?

Today I will remember:
• I will fear the Lord by respecting Him today.
• I will serve Him wherever He takes me.
• I will count my blessings and consider all He has done.

*Lord, may I live counting the good and praising You
for Your present help in my everyday, ordinary life.*

---

190 Matthew 6:34.

THANKING GOD FOR ALL THINGS

Always giving thanks to God the Father for everything,
in the name of our Lord Jesus Christ.
EPHESIANS 5:20

This verse has been the subject of many conversations. How can we thank God for everything when some things are not good? What we need to remember is that though all things are not good in and of themselves, God is good. And God is working all things together for the good—all things, not just the things we understand.[191] This is where human wisdom can leave us speechless and empty. If we can't make sense of it, we ignore it. But all Scripture has been inspired by God and is useful to teach us how to live.[192] It's clear that we are to live a life of thanksgiving, even when—perhaps especially when—it doesn't make sense.

From jail, the apostle Paul encouraged his upset followers by saying, "What has happened to me will be for my deliverance."[193] He had a way of trusting God in the most unfavorable of circumstances. He seemed to know that God is always working, and that a bad situation will not stop God from His desired outcome.

I have seen this in my life too. Hard has been the unlikely pathway to holy more than once. I have come to know that things happen *to* me so that something can happen *in* me. It's because of that reality that I can thank God in and for all things. Aligning to biblical truth has rewards as we follow Him.

Today I will remember:
- I am to always give thanks—even when I don't understand what God is doing.
- I am to thank God for all things in the name of Jesus.
- God is always at work in my life; therefore, I can trust Him.

Lord, may I thank You in all things and for all things,
even when I don't understand what you are doing in my life.

---

191 See Romans 8:28.
192 See 2 Timothy 3:16.
193 Philippians 1:19.

GRATITUDE SETS OUR HEARTS UPWARD

For where your treasure is, there your heart will be also.
MATTHEW 6:21

I have loved being a mother. Of all the treasures in life, my children are on the top of the list. Raising kids often found me at games, concerts, and plays. Whatever was important to my kids became important to me. I took an interest in things that never excited me before. Because my kid's hearts were in it, this momma's heart followed. Whatever we treasure will become our priority.

Jesus, in the Sermon on the Mount, was teaching about the difference between earthly and heavenly treasures. He was actually speaking about priorities as He pointed out how the heart will be with what's most important to us. Whatever we focus on determines our actions and how we live. When we focus on earthly success or material possessions, our hearts will be set on all we can do to attain them.

How does this relate to living gratefully? As we begin to stretch ourselves to be grateful each day, we are setting our heart on God and His goodness. We are putting our heart where our treasure is. When we prioritize thanking God, our actions will be aligned with honoring God with our lives here on earth. The more grateful we are and the more we practice thanking God in our everyday lives, the more connected to God we become as our focus changes. What can you thank God for today?

Today I will remember:
- My heart will follow what is important to me.
- If I seek first the Kingdom of God, everything else will follow.
- Being grateful aligns my heart with where my treasure is.

Lord, may my heart be set on heaven as I walk these streets on earth. May my life be transformed by being grateful and having a heart set on You.

WHERE GOD LEADS

*But thanks be to God, who in Christ always leads us as
captives in Christ's triumphal procession and uses us to
spread the aroma of the knowledge of him everywhere.*

2 CORINTHIANS 2:14

Sometimes life take a turn and we end up on a different path than we anticipated.
That is what happened with the apostle Paul when Titus didn't meet him in Troas
as planned.[194] Paul had no peace when didn't find him there, and he moved on to
Macedonia. His trip didn't go as planned. Yet rather than this resulting in drama,
there was thanksgiving. Rather than overthinking, there was a solid assurance that
God was with him and God would lead him.

God always leads his people in triumph. From day to day, situation to situation,
amidst open doors and closed ones, God's people are led by God, and that's something to be thankful for.

In a Roman triumphal procession, the general would display his treasures and
captives in a cloud of incense. To the victors the smell was sweet, but to the captives
it was the smell of death. When we walk with Christ, our lives bring the fragrance of
life. It is Christ in us, and as we praise Him and continue to acknowledge His faithful
presence with us, our lives will continue to be one of overcoming even with twists,
turns, and unanticipated directional changes. Can you thank God in the midst of
change today? Can you trust that God is leading you into triumph—placing you
where you need to be?

Today I will remember:
- God is always leading me—I don't have to fear change.
- God leads me in triumph and glory—I can trust His adjustments.
- God spreads the fragrance of Christ through my life—it's Christ in me.

*Lord, may I follow Your lead and not be concerned by change and disruption.
Rather than drama, I long to learn to thank You wherever You lead.*

A CHANGE OF FOCUS

They are new every morning; great is your faithfulness.
LAMENTATIONS 3:23

Cancer is a word nobody wants to hear pronounced over them. But for some, cancer has become a life spin that leaves them clinging to their pillow, not wanting to get out of bed to face another day or another treatment. I know because I've been there. Whether it's cancer, marital discord, relational problems, financial collapse, job loss, shattered dreams, or any other hard situation—the discouragement is real and the only way to find courage is to focus on God's faithfulness. This focus will not erase the situation but will reframe the experience. A focus on thankfulness helps you remember that you can expect to get through with God's help.

Living gratefully often requires remembering times in the past when God showed up and was faithful to you. Often, He shows His faithfulness in the final hour, and remembering this can help you thank Him once again as you face new problems in a new day. God's faithfulness does not run out. It's new—brand new—every single morning. When you open your eyes, faithfulness greets you. You can count on it and so can I. Today, as I remember ringing that bell at the cancer treatment center and God getting me through the fear and discouragement of my cancer journey, I will thank Him for His faithfulness that met me each and every day and continues to do so. Someone needs to be encouraged with this reminder today—maybe it's you.

Today I will remember:
- God's faithfulness meets me each new day.
- I will thank God that He is always faithful.
- I will encourage myself and others to thank God for His faithfulness even in the worst of times.

Lord, I don't have to fear the future, for Your faithfulness will meet me there with the rising of each morning sun. I am grateful.

PEACE AND RELEASE

Do not be anxious about anything, but in every situation, by prayer and petition, with thanksgiving, present your requests to God. And the peace of God, which transcends all understanding, will guard your hearts and your minds in Christ Jesus.

PHILIPPIANS 4:6-7

Anxiety is real. For some it's a chemical response, but for others it's a learned life response. The apostle Paul spoke in general to those who are worried and troubled. *Anxious* in the original Greek text means to be troubled with constant cares. You can read this as a strong exhortation or a gentle leading. In either case it is an invitation from a loving God to a place of peace and release.

It is estimated that 264 million people in America suffer with feelings of anxiety. In a world filled with unrest, economic problems, political divisions, and rapid rising crime, it's no wonder people are troubled. There are real reasons to be. And there is a real God who wants to meet us right where we are to calm our anxious hearts. Thanksgiving is part of that equation.

When you are anxious, stop and halt the thoughts. Then take what is troubling you to prayer, spill the details, and thank God for this opportunity to trust Him more. Though it sounds simplistic, this biblical wisdom works. The peace of God is better than relief from a bottle, pastry, or shopping spree. The peace that comes from God is something we can't fully understand without experiencing it. God is inviting each of us into that experience with Him.

Today I will remember:
- I am not to be troubled or anxious—stop the thoughts.
- I am to pray, giving God the details—pour it all out.
- I am to live in thankfulness because He hears, He answers, and He is for me.

Lord, teach me to stop the troubling thoughts when they come.
I desire to be a woman of peace, prayer, and thanksgiving.

COME INTO GOD'S PRESENCE

Let us come before him with thanksgiving
and extol him with music and song.

PSALM 95:2

Praise and thanksgiving are two lifestyle habits that are overlooked. It takes humility to come into God's presence with thanksgiving. It takes a surrender of self to make a joyful noise if you don't like to sing. But both thanksgiving and worship are part of the spiritual journey of walking with Jesus.

The first time I heard about praising in adversity and sitting alone with God, I thought it sounded crazy. A Christian in ministry, I hadn't been exposed to people who actually waited on God, practiced His presence, or burst out in songs of praise as part of their regular life. I was missing out. When I began to practice coming into His presence—sitting quietly and recalling all the things I had to be thankful for—it led to singing out from my heart songs of love and praise to God. In hard times, I listen to recorded music of thanksgiving. I now know the power of sitting in thanks before making any requests. The truth is, the more I live in thanksgiving, the fewer requests I have. Being thankful imprints the heart, and somehow you know it's all going to be ok, because God is with you.

Today I will remember:
• Prioritize getting quiet before God—driving alone, sitting with Him, walking.
• Thank Him for every detailed thing that comes to mind.
• Sing. He doesn't care about the voice; He is about the heart.

Lord, make me a woman who rests in Your
presence with a heart of gratitude and praise.

THANKING GOD BY FAITH

I will give thanks to you, Lord, with all my heart;
I will tell of all your wonderful deeds.

PSALM 9:1

Wonderful things are usually experienced after hardship. We cry out and God shows up. He shows up not like a genie in a bottle, but like the true God He says He is—healer, deliverer, lover, protector, and provider—to name a few.

Last summer our friend had a freak fall while vacationing in Hawaii. His brain injury was severe. For weeks it didn't look like he would make it. His wife, Jean, trusted and prayed. She thanked God in advance of the miracle.

Today she can tell of the wonderful kindness of a God who heard and answered. Her husband is better every day and his recovery is a miracle. But before the miracle, his wife gave thanks to the Lord with all her heart. She thanked God with no outcome in sight, though she was alone and away from home, while dealing with medical things she didn't fully understand, and even as she told their children that things were not looking good. She is a living example of a true worshipper. She was steadfast. God was faithful. The rest is history and the telling of God's wonderful work.

This story convicts me. I realize that I don't thank God enough in advance, but rather wait until I'm sure of the outcome. Thanksgiving involves praising God by faith—in the storms, in the hardships, in the good and the bad—always. My friend Jean models that before everyone who knows her. I am grateful for her testimony and how it instructed my own heart.

Today I will remember:
* Giving thanks to God daily is a priority.
* I will continually pour out my heart to Him.
* I will testify of the wonder of who He is and how He works.

Lord, with all my heart I long to be a woman who thanks You without knowing
the outcome and who trusts You fully regardless of how things turn out.

WORTHY TO BE PRAISED

Enter his gates with thanksgiving and his courts with praise;
give thanks to him and praise his name. For the Lord is good and his
love endures forever; his faithfulness continues through all generations.

PSALM 100:4-5

Is your worship genuine, or are you going through the motions? There isn't a right or wrong answer, and maybe your reality is that it depends on the day. That's true for me too. Some days I am filled with praise, and others I'm pitifully discouraged. God loves me the same in both.

Rather than seeing Scripture as a means of good or bad performance, let's look at it for what it is—instruction for living a godly life. When viewing it as such, I can evaluate what in my daily walk can be surrendered to God and what areas I can grow in. None of us ever arrives; we will be growing until our very last breath.

God alone is worthy of being worshipped. We are not to be the center of our universe, and neither are our children, our grandchildren, or our careers. God alone is worthy of the center spot in our lives. This psalm tells us to remember how dependable God is, how loving and faithful. When we remember that, our worship will be filled with joy and praise. When we forget and our eyes are on ourselves, our worship dries up and we go through the motions. This is a psalm about remembrance of God's faithfulness as much as it is about entering into God's house with praise. We each choose how we will live.

Today I will remember:
- I am to come before God with thanksgiving and praise.
- The Lord is good, and His love endures forever.
- His faithfulness endures to the next generation.

Lord, be the center of my life, the reason for my praise, and the foundation
for my family into the next generation. Thank You for loving me.

WATCH AND BE THANKFUL

Devote yourselves to prayer, being watchful and thankful.
COLOSSIANS 4:2

Have you ever grown tired of prayer? Paul says we should devote ourselves to prayer and watch for the answers. This persistence is an expression of our faith that God hears our prayers, and the waiting for answers helps us remember that He ultimately knows best.

I had been a Christian for a long time before prayer became a serious part of my everyday life. It started with a little 40-day prayer challenge. Before that I prayed as needs came up, but daily prayer and intercession was only something I thought I should get to—and never did. After all, aren't we all busy? Now I realize that the excuse of no time for daily prayer was keeping me from the biggest blessing. What started small became something I looked forward to. Sometimes I sat to pray, and other times I laced my shoes and walked. At month's end I would highlight the answered prayers and move unanswered prayers to the next month's list.

One of my daily prayers was for our daughter who struggled with infertility to be able to conceive a child. I prayed daily for months. When they told us she was pregnant, I freaked out. I seriously went wild. I was amazed that God answered. The first year of this practice I saw God do things I will always hold on to. God answers the prayers of His people. We pray, we watch, and we thank Him.

Today I will remember:
- I am to devote myself—to commit by giving time to—prayer.
- I am to watch for God's answers, keeping track of His work.
- I am to thank Him for His faithfulness in all things.

Lord, may I never forget how You meet us when we pray and answer us when we call out to You. I want to be devoted to prayer in every season of my life.

December

LIVING HOPE

"If we keep telling the Christmas story, singing the
Christmas songs, and living the Christmas spirit,
we can bring joy, hope, and happiness to this world."
Norman Vincent Peale[195]

---

195   Reader's Digest, "Religious Christmas Quotes," https://www.rd.com/list/religious-
christmas-quotes/.

HOLIDAYS AND HOLY DAYS

*The Spirit of the Sovereign Lord is on me, because the
Lord has anointed me to proclaim good news to the poor.*
ISAIAH 61:1

December brings the sparkle of decor, the shimmer of brightly lit trees, the smell of fresh-baked cookies, and days filled with holiday music. There are many things to like about the season, but there are also things we don't like at all. Things like crowds, missing loved ones who are no longer with us, rude people trying to cram all their holiday lists into one day, and too much to do with too little time. I am exhausted by the time the day arrives, and somewhere along the way the joy and sparkle begin to fizzle.

What if the month of December could be different? What if this traditionally hectic holiday month could be a true celebration of the heart? Let's make this month a time of remembrance, where each day we remember the gift that came through the birth of Jesus Christ.

The promise of the Savior was meant to penetrate everything about us. When we focus on the true gifts of Christmas, our dark December days bring real joy and life-changing peace. Jesus came not only to bring the peace our hearts long for, but to bring good news to the poor. We can have all the material things we desire but be poor in spirit. We can reach the end of the year and find ourselves disappointed and brokenhearted. Jesus came for us—the poor in heart who need good news for daily living.

Today I will remember:
- The holidays can turn into a month of holy days.
- Remembering who Jesus is and why He came shifts our focus.
- Jesus came to bring good news to the poor.

*Lord, may the crazy cycle of December be stopped this year before it starts.
Draw my heart to remembering You, Your story, and the miracle of Christmas.*

FORGET NOT

Praise the LORD, my soul, and forget not all his benefits.
PSALM 103:2

There doesn't seem to be much room for creating a different December amidst the hustle and bustle. For many, the joy of Jesus is forgotten, with the exception of church services and children's pageants. If our heart grows tired and hard from too much stress, it will affect everyone around us. It starts with us. One woman at a time, let's remember the reason we celebrate. One woman at a time, let's count the joys and pass on the heartbeat of God to those around us. We can carry joy or we can grumble our way through the month. Whatever we choose will affect us and those around us, so let's choose something beautiful and different by choosing to remember.

The psalmist says, "forget not all his benefits." When I read that, the two words that stand out to me are *forget not*. It's so easy to forget things, and if what we are forgetting is who our God is and what He promises, we will lose the joy of our relationship with Him. Let's start the month with the benefits mentioned by the psalmist: "Who forgives all your sins and heals all your diseases, who redeems your life from the pit and crowns you with love and compassion, who satisfies your desires with good things so that your youth is renewed like the eagles.[196]

Forgiveness, healing, redemption, love, compassion—these are examples of a good God giving good things according to our need. These are the true gifts of Christmas.

Today I will remember:
- I am to pay attention to His benefits.
- I am to remember and "forget not" His goodness.
- My soul—my mind, will, and emotions—remember and praise God.

Lord, as I go through this month, making it a time of holy remembrance, draw me close to You in praise and thanksgiving. You are the true gift of Christmas.

FIND THE GOOD IN TODAY

Whatever is true, whatever is noble, whatever is right, whatever is pure,
whatever is lovely, whatever is admirable—if anything is excellent or
praiseworthy—think about such things. ...And the God of peace will be with you.

PHILIPPIANS 4:8-9

As the month rolls out, let's start each day by looking for five good things to recognize and thank God for. Gratitude is the gift we give back to God, thanking Him and taking notice of all the things in life that bring joy and reflect goodness. Jot them down—little things and big things—noticing the beauty that might get overlooked. Gratitude doesn't have to be about lofty things. Perhaps it's the simple ordinary things remembered that make the most difference.

Things like: Coffee with pumpkin creamer, baby sleeping all night, fireplace that lets me have a cozy fire, chocolate chip cookies and I only ate one, my health, God is with me, Jesus came to give me life, light, and love! When we look for good and thank God, we ambush negativity. One thing is certain: If you and I spend the month counting our daily gifts in gratitude, we will have peace—the peace of God kind of peace. This last month of the year has holidays, holy days, and hectic lives all wrapped up in four short weeks. If we aren't careful, we will miss remembering the gifts of Christmas that give us hope. Listing just five things we're grateful for every day will breathe something new into our season.

Today I will remember:
- I am to look for good and dwell on the good.
- I can find good in simple, ordinary things.
- When I dwell on the good, the holidays become holy days.

Lord, may this month be one of noticing the good around me
instead of wishing for more to make me merry. Untangle the parts
of Christmas that weigh me down rather than lifting You up.

THE FREEDOM OF THE CHRISTMAS STORY

He has sent me to bind up the brokenhearted...and provide for those who grieve.
ISAIAH 61:1, 3

Christmas isn't the most wonderful time of the year for everyone. Many are walking through the month just holding on. Hearts are broken from divorce, relational breakups, and loss of loved ones. There is nothing like that first Christmas without the person you thought would be there forever. I walked through some hard Christmases—the first without my parents, the first as a single mom, the first without holiday visitation of my kids—there were some dark Decembers in my story. I wish I had known to look for good and dwell there, but I chose to dwell on what I missed. I am glad Jesus understands our human pain. Jesus came for the hurting, the brokenhearted, and those suffering losses. He was sent by God to bind up those wounds.

Isaiah goes on, "To proclaim freedom for the captives and release from darkness for the prisoners, to proclaim the year of the LORD's favor and the day of vengeance of our God, to comfort all who mourn, and provide for those who grieve in Zion—to bestow on them a crown of beauty instead of ashes, the oil of joy instead of mourning, and a garment of praise instead of a spirit of despair."[197]

The good news is that Christmas is for everyone—especially for those who are hurting. The gift of Christmas isn't under the tree, it's wrapped in the heart. Be aware of those who are alone or grieving loss of any kind, and be the love of Christ to them in any way you can.

Today I will remember:
• Jesus came for the hurting—to bind up their wounds.
• Jesus gives us beauty instead of ashes.
• Jesus gives us a garment of praise instead of despair.

Lord, thank You for coming for us. You are the promised
Savior who came to rescue, redeem, and restore.

---

197   Isaiah 61:1-3.

A GOD WHO UNDERSTANDS

*For we do not have a high priest who
is unable to empathize with our weaknesses.*
HEBREWS 4:15

The rain whipped in front of the windshield, making it difficult to see the road ahead. But as we stopped at a red light, things got a little clearer and the bright lights of the Christmas sign at the corner church caught my eye. "Welcome, Prince of Peace!" was shining through the downpour, sending a message on that soggy December night—a night when people undoubtedly were taking cover in their homes, at a time of year when suicide hotlines are busier than ever, depression soars, and the most wonderful time of the year is often seen as much less than wonderful. The truth is, some people just try to get through December hoping that the next year will be better. As my thoughts flashed through a year that had been filled with illness and personal uncertainty, I thought of how Jesus met me right where I was every time. He is a God who suffered and understands weakness and pain. Oh yes, Jesus, the Prince of Peace, I welcome You!

I had heard those words that lit up the soggy night—Prince of Peace—many times over the years. But like a worn-out pair of shoes, those words had lost their shine. I didn't pay attention to the power of their meaning and had taken them for granted. Similarly, I've taken for granted the gift of Jesus understanding human weakness—and not just understanding, but then sympathizing with the things that break us.

Today I will remember:
• Jesus understands pain and suffering.
• Jesus cares about what breaks us.
• Jesus sees our weaknesses and leads us to a better place.

Lord, may I pay attention to everything around me that points me to You.

—◦ஃ◦✦◦ౘ◦—

OUR COUNSELOR

And he will be called Wonderful Counselor.
ISAIAH 9:6

One of my love languages is gifts. But the older I get, the less I need. So I like a gift that has lasting value. The birth of Jesus was that kind of gift. Jesus came into an imperfect world to bring salvation for people like us who struggle with real-life things like hardships, taxes, and grief. Under the dark starlit night, in a stinky barn, the prophecies were fulfilled. There would be no more gloom or darkness for the people in distress. A child would be born, a Son given, and the government would be on His shoulders.

The Christmas story is filled with hope, and Isaiah tells us that this Son would be called Wonderful Counselor, Mighty God, Everlasting Father, and Prince of Peace. Each name is a powerful descriptive of what the Messiah represented and a reason for joy. The greatest gift ever given is the gift of Jesus coming for us. Yes, Jesus came to be our guide through life, our Wonderful Counselor.

Counselor here comes from the Hebrew word *yaats*, which means to advise, resolve, guide, and purpose. Jesus came to bring light and help into our lives. Sit with that for a moment. And as you sit with this one name of Jesus, think about what this means to you in this season.

It was once said "Today is a gift—that's why it's called the present."

Today I will remember:
- Jesus came to be my Wonderful Counselor
- Jesus is my advisor, resolver, and guide. He leads me.
- Jesus came for people in distress, to give them light and increase their joy.

Lord, thank You for being my Wonderful Counselor. And, though I like celebrating You at Christmas, I am grateful for You every day of the year.

HE RESCUES HIS PEOPLE

He brought me out into a spacious place;
he rescued me because he delighted in me.
PSALM 18:19

A spacious place is a light place. It's a far cry from the dark spaces we experience when life is hard. In God's spacious place we are known and seen—especially when we are frustrated, hurting, and cramped. I wish I didn't know about the limiting place of depression, but I do. The truth is, I never thought I would see the light of a happy life again. Rejection and the death of a marriage lured me into the space of believing the worst about myself and my life. It was hard to believe God could rescue me.

But He did. *Rescue* means to save from a dangerous or distressing situation. God is our rescuer. I know that I am not the only one who has been in the pit because of life circumstances. Maybe you have been there too. But God is the One who rescues us from ourselves, others, and the hurt that wedges its way into our minds. Why does He rescue us? Because He delights in us. That is probably the best part of this verse—God delights in us you and me—we are imperfect women loved by a perfect God.

Today I will remember:
- God desires to bring me out of the cramped spaces into a life of freedom.
- God is always working in my life.
- God delights in me—He is pleased in who He made and who He is making me to be.

Lord, words fail to express my gratitude for how You reached into my
life and rescued me. Today, I stop to say thank You—Two common
words that are lifted to a God of uncommon love and power.

THE KEEPER OF MY WELFARE

And he will be called...Prince of Peace.
ISAIAH 9:6

The names of Jesus have become the catch phrases of Christmas. Greeting cards and banners display the words Wonderful Counselor, Mighty God, and Prince of Peace. Lean in, because the meaning behind these words can change our lives. *Prince* is from the Hebrew word *sar*, which means chief, captain, or keeper. *Peace* in the original can mean safety or welfare. With those together, I can declare that Jesus came to be the Prince of Peace, the Keeper of my Welfare, the Captain of my Safety. I often tell myself that Jesus is the keeper of my welfare, and this brings me back to a place of trust.

We can all have peace, but we are responsible for where our minds settle each day. If we stop allowing the negative habit of being troubled to rule us, we will have a peace that Jesus said is bigger than anything the world can throw at us. Maybe we've become immune to the words of Christmas. Then we wonder in the middle of our storms why our umbrella is leaking and we don't feel shelter. We have become immune to the words of truth and fail to nestle up under them. We can't expect to rant about our latest crisis and have peace wash over us. We must choose to believe God is who He says He is. True peace is not dependent on circumstances or how other people's poor choices affect us. Jesus is the Prince of Peace—it's settled.

Today I will remember:
- I choose what I allow my mind to focus on.
- Jesus watches over my welfare.
- I have peace when I choose to believe this.

Lord, thank You for being a God who watches over me—my keeper, captain, and chief. Truly You are the greatest gift I have ever received.

THE GOD WHO CARES

And he will be called...Wonderful Counselor.
ISAIAH 9:6

December is filled with joy or angst—and sometimes both. Decorations and twinkle lights make everything feel magical, but real life doesn't always sparkle. Problems don't go away simply because we have turned the page on a calendar. Real life still exists, and it gets magnified in the stress of trying to create a *Merry Little Christmas*. But even with real-life complexities, we can live a Spirit-filled life with Jesus as our Counselor. A. W. Tozer says, "The Spirit-filled life is not a special, deluxe edition of Christianity. It is part and parcel of the total plan of God for His people. There is nothing about the Holy Spirit queer or strange or eerie...the Holy Spirit is the spirit of Jesus, and is as gracious and beautiful as the Savior Himself."[198]

Jesus, the star of the Christmas season, is called a Wonderful Counselor, and as such He cares deeply about the hurts and hang-ups that people walk into December with. Jesus said, "But when he, the Spirit of truth, comes, he will guide you into all the truth. He will not speak on his own; he will speak only what he hears."[199] We are also told, "If any of you lacks wisdom, you should ask God, who gives generously to all without finding fault, and it will be given to you."[200]

Unwrap the generous gift of Christmas in the truth that Jesus is your Counselor—and He is indeed wonderful.

Today I will remember:
• I can go to Jesus with my questions and cares.
• Jesus came to be a Wonderful Counselor.
• Jesus will guide me into all truth.

Lord, may my heart be turned to You for counsel and direction.
Thank You for caring about what concerns me.

---

198 A.W. Tozer, *Gems from Tozer* (Camp Hill, PA: Christian Publications, 1979), 29.
199 John 16:13.
200 James 1:5.

OUR WARRIOR GOD

And he will be called...Mighty God.
ISAIAH 9:6

It often escapes our notice that God didn't send His Son amidst a dazzling production. There was no fanfare. Jesus was born in a plain farm field, on a dark night, with just a few shepherds. Kari West says, "Both the good news and the best gift arrived at night...Into our dark December comes this undeserved and unbelievable love gift from the Father. You and I are accepted just as we are—moody or merry; rich or poor; married, widowed or divorced.... This gift comes with an eternal, unchanging, non-negotiable, non-refundable guarantee."[201]

Imagine someone who is to be called Mighty God (Isa. 9:6) coming from such humble beginnings—and yet this was God's plan. "See, your king comes to you, righteous and victorious, lowly and riding on a donkey."[202] There is so much here—He is our powerful God, our warrior; He is strong. My kids were raised on superheroes, and here we see that Jesus came to be that hero for us all—He is giant and strong, coming to rescue us from the dangers and damaging effects of earthly life. This life isn't all there is, so hang on this Christmas and focus on the truth that a mighty God holds you and everything will be OK.

Today I will remember:
- Jesus came humbly to earth as part of God's plan.
- He came with salvation and is a warrior.
- The best gift arrived with humble beginnings and strong outcomes.

Lord, You are my champion. May I always
remember this and put my trust completely in You.

---

201 Kari West, *Dare to Trust, Dare to Hope Again* (Colorado Springs: David C Cook, 2001), 117.
202 Zechariah 9:9.

ROUND-THE-CLOCK CARE

He will be called...Everlasting Father.
ISAIAH 9:6

While we are busy making out wish lists for ourselves or our kids, Jesus wants us to know that He is everything we need in this life. He has the power to change our life from the inside out. He doesn't live in a church building anxiously awaiting Sunday visitors. The Bible is clear that once we've believed in the Lord Jesus and given our lives to Him, He lives within each one of us. "I am in my Father, and you are in me, and I am in you."[203]

Isaiah said that the coming King—the Messiah—would be an Everlasting Father. *Everlasting* in the original means duration, continue, advance. He is our loving Father who guides us into the next step and will stay with us for the duration of this journey. Everlasting also means "round the clock." I like that definition because I can remember that Jesus is my 24/7 Father. He is with me around the clock, giving me the next step, helping me advance.

Each of us has within us a void that only God can fill. Try as we might to fill it with other things, none of them can continually satisfy us. Once we fill up, we empty out just as quickly. Once we are on empty again, the cycle is repeated. Frustration mounts until we finally say, "Here, God, take all of me and fill me with Yourself." He wants us to have the assurance that He has everything we need, and He is in the business of restoring, reshaping, renewing, and rebuilding lives for His purposes, 24/7.

Today I will remember:
- God is with me around the clock.
- I cannot escape His presence with me.
- He fills the void that I've tried to fill with other things.

> *Lord, thank You for promising to be with me around the clock and for the duration of my journey. You are my everlasting, 24/7 Father.*

---

203 John 14:20.

GIVING GOD MY YES

But the angel said to her, "Do not be afraid, Mary; you have found favor with God. You will conceive and give birth to a son, and you are to call him Jesus. He will be great and will be called the Son of the Most High."

LUKE 1:30-32

Mary was young, poor, and female—all things that people in that day would count as being unusable for God—especially for any major task. Yet God chose Mary for one of the most stunning walks of obedience that He had ever demanded of anyone. She was afraid, just as we would be, but she said "yes" anyway. Do you ever feel unusable? God is not limited by our backgrounds. He often calls those who seem least likely so that He can equip them by His Spirit, filling them and working through them.

Mary found favor with God, but God's blessing brought her much pain. She would be ridiculed, her fiancé would be tempted to leave her, and her Son would be rejected and then murdered. But through her "yes," a Son would be born who is the hope of the world. Her submission was God's plan to bring about our salvation, and that is why she has been honored and praised for generations. Maybe God is asking for your "yes" and you are wavering. Today, think of Mary and how God called a poor young girl to complete His sovereign plan. What will your "yes" accomplish for His kingdom? In your family? In your community? When you don't think God can use you—remember Mary.

Today I will remember:

• When God calls me to obedience, I must move forward despite my fears.
• God equips those He calls.
• God can do amazing things through one woman saying "yes."

Lord, You have my "yes" today. May I remember Mary
and how You used an ordinary life in an extraordinary way.

THE GOD OF DETAILS

You are to call him Jesus. He will be great and will be called the Son of the
Most High. The Lord God will give him the throne of his father David, and
he will reign over Jacob's descendants forever; his kingdom will never end.

LUKE 1:31-33

God is in the details. He was writing the Kingdom story all the way down to the name of the baby Mary would carry. The name Jesus is a Greek form of the Hebrew name Joshua. It was a common name back then, meaning "the Lord saves." Just as Joshua had led Israel into the Promised Land, so Jesus would lead His people to eternal life. The people in that day took names seriously and noted the symbolism and power of a name. In Jesus' name people were healed, demons were banished, and sins were forgiven. Much earlier God promised David, "Your house and your kingdom will endure forever before me; your throne will be established forever."[204] This promise was fulfilled through the birth of Jesus. It's all about the details!

Have you seen God working in the details of your life? Once I began noticing God at work behind the scenes, my faith grew and my life changed. I still had all the same problems and hurts as before, but I was certain that God was at work and that every little detail in my life was being written in the story—ordained by Him before I ever took my first breath. When we start believing that God is in the details, we will see God in everything.

Today I will remember:
• God is in the details of my life.
• God is always at work behind the scenes.
• God is fulfilling His plan and writing my story.

Lord, seeing You in everything changes everything.
May I never forget that You are always at work,
and in remembering, may I trust You completely.

---

204 2 Samuel 7:16.

THE GOD OF POSSIBLE

For nothing will be impossible with God.
LUKE 1:37, ESV

My friend was diagnosed with a rare stage 4 cancer. The doctors said she was dying. She believed God was going to heal her, aware that nothing—NO THING—is impossible for God. That was over ten years ago. Today she is alive, well, and serving God. There are many details to the story, but the bottom line is that God is in every detail. When I think of her story, I'm reminded of two Scriptures. Job reminds us, "A person's days are determined; you have decreed the number of his months and set limits he cannot exceed."[205] And before raising Lazarus from the dead, Jesus said, "This sickness will not end in death. No, it is for God's glory so that God's Son may be glorified through it."[206] In God's Kingdom calendar, it was not my friend's time, and her story has brought much glory to God and attention to the truth we see here—that nothing is impossible with God.

Are you in an impossible situation? Jesus said, "If you have faith as small as a mustard seed, you can say to this mountain, 'Move from here to there,' and it will move. Nothing will be impossible for you."[207] For those of us who think our faith isn't big enough for our problems, we can find hope in mustard-seed faith. In the Christmas story we are not told Mary had great faith. We are told that she was afraid, and yet she said yes and believed. Christmas is believing that with God, all things are possible.

Today I will remember:
• All things are possible with God.
• God is in the details of my story, all to bring Him glory.
• God has a plan for my one and only life—and I can say yes to His plan.

Lord, I love the word impossible because it reminds me
that its meaning is cancelled from Kingdom thinking.
May I always believe that You are the God of the impossible.

---

205 Job 14:5.
206 John 11:4.
207 Matthew 17:20.

NO HOLDING BACK

"I am the Lord's servant," Mary answered, "May your word to me be fulfilled."
LUKE 1:38

When God asks us to follow Him in obedience, we don't know what the outcome of our "yes" will be. Certainly there were many obstacles for Mary. A young unmarried girl who became pregnant in those days risked being discarded by everyone unless the father of the child agreed to marry her. If her own father rejected her, she would be forced into begging or prostitution to earn a living. In this case, Mary also risked being seen as crazy or mentally unstable with her story of a visit from an angel and being pregnant by the Holy Spirit.

Mary said yes before knowing the outcome. We often wait for the bottom line, doing all the calculations before we give God our firm "yes," and even then, we often waver. Maybe what holds us back is the risk or the fear of the unknown. Young Mary identified herself as His—the Lord's servant. That seemed to be the bottom line for her. She said, "I am Yours, so here I am!" That is the kind of yielded spirit God will develop in us as we identify as a woman belonging to God and created for His purpose. This is how we can move forward in faith, regardless of what God asks of us or calls us to do. I want to have the heart of Mary that says, *Lord be it unto me as You have said.*

Today I will remember:
• I am the Lord's, created for His purposes.
• When God asks me to do something, I will yield.
• Saying yes to God takes faith and honors Him.

> *Lord, forgive me for the many times that fear has held me back. I desire to be fully yielded and available to You and Your plans for me. May it be so, for I am Yours.*

THE BIGGER STORY

An angel of the Lord appeared to him in a dream and said,
"Joseph son of David, do not be afraid to take Mary home as your wife,
because what is conceived in her is from the Holy Spirit...You are to give
him the name Jesus, because he will save his people from their sins."

MATTHEW 1:21

There are two sides to every story. Joseph and Mary were pledged to be married when his whole world changed. Imagine being Joseph. Your fiancée is pregnant, and the baby isn't yours. What do you do? "Joseph, since he was a righteous man..."[208] The choices that Joseph ends up making are entirely because he is a man of integrity and wants to honor God. Engagements could only be broken through death or divorce—even though sexual relations were not yet permitted. Joseph could marry her, divorce her, or watch her be stoned to death.

Then the angel appeared to Joseph. The son to be born would be the long-awaited Savior of the world. And so Joseph followed God into the journey of being part of a bigger story. God calls us to follow Him too. We are narrow and small in our thinking, while God speaks large dreams to our hearts that require faith and following. The main point of the story is about God's bigger plan—the baby—the One who would live and die for the salvation of all who believe in Him.

What is God asking you to follow Him in today?

Today I will remember:
• God has a bigger story and a sovereign plan.
• His plan is to offer salvation to all people through His son Jesus Christ.
• Both Joseph and Mary yielded to God.

Lord, may I be yielded to You in this life,
so that I can be part of Your work and story too.

---

208 Matthew 1:19, NASB.

GOD WITH US

*All this took place to fulfill what the Lord had said through
the prophet: "The virgin will conceive and give birth to a son,
and they will call him Immanuel" (which means "God with us").*

MATTHEW 1:22-23

Mary and Joseph named the baby Jesus—meaning "the Lord saves"—because He would save the world from sin and death. But years before, the prophet Isaiah called Him Immanuel—meaning "God with us"—because Jesus would be God in the flesh, literally dwelling among the people. The gift of Christmas is not only our rescue from sin and death, but the gift of His presence. More than words on a Christmas card, Immanuel—God with us—can be a comfort during any season of life. Especially Christmas. No circumstance can take His presence away from us—not even death, divorce, or distance from loved ones.

Many people feel alone during the holidays, as merriment can magnify the losses or distance we experience when we can't spend the holidays with those we love. No matter how we are feeling, we are never alone. When you feel lonely, stop and thank God that He promises to be with you. Thank Him that His presence enfolds you in love and that He is watching over you constantly. Begin accepting every day as a gift from His hand and as a custom-designed provision just for you. Because He is with you, He can be found in every situation.

Today I will remember:
- I can trust that Immanuel will always be with me.
- When I feel lonely, I can call out to God.
- Though unseen, I can trust that God's presence is near.

*Lord, draw me closer to You when I am feeling lonely or distant
from others. Show me what I can do to live fully in Your presence.*

NOTICING GOD AT WORK

Mary treasured up all these things and pondered them in her heart.

LUKE 2:19

After Mary gave birth to Jesus, angels appeared to shepherds nearby, telling them the good news—the Messiah was born! Word spread, and amidst all the excitement and activity Mary was quiet, thinking deeply about what had just happened. She was an ordinary woman who was part of an extraordinary miracle. Scripture tells us she *treasured* all of the things and *pondered* them in her heart. That night, beside the manger, Mary's heart was forever changed.

As a woman, I relate to Mary being sentimental. I remember the details of when I had my first baby. The pain, the rush of emotions, and all the activity—then the calm of gratitude and wonder. I cried tears of gratefulness and joy and was amazed at the perfect baby boy in my arms. God was faithful, I was tired, but my heart was forever changed.

The scene at the manger was thousands of years ago, but our lives have been forever changed too. We all have needed some good news, and Jesus is the good news. Christmas isn't found under a tree, with the perfect gift or the perfect decorations— it is found in the heart. Perhaps it's time to slow down, find moments to ponder the miracle of Christmas, and consider how we can now bring that miracle to others. Sometimes the holidays look different than we hoped, but they can always be filled with wonder when we carry Christmas in our hearts.

Today I will remember:
- It's important to take note of God's work around us.
- Finding time to be with God during this season is the priority.
- Christmas is in the heart, not under the tree.

Lord, forgive me for the times I rush away from the wonder of Your work.
May I take the time to remember and thank You for all You've done.

MY HIDING PLACE

*I wait quietly before God, for my victory comes from him. He alone
is my rock and my salvation, my fortress where I will never be shaken.*

PSALM 62:1-2, NLT

My kids loved to make Christmas lists. Now our grandchildren make Amazon wish lists. Times have changed, but one thing never changes—kids love to dream and create. Some of the best gifts for kids don't cost anything. Our kids liked making forts and tents out of blankets stretched out across chairs, tables, or whatever they could find. Under those blankets was a fortress where they weren't bothered by anything else—life was good when they were playing beneath those blanket walls.

A fortress, by definition, is a secure place. The psalmist said God was his fortified place, where he wasn't shaken by all the problems of the world. For some reason, problems loom larger during the holidays when everyone is expected to be merry. "The season becomes more of a burden than a blessing. Wherever we turn we see people trying to cram an old-fashioned, picture-perfect holiday into their schedule. The frenzy is contagious. We are haunted by our own Christmas past."[209]

The frenzy must stop so we can quiet our hearts before God. All victory and power come from him. You can't fix a worn-out heart with more activities, but you can find new strength when God becomes your hiding place. He is your fortress, the place where you gain strength for the daily battles of life.

Today I will remember:
- I am to quiet my heart before God.
- He is my fortress and place of victory.
- I will not be shaken when I hide myself in Him.

*Lord, in the busy of the season, remind me to quiet my heart before You—even
if it's just a five-minute break from the frenzy to spend time hidden in You.*

---

209 Kari West, *Dare to Trust, Dare to Hope Again*, 116.

LIVING LOVED AT CHRISTMAS

So the Word became human and made his home among us.
He was full of unfailing love and faithfulness.

JOHN 1:14, NLT

The Christmas season is not in the Bible—it's our tradition. We pull out our decorations, hang the twinkle lights, and put on our Christmas playlists. There is nothing like fresh-baked cookies and the sounds of the holidays. Christmas is the designated day to celebrate the birth of the Savior—Jesus Christ. But Jesus didn't have a holiday playlist, was never in a Christmas parade, never hung a stocking or decorated a tree. Jesus died at thirty-three, never experiencing any of the hoopla that we call Christmas. What Jesus did do was love people, and He did it lavishly.

He spoke to a divorcee, allowed a prostitute to wash his feet, and He celebrated the sacrifice of a poor widow who gave all she had. Into our own Christmas season, Jesus reaches out to us where we are with the undeserved gift of His love.[210]

The greatest gift came wrapped up in being loved as we are—moody or merry—not who we think we should be. There might be some New Year's goals around the corner, but nothing we do can make Jesus love us more than He does this very moment. We live out of a place of love, not trying to earn love by changing or achieving.

Today I will remember:
- Jesus came and made His home among us.
- He is full of love and unfailing faithfulness.
- The greatest gift is the gift of God's unfailing love.

Lord, Your love is more than I can comprehend. May I live
in Your love and love others the way You love them.

THE GREATEST SERMON

God showed how much he loved us by sending his one and only Son into the world so that we might have eternal life through him. This is real love—not that we loved God, but that he loved us and sent his Son.

1 JOHN 4:9-10, NLT

The greatest sermon ever told took place in a plain farm field, beneath a starlit sky, in front of a few ordinary shepherds. Why wasn't He born in a beautiful palace instead of a dirty stable? God is in the details, and there was no room at the inn for a reason. God didn't send the gift of His Son in fancy packaging, but rather in humble beginnings that speak to the plan of God. "Though he was rich, yet for your sake he became poor, so that you through his poverty might become rich."[211]

Jesus was sent for all people—rich and poor, powerful and helpless, famous and obscure. He loves us all, no matter who we are. He willingly left heaven's glory to walk among us and show us His love. No matter what hardships we face, Jesus knows what we're going through and holds the details of our lives too. Don't leave Him in the stable this Christmas, but welcome Him into your heart and life. We can trust Him with the details of our story. The angel declared, "A Savior has been born to you; he is the Messiah, the Lord."[212] Christmas began by a trough, in the dirt.

Today I will remember:
- God showed His love by sending Jesus.
- Real love is God pursuing us through sending Jesus.
- Because of His love, we can trust Him with the details of our story.

Lord, I am amazed at Your attention to detail. The same author of the Christmas story is now writing mine. I trust You and receive the gift of Your love.

---

211 2 Corinthians 8:9.
212 Luke 2:11.

THE GOD WHO SAVES

From the LORD comes deliverance.
May your blessing be on your people.

PSALM 3:8

Tucked under the holiday food table watching the adults get drunk on Christmas Eve was awful. The craziness went on until midnight—when it was time for presents. Intoxicated adults do not leave children with happy holiday memories. That was my life—a mother who was miserable and a father who drank too much. They were good people; they just didn't know Jesus. Growing up in angst left me wanting more. I accepted Jesus as my Savior right before college, on a Monday night at Calvary Chapel Costa Mesa—during what we now call the Jesus Revolution. My parents waited for it to fizzle out, but instead of fizzling my faith grew.

Newly retired, my Dad seemed empty too—though he never voiced it. My parents watched my life change from party girl to Jesus girl. Soon they both accepted Christ. My father never looked back and never drank another drop of alcohol. It was a miracle in our midst because we all knew Daddy was an alcoholic. No one told him not to drink, he just knew God had saved him from himself and his vices. My miserable mom became filled with joy, and their marriage was made completely new by God. They were baptized at Pirates Cove in Orange County a few months after I was. God was making all things new—He delivered us. Life wasn't perfect, but our lives had meaning beyond ourselves.

I miss my parents every Christmas. They are my history and part of my story, and I love them deeply and thank God for saving us. Jesus changed our story because that is what Jesus does—He seeks and saves the lost.

Today I will remember:
• God is a deliverer.
• God sent Jesus to redeem lives.
• A life redeemed is a life blessed.

Lord, there aren't enough words...thank You
for delivering my family and breaking the chains.

─◇ ⁊ ◈◈◈ ℥ ◇─

DON'T MISS THE SPARKLE

*Abraham called that place The LORD Will Provide. And to this day
it is said, "on the mountain of the LORD it will be provided."*
GENESIS 22:14

It was November, the cancer diagnosis was grim, and her "last" December was a "black Christmas"—no lights, gifts, or sparkle. But she didn't die. A few years later her cancer returned, and she was given only weeks to live. This time she was determined to make the last Christmas her best. She told everyone she knew, "Don't miss the sparkle," realizing her earlier "black Christmas" was a waste. If it truly had been her last, she would have thrown it away. Not this time—this truly was her last, and she lived it with joy.

We don't realize the brevity of life, and as a result we get stuck in problems and emotions. We get in our own way and miss the joy. My sweet friend died shortly after that Christmas, and she left a legacy. Watching her live joy in the hard changed us all, and "don't miss the sparkle" became something we still say to remind ourselves to live looking up. In my mind's eye, I still see the lighted wreath around her wheelchair and the memory of her gifting her closest friends a private concert in our church chapel. She went out making a difference; God provided her what she needed to make her last days some of her best.

Is it a black Christmas? If so, God cares and wants to provide joy in your pain and darkness. When we look up, we find living hope and see the light hope outside of ourselves.

Today I will remember:
• The Lord God is my provider.
• He provides in the good and bad times.
• I can choose to trust Him, and He will provide joy in the hard places.

*Lord, help me not to be so wrapped up in myself or my feelings that I miss the life
you've given me. May each day be a reminder of the gift of Your provision.*

WHEN CHRISTMAS IS HARD

In all their distress he too was distressed....In his love and mercy
he redeemed them; he lifted them up and carried them.

ISAIAH 63:9

We were excited because our blended family would be together for Christmas. As I checked off lists and wrapped presents, the anticipation mounted. Then the call came on Christmas Eve—they weren't coming. The kids were not being put on a plane. No reason—no explanation—just pain.

My sweet husband was determined to go to the airport on Christmas morning and wait for them. He had faith they would show up. But they didn't. The rest of us tried to hold off gifts until they came, but they never came. There was pain all around. There were tears as my husband packed up their gifts to send by mail. He carried the cross of his pain in such a way that it was formed into love—love for a God who was holding him up. He didn't run from the suffering; he was transformed by it. It wasn't the merriest Christmas, but this is real life.

Friends, some Christmases are hard. The truth of Christmas—Jesus coming to rescue and save us—is real even in the most disappointing of circumstances. That Christmas broke my husband's heart, but God held his heart, and what could have been a hard heart turned into holy transformation. Christmas is about Jesus, and He is about love and forgiveness. We are broken people, but Jesus came for us all. And that is the bottom line of Christmas.

Today I will remember:
- God cares when I am distressed.
- He lifts me up and carries me.
- Hard circumstances, though not invited, can be holy and transformative.

Lord, thank You for caring about us in our distress. Thank you for carrying us and
lifting us up. Most of all, thank You for the transforming work of Your love.

THE GIFT OF CHRISTMAS

Glory to God in the highest heaven,
and on earth peace to those on whom his favor rests.
LUKE 2:14

"Jesus was born into a world much like our own. People were wrapped up in their own agendas, registering for the census, finding lodging, feeding donkeys, and tending sheep. They were also divorcing their wives and burying their dead. There was discrimination, high taxes and political upheaval."[213] Into such a world, He came to purchase our freedom by His blood on the cross. This is our hope today.

But at Christmastime we settle into what we know, not thinking of the power of the story. We love our comforts and our plans. Nothing is wrong with that, but this is a sacred holiday. Do not let it pass without asking God for a fresh perspective on your life. "Dare to look up this holiday season and ask for something new. Ask the Lord Himself to reveal a fresh revelation of His love, one that leaves you undone and renewed, all at the same time. Ask Him for new levels of awe and wonder that you might go forward into your future, unafraid, full of hope."[214] May this Christmas launch you into your next season with the full assurance that you are God's own child.

Let every heart prepare Him room!

Today I will remember:
- This is a sacred holiday. I am to give God praise.
- He came to bring peace on earth and favor to His people.
- I am to ask God for more of Him and the wonder of His love.

Lord, I praise You, Almighty God, for coming to earth and paying the price for us. Give me a fresh revelation of Your love and a hope for my future in You.

---

213 Kari West, *Dare to Trust, Dare to Hope Again*, 117.
214 Susie Larson, *Prepare Him Room* (Minnesota: Bethany House, 2021), 183.

EACH NEW DAY

In the morning, LORD, you hear my voice; In the morning
I lay my requests before you and wait expectantly.

PSALM 5:3

And just like that—it's over. Switching gears isn't always easy, and you many find yourself in the post-Christmas slump. Some years I've wanted to make Christmas last longer by keeping the decor up and playing Christmas music until the New Year. But other years I can't wait to get rid of the mess, wrappings, treats, and decor—it was fun while it lasted, but now it's over. Regardless of which category you fall into, this is the time we might be a little worn out from decking the halls or depleted from grieving our losses. Perhaps the next several days are a good time for reflection and prayer.

The psalmist writes about coming to God in the morning. This is obviously not a silent encounter because the Lord hears his voice. Does the Lord hear your voice in the morning? Or do you pray only when things are stressful? The psalmist prays every morning, laying his requests before God and then waiting for God to answer. This is what we need now as the year winds down and the New Year waits. Hopefully the Christmas season had us focused on the beauty of Jesus in such a way that we open the page of a new calendar with hope. "And when you pray to God regularly, irregular things happen on a regular basis."[215]

Today I will remember:
- I am to seek God each morning.
- I am to lay my needs and requests before Him each day.
- When I seek God regularly, things happen.

Lord, may You hear my voice each morning and receive my
prayers. It is my desire to seek You and be close to You.

---

215 Mark Batterson, *The Circle Maker* (Grand Rapids, Michigan: Zondervan, 2012), 15.

CALL ON THE SAVIOR

Then you will call on me and come and pray to me, and I will listen to you.
You will seek me and find me when you seek me with all your heart.

JEREMIAH 29:12-13

Maybe this has been a hard year for you or someone you love. Life has seasons, and some of them are harder than others. We can get lost along the way—even as Christians. We lose focus and need help finding our way back. In each season, we can trust that God is always working toward our journey back to freedom and to Him. God's plan is always to lead us back to Himself and a place of prayer and seeking.

Jeremiah said, "'I know the plans I have for you,' declares the Lord, 'plans to prosper you and not to harm you, plans to give you hope and a future.'"[216] He was a leader who stirred up hope. They were held down, held back, and most likely discouraged. Yet God promised to bring them back because despite the captivity, God knew the plan. Part of the plan was to become people who didn't forget God's goodness, people who sought God with all their hearts, calling on Him in regular prayer. What is the message to us today? When we call on God, He hears and listens. When we seek God, we will find Him.

God's plans for us are always good. That doesn't mean that we won't suffer or go through hard seasons. But it does mean that God is working in us—and in the details—even when things are hard.

Today I will remember:
- When I pray, God listens.
- When I seek God, I will find Him.
- He has a future plan for me, and it is good.

Lord, may I be a woman who seeks You with
all my heart and calls on You for every need.

GIVE OTHERS COURAGE

*But encourage one another daily, as long it is called "Today,"
so that none of you may be hardened by sin's deceitfulness.*
HEBREWS 3:13

If today were your last, would you want to be kind, loving, and encouraging? Though we don't know about tomorrow, we have today to show practical love. Sometimes our focus is off and our attitude is ugly. In that state of mind, we might not want to encourage people. We live in a world with people who hurt us and get on our very last nerve. It's easier to harden our hearts than encourage others. But all people need community, encouragement, and love. We are commanded to learn the walk of loving others and let God's love flow through us to them. Rather than hardening our hearts when others don't live up to our expectations, here are three practical things we can do:

• Do good to them—this takes action.
• Bless them and speaking kindly to them—this takes humility.
• Pray for them—this takes commitment.

Action, humility, and commitment will also take a growing selflessness on our part. As you close out this year, ask yourself if there is anyone in your life who keeps hurting you or someone that you need to forgive. Ask yourself if there is anyone you need to apologize to. Getting your relational affairs right before God is the best way to prepare for the New Year. Acknowledging the condition of your heart is the first step of living in faith and truth.

Today I will remember:
• I am to encourage other people daily.
• Thinking of others helps keep my heart soft before God.
• Encouraging others is an act of humility and kindness.

*Lord, today I yield myself to You to be a vessel of encouragement and love.
Show me ways to be kind and encouraging in meaningful ways.*

SEASONS OF LIFE

Forget the former things; do not dwell on the past.
ISAIAH 43:18

Each season of a woman's life will require transition and change. Moving from one stage to the next is not easy because we want to hold tightly to the past. But our twenties are going to look different than our forties, sixties, and beyond. We must move forward and learn to do so gracefully. Our pasts may have held some amazing things, and it's hard to believe that those times are truly over. But if we don't let go of where we were, no matter how good it was, we will never get to where God is taking us now.

Not holding on to the past is a biblical theme. The Israelites had expectations of God and how He works. But their expectations were preventing them from seeing what God was actually doing, and this stopped them from comprehending what He had planned for their future. Rather than telling them to forget everything they ever learned or lived, the instruction was to not allow the past to hinder what God was doing in the present. "See, I am doing a new thing! Now it springs up; do you not perceive it?"[217]

In a similar vein, Paul said, "I focus on this one thing: Forgetting the past and looking forward to what lies ahead..."[218] Forgetting what lies behind is meant to spur us into a more trusting relationship and open us up to the new things that God is currently doing in our lives.

Today I will remember:
- God worked in my past, but that season is over.
- Putting my past behind me allows me to be open to God today.
- I am to press forward to the new thing that God has for me now.

Lord, help me to accept where I am today,
let go of my past, and have hope for the future.

---

217 Isaiah 43:19.
218 Philippians 3:13, NLT.

PRACTICE STEPS

Only let us live up to what we have already attained.
PHILIPPIANS 3:16

Christian maturity is not learning the whole Bible but living in the guidance of Scripture one verse at a time. If we never walk by faith in what we are learning, we will have learned nothing. The Holy Spirit works in us, and we can either live up to those changes or be sidetracked. Our personal journey is sacred, and God desires to grow us every step of the way. Living in what God has made real to us is the most important discipline, and it is ongoing.

Every year about this time I take an inventory of where I've been and where I am. As the year comes to a close, I solidify a word and verse to take into the new year. One year my theme was trust, and my verse was "Trust in the LORD with all your heart and lean not on your own understanding."[219] I took both the word and the verse into every day of the new year, and at year's end I reflected on what God had taught me. The things I learned made up a powerful list—one item being, "My heavenly Father knows what I need."[220] Going forward, it was important to remember and work on living in those truths. There have been years that I have grown more from one verse applied than I ever did from hundreds of verses read. Paul knew the power of living up to what we know—let's make it our practice too.

Today I will remember:
• Pressing forward is letting go of the past, but not past lessons.
• When God teaches me a truth, I am accountable to live in it.
• Living up to what I have attained is walking by faith in the truths I am learning.

Lord, thank You for the lessons I've learned that have become part of me. I want to grow until my very last breath.

---

219 Proverbs 3:5.
220 See Matthew 6:8.

A NEW SLATE

Search me, God, and know my heart; test me and know my anxious thoughts.
See if there is any offensive way in me, and lead me in the way everlasting.
PSALM 139:23-24

As the year closes, let us remember that every day is a new beginning—a fresh page in our story. The psalmist asked God to search his heart, and this is a practice that we can take into each new day. When I look at this passage, I see a simple path to applying this to my life. It has become a daily practice and prayer that is in four parts.

Search me—Lord, look within me and see if there is anything offensive to You.
Cleanse me—from all sin and wrongdoing against You or others.
Fill me—afresh with Your Holy Spirit and grace for today.
Use me—Pour out from my life, using me as Your vessel today.

There is something centering about praying this Scripture. I amplify each aspect as needed. For instance, on *cleanse me* I may have things I need to repent of that morning. I like to think of myself as a vessel that is getting washed out and wiped cleaned from yesterday and prepared to be refilled and used today. This is the new page. We only get so many pages in this story of ours, so let's connect to God, use each day wisely, and watch God move through us to others. There is no greater joy.

Today I will remember:
• Every day is a new opportunity to seek God.
• Asking God to search us and cleanse us is a privilege.
• Trusting God to lead us forward is freeing.

Lord, thank You for the days You've given me this year—the lessons You've
taught and the Scripture You've made real. May my heart be yielded before
You and my life available for being Your instrument in this world.

ABOUT THE AUTHOR

Debbie Alsdorf

Debbie Alsdorf is a ministry leader and author with a mission to help women live a better story by leading them to the heart of God's love and the truth of His word. She has been a women's ministry leader for over thirty years, a biblical lay counselor and the author of many books, studies and curriculums. She has been featured on radio, podcasts and television and is a Bible teacher on the Aspire Women's Event Tour. She and her husband Ray have raised a blended family and now love on ten grandchildren.